BLACK AMERICANS:
A Statistical Sourcebook

1999 Edition

Louise L. Hornor
Editor

ISBN 0-929960-26-2

printed in the United States of America

Printed on recycled paper.

Information Publications
3790 El Camino Real, Suite 162
Palo Alto, CA 94306
650-965-4449

BLACK AMERICANS:
A Statistical Sourcebook

Introduction

Black Americans: A Statistical Sourcebook is the second in a series of statistical sourcebooks covering significant topics in American life, and this is its tenth year of annual publication. Black Americans resulted from the view that, despite the fact that there is coverage of Black Americans in an assortment of reference sources, there is a need for a single volume statistical reference devoted entirely to this important segment of the population.

Black Americans provides an extensive collection of tables which display information on a wide variety of topics. With a few exceptions, each table presents information about the Black population, the White population, and a total for Americans of all races and ethnic groups. The purpose in doing so is not to advance a specific perspective about Black Americans but to provide a context within which the tabular data can be more fully understood and evaluated.

Presenting data by race and ethnicity always puts one at risk of being labeled racist. Although undoubtedly there will be persons on both sides - those who see Black Americans as a propagandistic derogation of the Black community and those who feel that the book eloquently proves the inherent prejudice of our culture - the intent here is to serve neither cause. In fact, Black Americans is not intended to serve any cause or advance any point of view but to serve as a reportorial resource, providing access to federal government information. By researching and presenting this sometimes difficult to find, hard to understand information, Black Americans can serve students, business persons, social scientists, researchers, and others who need basic data about Black Americans.

The use of the term 'Black' itself can also be a cause for controversy. A number of terms have been used by Black Americans to name themselves, and in fact, as this is written there seems to be some evidence that 'African-American' is coming to replace the term Black. Black is used here solely because it is the word currently used by the federal government in gathering data. Federal usage has changed over the years, and as it continues to change, those changes will be reflected here.

The next sensitive question is, just who is Black? For federal data collection purposes, Black persons are those who say they are Black (or, in some surveys, Negro, or Afro-American). For statistical reporting purposes, being Black is based solely on self-identification.

The federal government considers Black to be a racial group, like White, Asian, etc. However, being of Hispanic origin, or identifying as Spanish is not counted as a racial group. For almost all federal data collection programs, persons may be of any race <u>and</u> also of Hispanic origin. The major exception concerns some U.S. Department of Education data which counts Hispanics separately from non-Hispanic Blacks, and non-Hispanic Whites. As a general guideline, it is believed that the overwhelming majority of persons identifying themselves as Hispanic for federal data collection purposes also are counted as White, although there are persons who are both Black and Hispanic.

Organization

The main portion of this book has been divided into eight chapters of tables:

Chapter 1: Demographics & Characteristics of the Population

Chapter 2: Vital Statistics & Health

Chapter 3: Education

Chapter 4: Government, Elections, & Public Opinion

Chapter 5: Crime, Law Enforcement, & Corrections

Chapter 6: The Labor Force, Employment & Unemployment

Chapter 7: Earnings, Income, Poverty, & Wealth

Chapter 8: Special Topics

The tables in each chapter represent results of a comprehensive review of all available federal government statistical information on the Black population. This material was edited and organized into chapters and arranged in a sequence roughly following the pattern found in publications of the U.S. Bureau of the Census.

Each table presents pertinent information from the source or sources in a clear, comprehensible fashion. As users of this book will likely be a diverse group ranging from librarians to business planners, from social scientists to marketers, all with different uses for the same data, the information selected for presentation was chosen for its broad scope and general appeal.

The Sources

All of the information in Black Americans comes from U.S. Government sources either originally or by way of republication by the federal government. In turn, most of the federal information is from the U.S. Bureau of the Census. Without question, the Bureau is the largest data gathering organization in the nation. It collects information on an exceptionally broad range of topics, not only for its own use and for the use of Congress and the Executive, but also for other federal agencies and departments. The reach of the Bureau is wider than most people realize. It encompasses the decennial Census of Population, the Current Population Survey, and the Annual Housing Survey. In cooperation with other agencies, the Bureau extends to the Consumer Expenditure Survey, the National Crime Survey, the National Family Growth Survey, and many others. The fact that the Bureau is responsible for so much of the federal government's data collection adds uniformity to the statistical information published by different agencies. Although the uniformity is not complete, there is enough to make the work of data users a lot easier.

The influence of the Bureau of the Census extends beyond federal government data collection. Because of the sheer volume of data it collects, many private data collectors have adopted some of its procedures and terminology. This has the added value for researchers of making private and public data more compatible.

Observant readers will note that the source of many tables is a Census publication, Statistical Abstract of the United States. There are a number of reasons for this. First, due to federal budget cuts, a growing quantity of information used in Statistical Abstract has never been published elsewhere before or it has never been published in such a detailed way. Second, as the preeminent federal data publisher, the Census Bureau has access to a wealth of raw data in machine readable form. It is able to aggregate data geographically on regional lines and break out other detail such as age, sex, race, etc., using its own parameters for publication. Thus, even when information is published elsewhere, the manner of presentation in Statistical Abstract is likely to be unique. Data from this source is presented in a more general way so as to be useful to many different types of data users.

On all tables where Statistical Abstract is cited as the source, the original source also has been checked for additional information. To make more detailed research easier, Statistical Abstract's own source (if it is not the Bureau itself), is listed as well.

Types of Information

Regardless of its source, there are basically two types of data presented in the tables of this book.

The first is complete count data. For example, the five questions asked of all Americans by the Bureau of the Census in its decennial census was an attempt at a complete count of a given universe.

The second type of data is survey information. Here a fairly large, specifically chosen segment of a population is studied. This sample is drawn to be statistically representative of the entire population or universe. Information about housing units and money income are some of the items in this book based on this type of survey information. Of course, survey information is only as good as the survey itself; therefore, the reader should always be the judge of the significance and accuracy of the material presented as it applies to his or her own research. Although specific survey methodology is not discussed here, a full reference to each source is made on every table. Interested readers may consult the original source materials, which in most cases contain a detailed explanation of survey methodology.

The Tables

This section details how the tables have been prepared and presented. Table titles are the first source of valuable information:

Table 2.01 Births and Birth Rates, by Age of the Mother, 1997

The table number contains the chapter number to the left of the decimal and the location of the table within the chapter to the right of the decimal. Thus Table 2.01 is the first table of Chapter 2. With a few exceptions, tables have been arranged within a chapter to present the oldest, most general information first, followed by newer, more specific information. This pattern is mirrored in the tables themselves, which present the oldest, most general information at the beginning.

In a table title, the word or words before the first comma identify the general topic of the table. Following the first comma is descriptive wording which identifies the detail presented about the general topic; i.e., the data is presented by age, sex, marital status, etc., in this case, by age. After the description of the presentation of the data, the years for which data is presented are shown.

It should be noted that both the table titles and the tables themselves retain the original terms of the source material. This has the advantage of making the book compatible with the original sources.

To further facilitate use, every table in the book presents data in two, three, five, or six columns. The left-most column or columns are for the Black population; the center column or columns are for the White population; and the right-hand column or columns present data for all races.

Along the left margin of each table appears a column of line descriptors. Here, after a general heading, subgroups of the heading (usually indented) are shown. Two principles cover arranging and presenting the line descriptors: the oldest, most general information appears first, progressing to the newer, more specific; and quantities appear first, followed by percentages, medians, means, and per capita amounts.

Wherever available and appropriate, a time span of data is presented, usually going back five to ten years. This provides readers with a historical context for the information. However, readers should be cautioned that the years selected have been chosen from no special knowledge of the subject, nor to make any specific point. Thus the fact that there has been a decrease or increase in a given indicator for the period displayed does not mean that the same trend will continue, or that it represents the continuation of a historical trend, or even that which appears to be a trend within this period actually is one. The time span and specific dates have been chosen largely to create a congruity of data, and a basis of comparison between different categories of information.

Table Notes

At the bottom of each table three key paragraphs appear: Source, Notes, and Units. The **Source** paragraph lists the source of the data presented in the table. When more than one source was used, the sources are listed in the same order in which the data itself appears in the table. As all sources are government publications, the issuing agency is listed as the author. All citations provide both the page and table number in the source from which the material was taken. This bibliographic detail on each table makes a separate bibliography at the end of the book unnecessary. A Superintendent of Documents Classification Number is also provided. This number is used as a locator number in most government depository libraries, and documents are shelved or filed according to it, just the way books in some public libraries are organized by the Dewey Decimal System.

In some cases, the data has been downloaded from government sites on the World Wide Web. In this case, the Universal Resource Locator (URL) is given.

The paragraph of **Notes** includes pertinent facts about the data, the time of year covered by the survey, and the scope of the survey universe. One general note can be made here at the outset about all tabular data: detail (subgroups) may not add to the total shown, due to either rounding or the fact that only selected subgroups are displayed.

The final paragraph of a table, **Units,** identifies the units used, specifically stating that the quantity is millions of persons, thousands of workers, dollars per capita, etc. Readers are urged to pay special attention to this especially when a median, mean, percent, rate, or a per capita amount is provided.

The Glossary

It is important to be clear about terminology in a work such as this. Not only does the government have overtly specialized terms which clearly require a definition or explanation, but many government agencies use ordinary words in specialized ways. There are real differences between: a household and a family; a family and a married couple; the resident population and the civilian non-institutional population; a service industry and a service occupation; an urban area and a metropolitan area; to name just a few. All specialized terms are defined either in the table or in the glossary. Needless to say, it is absolutely vital to understand the meaning of all terms used in a table before drawing any conclusions from the data. When in doubt, consult the glossary.

For many tables, it is not possible to fully define a term or concept in the table notes, so the glossary serves as an important tool in using the tables. All terms that appear in either the title or text of a table which may be unclear or are used in a special way are defined in the glossary. Wherever possible, the definition is adapted (and in many cases taken verbatim) from the definition provided in the source publication. Not all source materials provide definitions, so sometimes a definition has been constructed by reviewing and summarizing explanatory and supplementary material from the source.

In compiling the glossary the intention was to provide short clear definitions, including only as much background material as necessary to make a term understandable. However, in practice this resulted in compromises. For certain terms (such as metropolitan area concepts), some methodological background is essential in order to achieve an understanding. Where such background is vital it has been included. Readers requiring additional technical or methodological detail are referred to the sources for more complete explanations.

The Index

Every key term from the tables has been indexed. Readers should note that the index provides table numbers as opposed to page numbers.

A Suggestion on How to Use This Book

One way to use this book is by locating the subject of general interest in the Table of Contents, and turning to that chapter. While the Table of Contents is detailed enough to narrow a search and the index can speed access to specific items, sometimes paging through the dozen or so tables in a given field uncovers unanticipated information of genuine importance. It is just this type of serendipity that has lead to the inclusion of information in this book, and sometimes such an unexpected find can greatly enhance a research project.

A Final Word

As this book is updated on an annual basis, questions, comments, and criticisms from users are vital to making informed editorial choices about succeeding editions. If you have a suggestion or comment, be assured that it will be both appreciated and carefully considered. If you should find an error here, please let us know so that it may be corrected. Our goal is to provide accurate, easy to use, statistical compendiums which serve our readers' needs. Your help enables us to do our job better.

Chapter 1: Demographics & Characteristics of the Population

Table 1.01 Resident Population and Median Age, 1790 - 1997

	Black		White		All Races	
	total	median age	total	median age	total	median age
1790 (August 2)	757	na	3,172	na	3,930	na
1800 (August 4)	1,002	na	4,306	16.0	5,308	na
1820 (August 7)	1,772	17.2	7,867	16.5	9,638	16.7
1840 (June 1)	2,874	17.3	14,196	17.9	17,069	17.8
1860 (June 1)	4,442	17.7	26,923	19.7	31,443	19.4
1880 (June 1)	6,581	18.0	43,403	21.4	50,156	20.9
1900 (June 1)	8,834	19.4	66,809	23.4	75,995	22.9
1920 (January 1)	10,463	22.3	94,821	25.6	105,711	25.3
1940 (April 1)	12,866	25.3	118,215	29.5	131,669	29.0
1960 (April 1)	18,872	23.5	158,832	30.3	179,323	29.5
1970 (April 1)	22,581	22.4	178,098	28.9	203,302	28.0
1980 (April 1)	26,683	24.9	194,713	30.9	226,546	30.0
1985 (July 1)	28,870	26.6	202,769	32.4	235,736	31.4
1986 (July 1)	29,306	26.9	204,301	32.7	241,096	31.7
1987 (July 1)	29,736	27.2	205,820	33.0	243,400	32.1
1988 (July 1)	30,202	27.3	207,377	33.1	245,807	32.3
1989 (July 1)	30,788	27.7	209,326	33.6	248,762	32.6
1990 (April 1)	29,986	na	199,686	na	248,710	32.8
1991 (July 1)	31,164	28.1	210,899	34.1	252,177	33.1
1992 (July 1)	31,635	28.5	212,912	34.4	255,082	33.4
1994 (July 1)	32,672	29.0	216,470	35.0	260,341	34.0
1995 (July 1)	33,141	29.2	218,085	35.3	262,755	34.3
1996 (July 1)	33,503	29.5	219,749	35.7	265,284	34.6
1997 (July 1)	33,947	29.7	221,334	36.0	267,636	34.9

SOURCE: U.S. Bureau of the Census, Statistical Abstract of the United States, 1989, p. 17, table 21; 1990, p. 17, table 19; 1991, p. 12, table 12, p. 22, table 27; 1992, p. 14, table 12, p. 15, table 14, page 23, table 24; 1994, pp. 22-23, table 22; 1995, pp. 22-23, table 22; 1996, pp. 22-23, table 22; 1997, pp. 22-23, table 22, 1998, pp. 22-23, table 22.C 3.134:(year)

U.S. Bureau of the Census, Current Population Reports: Population Profile of the United States 1989, Series P-23, # 159, p. 31. C 3.186/8:989

NOTES: 'All Races' includes other races not shown separately. Data through 1940 excludes Alaska and Hawaii. 1985-1989 data are from the Current Population Survey.

UNITS: Population in thousands of persons; median age in years.

Table 1.02 Population Projections, by Age and Sex, 2000 - 2025

	Black	White	All Races
2000			
all ages	35,454	225,532	274,634
under 5 years old	3,127	14,724	18,987
5-13 years old	5,727	28,254	36,043
14-17 years old	2,414	12,412	15,752
18-24 years old	3,966	20,852	26,258
25-34 years old	5,172	29,837	37,233
35-44 years old	5,649	36,762	44,659
45-54 years old	4,111	31,247	37,030
55-64 years old	2,406	20,600	23,962
65-74 years old	1,675	15,846	18,136
75-84 years old	890	11,131	12,315
85 years old and over	317	3,866	4,259
Male	16,811	110,799	134,181
Female	18,643	114,734	140,453
2005			
all ages	37,734	232,463	285,981
under 5 years old	3,244	14,618	19,127
5-13 years old	5,813	27,716	35,850
14-17 years old	2,735	13,177	16,986
18-24 years old	4,233	22,306	28,268
25-34 years old	5,212	28,705	36,306
35-44 years old	5,499	34,201	42,165
45-54 years old	4,909	34,574	41,507
55-64 years old	2,995	25,334	29,606
65-74 years old	1,781	15,844	18,369
75-84 years old	959	11,553	12,898
85 years old and over	354	4,434	4,899
Male	17,874	114,350	139,785
Female	19,860	118,113	146,196

continued on the next page

Table 1.02 continued

	Black	White	All Races
2010			
all ages	40,109	239,588	297,716
under 5 years old	3,454	15,142	20,012
5-13 years old	5,962	27,087	35,605
14-17 years old	2,737	12,951	16,894
18-24 years old	4,674	23,489	30,138
25-34 years old	5,489	30,099	38,292
35-44 years old	5,236	30,646	38,521
45-54 years old	5,326	35,911	43,564
55-64 years old	3,801	29,845	35,283
65-74 years old	2,033	18,101	21,057
75-84 years old	1,002	11,208	12,680
85 years old and over	396	5,108	5,671
Male	18,981	118,000	145,584
Female	21,129	121,588	152,132
2025			
all ages	47,539	262,227	335,050
under 5 years old	3,964	16,630	22,498
5-13 years old	6,990	29,949	40,413
14-17 years old	3,104	13,166	17,872
18-24 years old	5,053	22,702	30,372
25-34 years old	6,514	32,831	43,119
35-44 years old	6,017	32,869	42,391
45-54 years old	5,007	29,010	36,890
55-64 years old	4,865	32,246	39,542
65-74 years old	3,901	29,733	35,425
75-84 years old	1,582	16,969	19,481
85 years old and over	541	6,122	7,046
Male	22,473	129,596	164,119
Female	25,066	132,631	170,931

SOURCE: U.S. Bureau of the Census, Statistical Abstract of the United States, 1996, p. 25, table 24; (data from U.S. Bureau of the Census, *Current Population Reports*, Series P-25). C 3.134:996

NOTES: 'All Races' includes other races not shown separately. Population projections as of July 1, of the year shown.

UNITS: Estimates of the total population in thousands of persons, includes armed forces overseas. Based on Series 14 - Middle Series.

Table 1.03 Resident Population, by Age and Sex, 1980, 1985, 1997

	Black	White	All Races
1980			
Both sexes			
total	26,683	194,713	226,546
under 5 years old	2,459	13,414	16,348
16 years old and older	18,425	149,121	171,196
65 years old and older	2,092	23,162	25,549
male			
total	12,612	94,924	110,053
under 5 years old	1,240	6,882	8,362
16 years old and older	8,454	71,559	81,766
65 years old and older	849	9,316	10,305
female			
total	14,071	99,788	116,493
under 5 years old	1,220	6,532	7,986
16 years old and older	9,971	77,562	89,429
65 years old and older	1,243	13,846	15,245
1985			
Both sexes			
total	28,887	202,768	238,740
under 5 years old	2,706	14,636	18,037
16 years old and older	20,380	157,584	183,010
65 years old and older	2,343	25,743	28,530
male			
total	13,683	99,006	116,161
under 5 years old	1,370	7,509	9,230
16 years old and older	9,374	75,820	87,631
65 years old and older	940	10,390	11,529
female			
total	15,204	103,762	122,579
under 5 years old	1,335	7,127	8,806
16 years old and older	11,006	81,764	95,379
65 years old and older	1,403	15,353	17,002

continued on the next page

Table 1.03 continued

	Black	White	All Races
1997			
Both sexes			
total	33,947	221,334	267,636
under 5 years old	2,892	15,184	19,150
5-13 years old	5,498	27,620	34,949
14-17 years old	2,389	12,231	15,429
85 years old and older	292	3,504	3,871
male			
total	16,121	108,893	131,018
under 5 years old	1,467	7,789	9,801
5-13 years old	2,790	14,168	17,896
14-17 years old	1,221	6,318	7,950
85 years old and older	86	998	1,112
female			
total	17,826	112,441	136,618
under 5 years old	1,425	7,396	9,349
5-13 years old	2,707	13,453	17,053
14-17 years old	1,169	5,913	7,479
85 years old and older	207	2,507	2,759

SOURCE: U.S. Bureau of the Census, Statistical Abstract of the United States, 1985, p. 28, table 30; 1987, p. 18, table 20; 1996, p. 21, table 21; 1998, p. 21, table 21 (data from US. Bureau of the Census, *Current Population Reports*, Series P-25). C 3.134:(year)

NOTES: 'All races' includes other races not shown separately.

UNITS: Resident population in thousands of persons.

Table 1.04 Components of Population Change, 1980, 1985, 1993, 1997; Projections, 2000

	Black	White	All Races
1980			
population on January 1	26,680	194,834	226,451
+ births during year	590	1,580	3,612
- deaths during year	233	1,739	1,990
+ net civilian immigration	75	431	845
net population increase	**452**	**1,580**	**2,582**
1985			
population on January 1	28,802	202,464	238,207
+ births during year	609	2,983	3,750
- deaths during year	244	1,816	2,083
+ net civilian immigration	58	352	648
net population increase	**422**	**1,521**	**2,316**
1993			
population on January 1	31,939	213,961	na
+ births during year	673	3,169	na
- deaths during year	282	1,950	na
+ net civilian immigration	111	539	na
net population increase	**502**	**1,757**	**na**
1997			
population on January 1	33,739	220,577	na
+ births during year	599	3,091	na
- deaths during year	278	2,015	na
+ net civilian immigration	112	554	na
net population increase	**433**	**1,630**	**na**
2000 (projected)			
population on January 1	35,225	224,818	na
+ births during year	685	2,986	na
- deaths during year	319	2,058	na
+ net civilian immigration	90	491	na
net population increase	**457**	**1,419**	**na**

SOURCE: U.S. Bureau of the Census, Statistical Abstract of the United States, 1991, p. 14, table 14; p. 15, table 16; 1994, p. 19, table 19; 1998, p. 20, table 20. C 3.134:(year)

NOTES: 'All races' includes other races not shown separately.

UNITS: Population in thousands of persons.

Table 1.05 Population Projections, 1995 - 2050 (revised)

	Black	White	All Races
1995	33,144	218,078	262,820
1996	33,611	219,641	265,253
1997	34,075	221,163	267,645
1998	34,537	222,648	270,002
1999	34,997	224,103	272,330
2000	35,454	225,532	274,634
2005	37,734	232,463	285,981
2010	40,109	239,588	297,716
2015	42,586	247,193	310,134
2020	45,075	254,887	322,742
2025	47,539	262,227	335,050
2030	50,001	269,046	346,899
2035	52,507	275,470	358,457
2040	55,094	281,720	369,980
2045	57,785	288,016	381,713
2050	60,592	294,615	393,931

SOURCE: U.S. Bureau of the Census, Current Population Reports: Population Projections of the United States By Age, Sex, Race, and Hispanic Origin, 1995 - 2050, Series P-25, #1130, pp. 32-34, table 1.
C 3.186: P-25/1104

NOTES: 'All Races' includes other races not shown separately. Population projections as of July 1, of the year shown.

UNITS: Estimates of the total population in thousands of persons, includes armed forces overseas. Based on Series 14 - Middle Series.

Table 1.06 Resident Population, by State, 1970 and 1980

	1970			1980		
	Black	White	All Races	Black	White	All Races
Alabama	903	2,534	3,444	996	2,873	3,894
Alaska	9	237	300	14	310	402
Arizona	53	1,605	1,771	75	2,241	2,718
Arkansas	352	1,566	1,923	374	1,890	2,286
California	1,400	17,761	19,953	1,819	18,031	23,668
Colorado	66	2,112	2,207	102	2,571	2,890
Connecticut	181	2,835	3,032	217	2,799	3,108
Delaware	78	466	548	96	488	594
District of Columbia	538	209	757	449	172	638
Florida	1,042	5,719	6,789	1,343	8,185	9,746
Georgia	1,187	3,391	4,590	1,465	3,947	5,463
Hawaii	8	298	769	17	319	965
Idaho	2	699	713	3	902	944
Illinois	1,426	9,600	11,114	1,675	9,233	11,427
Indiana	357	4,820	5,194	415	5,004	5,490
Iowa	33	2,783	2,824	42	2,839	2,914
Kansas	107	2,122	2,247	126	2,168	2,364
Kentucky	231	2,982	3,219	259	3,379	3,661
Louisiana	1,087	2,541	3,641	1,238	2,912	4,206
Maine	3	985	992	3	1,110	1,125
Maryland	699	3,195	3,922	958	3,159	4,217
Massachusetts	176	5,478	5,689	221	5,363	5,737
Michigan	991	7,833	8,875	1,199	7,872	9,262
Minnesota	35	3,736	3,805	53	3,936	4,076
Mississippi	816	1,393	2,217	887	1,615	2,521
Missouri	480	4,177	4,677	514	4,345	4,917
Montana	2	663	694	2	740	787
Nebraska	40	1,433	1,483	48	1,490	1,570
Nevada	28	448	489	51	700	800
New Hampshire	3	733	738	4	910	921
New Jersey	770	6,350	7,168	925	6,127	7,365
New Mexico	20	916	1,016	24	978	1,303
New York	2,169	15,834	18,237	2,402	13,961	17,558

continued on the next page

Table 1.06 continued

	1970			1980		
	Black	White	All Races	Black	White	All Races
North Carolina	1,126	3,902	5,082	1,319	4,458	5,882
North Dakota	2	599	618	3	626	653
Ohio	970	9,647	10,652	1,077	9,597	10,798
Oklahoma	172	2,280	2,559	205	2,598	3,025
Oregon	26	2,032	2,091	37	2,491	2,633
Pennsylvania	1,017	10,738	11,794	1,047	10,652	11,864
Rhode Island	25	915	947	28	897	947
South Carolina	789	1,794	2,591	949	2,147	3,122
South Dakota	2	630	666	2	640	691
Tennessee	621	3,294	3,924	726	3,835	4,591
Texas	1,399	9,717	11,197	1,710	11,198	14,229
Utah	7	1,032	1,059	9	1,383	1,461
Vermont	1	443	444	1	507	511
Virginia	861	3,762	4,648	1,009	4,230	5,347
Washington	71	3,251	3,409	106	3,779	4,132
West Virginia	67	1,673	1,744	65	1,875	1,950
Wisconsin	128	4,259	4,418	183	4,443	4,706
Wyoming	3	323	332	3	446	470

NOTES: U.S. Bureau of the Census, Statistical Abstract of the United States, 1972, p. 12, table 12; p. 28, table 30. C 3.134:972
U.S. Bureau of the Census, Census of Population: General Population Characteristics: United States Summary PC80-1-B1, p. 1-125, table 62. C 3.223/6:980/B1

UNITS: 'All Races' includes other races not shown separately.

UNITS: Population in thousands of persons.

Table 1.07 Resident Population, by State, 1990 and Projections for 2020

	1990			2020		
	Black	White	All Races	Black	White	All Races
Alabama	1,021	2,976	4,041	26.0%	72.0%	5,231
Alaska	22	415	550	3.6	65.2	866
Arizona	111	2,963	3,665	2.7	85.0	5,713
Arkansas	374	1,945	2,351	14.4	83.1	3,005
California	2,209	20,524	29,760	8.0	71.0	47,953
Colorado	133	2,905	3,294	4.6	90.1	4,871
Connecticut	274	2,859	3,287	11.1	85.2	3,617
Delaware	112	535	666	24.7	70.7	871
District of Columbia	400	180	607	63.5	33.0	636
Florida	1,760	10,749	12,938	17.9	78.9	19,449
Georgia	1,747	4,600	6,478	30.2	66.9	9,426
Hawaii	27	370	1,108	3.2	47.9	1,815
Idaho	3	950	1,007	0.6	95.3	1,600
Illinois	1,694	8,953	11,431	18.4	75.2	13,218
Indiana	432	5,021	5,544	10.0	87.7	6,488
Iowa	48	2,683	2,777	3.0	94.6	3,038
Kansas	143	2,232	2,478	7.1	87.4	3,130
Kentucky	263	3,392	3,685	9.0	89.7	4,313
Louisiana	1,299	2,839	4,220	32.5	63.9	5,193
Maine	5	1,208	1,228	0.4	97.7	1,400
Maryland	1,190	3,394	4,781	32.6	59.6	6,289
Massachusetts	300	5,405	6,016	6.9	86.5	6,363
Michigan	1,292	7,756	9,295	19.2	77.0	10,377
Minnesota	95	4,130	4,375	2.4	90.1	5,426
Mississippi	915	1,633	2,573	35.2	63.1	3,100
Missouri	548	4,486	5,117	11.9	85.5	6,123
Montana	2	741	799	0.3	90.4	1,071
Nebraska	57	1,481	1,578	4.5	92.5	1,885
Nevada	79	1,013	1,202	7.7	81.3	2,145
New Hampshire	7	1,087	1,109	0.9	95.6	1,399
New Jersey	1,037	6,130	7,730	18.2	73.5	9,058
New Mexico	30	1,146	1,515	1.7	82.7	2,338

continued on the next page

Table 1.07 continued

	1990			2020		
	Black	White	All Races	Black	White	All Races
New York	2,859	13,385	17,990	21.1%	70.6%	19,111
North Carolina	1,456	5,008	6,629	23.5	72.3	9,014
North Dakota	4	604	639	0.8	90.8	719
Ohio	1,155	9,522	10,847	13.8	83.8	11,870
Oklahoma	234	2,584	3,146	7.3	80.0	4,020
Oregon	46	2,637	2,842	1.9	89.1	4,367
Pennsylvania	1,090	10,520	11,882	11.4	85.4	12,656
Rhode Island	39	917	1,003	5.2	88.6	1,090
South Carolina	1,040	2,407	3,487	31.7	66.5	4,685
South Dakota	3	638	696	0.6	83.7	863
Tennessee	778	4,048	4,877	17.5	80.6	6,434
Texas	2,022	12,775	16,987	12.6	82.9	25,592
Utah	12	1,616	1,723	0.7	90.9	2,749
Vermont	2	555	563	0.6	97.1	658
Virginia	1,163	4,792	6,187	21.6	72.5	8,388
Washington	150	4,309	4,867	2.6	84.8	7,960
West Virginia	54	1,792	1,856	2.7	95.6	1,852
Wisconsin	245	4,513	4,892	8.0	87.8	5,846
Wyoming	4	427	454	0.9	93.9	658

SOURCE: U.S. Bureau of the Census, Statistical Abstract of the United States, 1991, p. 22, table 27 (data from U.S. Bureau of the Census, *Current Population Reports*, Series P-25 and Census Press Release CB91-100). C 3.134:(year)

U.S. Bureau of the Census, Population Projections for States, by Age, Sex, Race, and Hispanic Origin: 1993 to 2020, tables 1 and 4. From *Current Population Reports*, P25-1111, downloaded from Census Bureau Bulletin Board. Telnet cenbbs.census.gov.

NOTES: 'All Races' includes other races not shown separately. 1990 data from the 1990 Census, 2000 data from projections by the US Bureau of the Census.

UNITS: Population in thousands of persons.

Table 1.08 Black Population of Selected Metropolitan Areas, 1996

	Black population	percent of total
New York-Northern New Jersey-Long Island, NY-NJ-CT-PA CMSA/NECMA	3,839	19.3%
Washington-Baltimore, DC-MD-VA-WV CMSA	1,840	25.7
Chicago-Gary-Kenosha, IL-IN-WI CMSA	1,656	19.3
Los Angeles-Riverside-Orange County, CA CMSA	1,306	8.4
Philadelphia-Wilmington-Atlantic City, PA-NJ-DE-MD CMSA	1,160	19.4
Detroit-Ann Arbor-Flint, MI CMSA	1,108	21.0
Atlanta, GA MSA	914	25.8
Houston-Galveston-Brazoria, TX CMSA	778	18.3
Miami-Fort Lauderdale, FL CMSA	688	19.6
Dallas-Fort Worth, TX CMSA	651	14.2
San Francisco-Oakland-San Jose, CA CMSA	573	8.7
Cleveland-Akron, OH CMSA	481	16.5
New Orleans, LA MSA	459	35.0
Norfolk-Virginia Beach-Newport News, VA-NC MSA	458	29.7
Memphis, TN-AR-MS MSA	452	41.9
St. Louis, MO-IL MSA	449	17.6
Boston-Worcester-Lawrence-Lowell-Brockton, MA-NH-NECMA	331	5.7
Richmond-Petersburg, VA MSA	280	29.9
Charlotte-Gastonia-Rock Hill, NC-SC MSA	270	20.4
Birmingham, AL MSA	259	28.9
Raleigh-Durham-Chapel Hill, NC MSA	248	24.2
Milwaukee-Racine, WI CMSA	243	14.8
Kansas City, MO-KS MSA	225	13.3
Tampa-St. Petersburg-Clearwater, FL MSA	224	10.2
Greensboro-Winston Salem-High Point, NC MSA	224	19.6
Jacksonville, FL MSA	223	22.1
Cincinnati-Hamilton, OH-KY-IN CMSA	222	11.5
Indianapolis, IN MSA	203	13.6
Pittsburgh, PA MSA	197	8.3
Orlando, FL MSA	195	13.8
Columbus, OH MSA	189	13.1
Jackson, MS MSA	182	43.3

continued on the next page

Table 1.08 continued

	Black population	percent of total
Baton Rouge, LA MSA	176	31.1
Nashville, TN MSA	176	15.7
San Diego, CA MSA	169	6.4
Seattle-Tacoma-Bremerton, WA CMSA	165	5.0
Greenville-Spartanburg-Anderson, SC MSA	161	17.9
Charleston-North Charleston, SC MSA	154	31.1
Augusta-Aiken, GA-SC MSA	149	32.9
Columbia, SC MSA	147	30.2
Mobile, AL MSA	145	28.0
West Palm Beach-Boca Raton, FL MSA	143	14.4
Shreveport-Bossier City, LA MSA	138	36.3
Dayton-Springfield, OH MSA	136	14.3
Buffalo-Niagara Falls, NY MSA	134	11.4
Louisville, KY-IN MSA	129	13.0
Minneapolis-St. Paul, MN-WI MSA	122	4.4
Denver-Boulder-Greeley, CO CMSA	119	5.2
Macon, GA MSA	119	38.0
Montgomery, AL MSA	116	36.7
Sacramento-Yolo, CA CMSA	115	7.0
Little Rock-North Little Rock, AR MSA	114	20.8
Oklahoma City OK, MSA	111	10.8
Phoenix-Mesa, AZ MSA	110	4.0
Las Vegas, NV-AZ MSA	109	9.1
Rochester, NY MSA	108	9.9
Columbus, GA-AL MSA	108	39.6
Lafayette, LA MSA	107	29.1
Austin-San Marcos, TX MSA	104	10.0
Hartford, CT NECMA	104	9.4
Savannah, GA MSA	104	36.6

SOURCE: U.S. Bureau of the Census, Statistical Abstract of the United States, 1998, p. 45, table 45. C 3.134:998

NOTES: Data based on the 1990 Decennial Census. Areas as defined by US Office of Management and Budget, December 31, 1992.

UNITS: Population in thousands of persons; percent as a percent of the total metropolitan area population.

Table 1.09 Marital Status, Persons 15 Years Old and Older, 1985, 1990, 1997

	Black		White		All Races	
	number	percent	number	percent	number	percent
1985						
All marital statuses	20,234	100.0%	157,090	100.0%	182,316	100.0%
single, never married	8,057	39.8	38,177	24.3	47,744	26.2
married, spouse present	7,015	34.7	92,465	58.9	102,229	56.1
married, spouse absent	1,603	7.9	3,960	2.5	5,770	3.2
widowed	1,794	8.9	11,404	7.3	13,484	7.4
divorced	1,764	8.7	11,084	7.1	13,089	7.2
1990						
All marital statuses	21,914	100.0%	163,417	100.0%	191,793	100.0%
single, never married	8,735	39.9	39,516	24.2	50,223	26.2
married, spouse present	7,619	34.8	95,337	58.3	106,513	55.3
married, spouse absent	1,683	7.7	4,191	2.6	6,118	3.2
widowed	1,730	7.9	11,731	7.2	13,810	7.2
divorced	2,146	9.8	12,643	7.7	15,128	7.9
1997						
All marital statuses	24,627	100.0%	173,296	100.0%	207,235	100.0%
single, never married	10,721	43.5	43,610	25.2	57,388	27.7
married, spouse present	7,764	31.5	96,790	55.9	109,331	52.8
married, spouse absent	1,916	7.8	5,057	2.9	7,420	3.6
widowed	1,646	6.7	11,668	6.7	13,749	6.6
divorced	2,580	10.5	16,171	9.3	19,347	9.3

SOURCE: U.S. Bureau of the Census, Current Population Reports: Marital Status and Living Arrangements, March, 1985, Series P-20, #410, p. 17, table 1; March, 1990, #450, p. 17, table 1; March, 1997(Update), #506, pp. 1-2, table 1. C3.186/6:(year); <www.census.gov/prod/3/98pubs/p20-506u.pdf>, accessed 15 October 1998.

NOTES: 'All Races' includes other races not shown separately.

UNITS: Number in thousands of persons 15 years old and older; percent as a percent of total (percents **not** standardized for age).

Table 1.10 Marital Status, Men 15 Years Old and Older, 1985, 1990, 1997

	Black		White		All Races	
	number	percent	number	percent	number	percent
1985						
All marital statuses	9,141	100.0%	75,487	100.0%	87,034	100.0%
single, never married	3,965	43.3	21,276	28.2	26,108	30.0
married, spouse present	3,554	38.9	46,261	61.3	51,114	58.7
married, spouse absent	663	7.3	1,666	2.2	2,439	2.8
widowed	324	3.5	1,744	2.3	2,109	2.4
divorced	636	7.0	4,540	6.0	5,264	6.0
1990						
All marital statuses	9,948	100.0%	78,908	100.0%	91,033	100.0%
single, never married	4,319	43.4	22,078	28.0	27,422	30.1
married, spouse present	3,862	38.8	47,700	60.4	52,924	58.1
married, spouse absent	627	6.3	1,842	2.3	2,360	2.6
widowed	338	3.4	1,930	2.4	2,282	2.5
divorced	802	8.1	5,359	6.8	6,045	6.6
1997						
All marital statuses	11,113	100.0%	84,540	100.0%	100,159	100.0%
single, never married	5,137	46.2	24,471	28.9	31,315	31.3
married, spouse present	3,955	35.6	48,479	57.3	54,666	54.6
married, spouse absent	668	6.0	2,381	2.8	3,257	3.3
widowed	340	3.1	2,264	2.7	2,690	2.7
divorced	1,014	9.1	6,945	8.2	8,231	8.2

SOURCE: U.S. Bureau of the Census, Current Population Reports: Marital Status and Living Arrangements, March, 1985, Series P-20, #410, p. 17, table 1; March, 1990, #450, p. 17, table 1; March, 1997(Update), #506, pp. 1-2, table 1. C3.186/6:(year); <www.census.gov/prod/3/98pubs/p20-506u.pdf>, accessed 15 October 1998.

NOTES: 'All Races' includes other races not shown separately.

UNITS: Number in thousands of men 15 years old and older; percent as a percent of total (percents **not** standardized for age).

Table 1.11 Marital Status, Women 15 Years Old and Older, 1985, 1990, 1997

	Black		White		All Races	
	number	percent	number	percent	number	percent
1985						
All marital statuses	11,092	100.0%	81,603	100.0%	95,282	100.0%
single, never married	4,092	36.9	16,901	20.7	21,636	22.7
married, spouse present	3,461	31.2	46,205	56.6	51,114	53.6
married, spouse absent	940	8.5	2,294	2.8	3,331	3.5
widowed	1,471	13.3	9,660	11.8	11,375	11.9
divorced	1,128	10.2	6,544	8.0	7,826	8.2
1990						
All marital statuses	11,966	100.0%	84,508	100.0%	99,838	100.0%
single, never married	4,416	36.9	17,438	20.6	22,718	22.8
married, spouse present	3,757	31.4	47,637	56.4	53,256	53.3
married, spouse absent	1,056	8.8	2,349	2.8	3,541	3.5
widowed	1,392	11.6	9,800	11.6	11,477	11.5
divorced	1,344	11.2	7,284	8.6	8,845	8.9
1997						
All marital statuses	13,514	100.0%	88,756	100.0%	107,076	100.0%
single, never married	5,584	41.3	19,139	21.6	26,073	24.4
married, spouse present	3,809	28.2	48,311	54.4	54,666	51.1
married, spouse absent	1,249	9.2	2,676	3.0	4,163	3.9
widowed	1,307	9.7	9,404	10.6	11,058	10.3
divorced	1,566	11.6	9,226	10.4	11,116	10.4

SOURCE: U.S. Bureau of the Census, Current Population Reports: Marital Status and Living Arrangements, March, 1985, Series P-20, #410, p. 17, table 1; March, 1990, #450, p. 17, table 1; March, 1997(Update), #506, pp. 1-2, table 1. C3.186/6:(year); <www.census.gov/prod/3/98pubs/p20-506u.pdf>, accessed 15 October 1998.

NOTES: 'All Races' includes other races not shown separately.

UNITS: Number in thousands of women 15 years old and older; percent as a percent of total (percents **not** standardized for age).

Table 1.12 Interracial Married Couples, 1980, 1990, 1997

	1980	1990	1997
All Married Couples	49,714	53,256	54,666
All Interracial Married Couples	651	964	1,264
All Black-White married couples	167	211	311
husband black, wife white	122	150	201
wife black, husband white	45	61	110
Other interracial married couples	484	753	953
husband black	20	24	56
wife black	14	9	1
husband white	287	436	577
wife white	163	284	319

SOURCE: U.S. Bureau of the Census, Statistical Abstract of the United States, 1989, p. 44, table 55. C 3.134:989
U.S. Bureau of the Census, Current Population Reports: Household & Family Characteristics, March 1990 Series P-20, #447, p. 143, table 13; March 1997 Series P-20, #509, p. 131, table 13. C3.186/6:(year)

NOTES: Data includes persons 15 years old and older.

UNITS: Thousands of married couples.

Table 1.13 Age, Educational Attainment, and Residence, 1985

	Black	White	All Races
Age			
Persons of all ages	28,151	199,117	234,066
persons:			
under 5 years old	2,699	14,610	17,958
5-14 years old	5,218	27,417	33,792
15-44 years old	13,590	93,852	110,948
45-64 years old	4,406	39,033	44,549
65 years old and over	2,238	24,205	26,818
Years of school completed			
All persons 25 years old and over	14,820	124,905	143,524
persons completing:			
0-8 years of school	3,113	16,224	19,893
1-3 years high school	2,851	14,365	17,553
4 years high school	5,027	48,728	54,866
1-3 years college	2,188	20,652	23,405
4 or more years college	1,640	24,935	27,808
Residence			
Northeast	5,296	43,185	49,276
Midwest	5,549	52,280	58,587
South	14,920	63,155	79,165
West	2,290	40,394	46,489
nonfarm	na	na	na
farm	na	na	na
inside metro areas	na	na	na
outside metro areas	na	na	na

SOURCE: U.S. Bureau of the Census, Statistical Abstract of the United States, 1987, p. 35, table 39, (data from U.S. Bureau of the Census, *Current Population Reports*, Series P-25). C 3.134:987
U.S. Bureau of the Census, Current Population Reports: Money Income of Households, Families and Persons in the United States, 1984, Series P-60 (#151), pp. 10-15, table 4. C3.186/22:984

NOTES: 'All Races' includes other races not shown separately.

UNITS: Population in thousands of persons.

Table 1.14 Age, Educational Attainment, and Residence, 1990

	Black	White	All Races
Age			
Persons of all ages			
persons:	30,332	206,853	245,992
under 18 years old	10,012	51,400	64,144
18-24 years old	3,568	20,767	25,311
25-44 years old	9,498	67,925	80,435
45-64 years old	4,766	40,281	46,536
65 years old and over	2,487	26,479	29,566
Years of school completed			
All persons 25 years old and over	16,751	134,687	156,537
persons completing:			
0-8 years of school	2,701	14,131	17,590
1-3 years high school	2,968	14,080	17,462
4 years high school	6,239	52,449	60,119
1-3 years college	2,952	24,349	28,075
4 or more years college	1,891	29,676	33,291
Residence			
Northeast	5,282	43,650	50,520
Midwest	5,991	52,399	59,428
South	16,499	66,004	84,044
West	2,561	44,800	52,000
nonfarm	30,276	202,339	241,374
farm	56	4,515	4,618
inside metro areas	25,402	158,087	191,169
outside metro areas	4,930	48,766	54,824

SOURCE: U.S. Bureau of the Census, Statistical Abstract of the United States, 1990, p. 38, table 43 (data from U.S. Bureau of the Census, *Current Population Reports*, Series P-25). C 3.134:990

U.S. Bureau of the Census, Current Population Reports: Poverty in the United States: 1988 and 1989, Series P-60, #171, p. 19, table 4; table 20, p. 149. C3.186/11:989

U.S. Bureau of the Census, Current Population Reports: Money Income of Households, Families, and Persons in the United States: 1988 and 1989, Series P-60, #172, pp. 124-145, table 29. C3.186/2:989

NOTES: 'All Races' includes other races not shown separately.

UNITS: Population in thousands of persons.

Table 1.15 Age and Residence, 1997

	Black	White	All Races
Age			
Persons of all ages			
persons:	34,458	221,200	268,480
under 18 years old	11,367	55,863	71,069
18-24 years old	3,715	20,259	25,201
25-34 years old	5,299	31,778	39,354
35-44 years old	5,499	36,736	44,462
45-54 years old	3,663	28,871	34,057
55-59 years old	1,220	10,458	12,190
60-64 years old	1,003	8,681	10,065
65 years old and over	2,691	28,553	32,082
Residence			
Northeast	6,273	42,997	51,202
Midwest	6,199	54,737	62,498
South	19,021	72,717	94,235
West	2,965	50,749	60,545
inside metro areas	29,435	175,164	216,143
outside metro areas	5,023	46,037	52,337

SOURCE: U.S. Bureau of the Census, Current Population Reports: Poverty in the United States: 1997, Series P-60, #201, pp. 2-4, table 2; pp. 24-26, table 5. <www.census.gov/prod/3/98pubs/p60-201.pdf,> accessed 15 October 1998.

NOTES: 'All Races' includes other races not shown separately.

UNITS: Population in thousands of persons.

Table 1.16 Selected Characteristics of Households, 1985

	Black	White	All Races
Marital status and sex of the householder			
All households, both sexes	9,480	75,328	86,789
male householder	4,665	53,868	60,025
married, wife present	3,077	43,444	47,683
married, wife absent	349	1,013	1,416
widowed	211	1,386	1,620
divorced	415	3,078	3,535
single, never married	623	4,947	5,772
female householder	4,815	21,461	26,763
married, husband present	392	2,199	2,667
married, husband absent	777	1,668	2,497
widowed	1,271	8,304	9,728
divorced	950	5,203	6,265
single, never married	1,425	4,087	5,606
Age of the householder			
All ages	9,480	75,328	86,789
15-24 years old	669	4,626	5,438
25-34 years old	2,470	17,010	20,013
35-44 years old	1,947	15,024	17,481
45-54 years old	1,488	10,792	12,628
55-64 years old	1,350	11,471	13,073
65 years old and over	1,556	16,406	18,155
Housing tenure			
All tenures	9,480	75,328	86,789
own housing unit	4,185	50,611	55,845
rent housing unit	5,295	24,667	30,943

continued on the next page

Table 1.16 continued

	Black	White	All Races
Size of the household			
All household sizes	9,480	75,328	86,789
one person	2,367	17,876	20,602
two persons	2,391	24,558	27,289
three persons	1,795	13,336	15,465
four persons	1,441	11,795	13,631
five persons	800	5,061	6,108
six persons	370	1,819	2,299
seven or more persons	317	882	1,296
persons per household	2.96	2.64	2.69
Residence			
All residences	9,480	75,328	86,789
Northeast	1,860	16,244	18,348
Midwest	1,863	19,599	21,697
South	4,924	24,283	29,581
West	834	15,202	17,163
inside metropolitan areas	na	na	na
outside metropolitan areas	na	na	na
nonfarm	na	na	na
farm	na	na	na

SOURCE: U.S. Bureau of the Census, Current Population Reports: Money Income of Households Families and Persons in the United States; March 1984, Series P-60, #151, pp. 10-14, table 4. C3.186/2:984
U.S. Bureau of the Census, Current Population Reports: Household& Family Characteristics, March 1985, Series P-20, #411, pp. 107-112, table 22. C3.186/17:985

NOTES: All Races' includes other races not shown separately.

UNITS: Number of households in thousands of households; persons per household, average.

Table 1.17 Selected Characteristics of Households, 1990

	Black	White	All Races
Marital status and type of householder			
All households	10,486	80,163	93,347
family households	7,470	56,590	66,090
married couple families	3,750	46,981	52,317
male householder, no wife present	446	2,303	2,884
female householder, no husband present	3,275	7,306	10,890
non-family households	3,015	23,573	27,257
male householder	1,313	9,951	11,606
-living alone	1,084	7,718	9,049
female householder	1,702	13,622	15,651
-living alone	1,525	12,161	13,950
Age of the householder			
All ages	10,486	80,163	93,347
15-24 years old	709	4,222	5,121
25-34 years old	2,625	17,137	20,472
35-44 years old	2,456	17,395	20,554
45-54 years old	1,606	12,404	14,514
55-64 years old	1,395	10,862	12,529
65 years old and over	1,695	18,144	20,156
Housing tenure			
All tenures	10,486	80,163	93,347
own housing unit	4,445	54,094	59,846
rent housing unit	5,862	24,685	31,895

continued on the next page

Table 1.17 continued

	Black	White	All Races
Size of the household			
All household sizes	10,486	80,163	93,347
one person	2,610	19,879	22,999
two persons	2,721	26,714	30,114
three persons	2,043	13,585	16,128
four persons	1,550	12,399	14,456
five persons	858	5,104	6,213
six persons	412	1,615	2,143
seven or more persons	293	877	1,295
persons per household	2.89	2.58	2.63
Residence			
All residences	10,486	80,163	93,347
Northeast	1,866	16,773	19,127
Midwest	2,092	20,339	22,760
South	5,622	26,155	32,262
West	906	16,896	19,197
inside metropolitan areas	8,816	61,155	72,331
outside metropolitan areas	1,670	19,009	21,016
nonfarm	10,464	78,556	91,710
farm	21	1,608	1,637

SOURCE: U.S. Bureau of the Census, Current Population Reports: Money Income of Households Families and Persons in the United States: 1988 and 1989, Series P-60, #172, pp. 9-11, table 1. C3.186/2:989

NOTES: All Races' includes other races not shown separately.

UNITS: Number of households in thousands of households; persons per household, average.

Table 1.18 Selected Characteristics of Households, 1997

	Black	White	All Races
Marital status and type of householder			
All households, both sexes	12,474	86,106	102,528
family households	8,408	59,511	70,880
married couple families	3,921	48,066	54,317
male householder, no wife present	562	3,137	3,911
female householder, no husband present	3,926	8,308	12,652
non-family households	4,066	26,596	31,648
male householder	1,876	11,725	14,133
-living alone	1,594	9,018	11,010
female householder	2,190	14,871	17,516
-living alone	1,982	12,980	15,317
Age of the householder			
All ages	12,474	86,106	102,528
15-24 years old	935	4,242	5,435
25-34 years old	2,752	15,344	19,033
35-44 years old	3,096	19,761	23,943
45-54 years old	2,371	16,400	19,547
55-64 years old	1,441	11,163	13,072
65 years old and over	1,878	19,196	21,497
Housing tenure			
All tenures	12,474	86,106	102,528
own housing unit	5,735	60,050	67,873
rent housing unit	6,529	24,635	32,954

continued on the next page

Table 1.18 continued

	Black	White	All Races
Size of the household			
All household sizes	12,474	86,106	102,528
one person	3,576	21,998	26,327
two persons	3,120	28,817	32,965
three persons	2,338	14,215	17,331
four persons	1,930	12,654	15,358
five persons	916	5,801	7,048
six persons	340	1,738	2,232
seven or more persons	253	883	1,267
Residence			
All residences	12,474	86,106	102,528
Northeast	2,286	16,926	19,810
Midwest	2,288	21,465	24,236
South	6,814	28,948	36,578
West	1,086	18,767	21,905
inside metropolitan areas	10,761	67,800	82,122
outside metropolitan areas	1,713	18,307	20,406

SOURCE: U.S. Bureau of the Census, Current Population Reports: Money Income in the United States: 1997, Series P-60, #200, pp. 1-3, table 1. <www.census.gov/prod/3/98pubs/p60-200.pdf> accessed 15 October 1998

NOTES: 'All Races' includes other races not shown separately.

UNITS: Number of households in thousands of households.

Table 1.19 Selected Characteristics of Family Households, 1985

	Black	White	All Races
Type of family			
All families	6,778	54,400	62,706
married couple families	3,469	45,643	50,350
male householder, no wife present	344	1,816	2,228
female householder, no husband present	2,964	6,941	10,129
Size of family			
All family sizes	6,778	54,400	62,706
two persons	2,261	22,711	25,349
three persons	1,730	12,743	14,804
four persons	1,358	11,517	13,259
five persons	762	4,894	5,894
six persons	366	1,704	2,175
seven or more persons	300	831	1,225
average per family	3.60	3.16	3.23
Number of related children under 18 years old			
All families	6,778	54,400	62,706
no children	2,887	28,169	31,594
one child	1,579	11,174	13,108
two children	1,330	9,937	11,645
three children	612	3,695	4,486
four children	223	1,049	1,329
five children	97	261	373
six or more children	50	115	171
average per family	1.14	0.88	0.92
average per family with children	1.99	1.83	1.85

continued on the next page

Table 1.19 continued

	Black	White	All Races
Number of earners			
All families	6,671	53,777	61,930
no earner	1,376	7,674	9,221
one earner	2,312	15,219	17,949
two earners	2,237	23,303	26,160
three earners	527	5,317	6,029
four earners or more	218	2,263	2,570
Housing tenure			
All tenures	6,778	54,400	62,706
own housing unit	3,271	40,865	45,015
rent housing unit	3,508	13,535	17,691
Residence			
All residences	6,778	54,400	62,706
Northeast	1,322	11,631	13,149
Midwest	1,345	14,309	15,839
South	3,561	17,953	21,781
West	550	10,507	11,938
nonfarm	na	na	na
farm	na	na	na
inside metropolitan areas	na	na	na
outside metropolitan areas	na	na	na

SOURCE: U.S. Bureau of the Census, Current Population Reports: Money Income of Households, Families, and Persons in the United States, 1984, Series P-60, #151, pp. 76-77, table 21. C3.186/2:984
U.S. Bureau of the Census, Current Population Reports: Household & Family Characteristics, March 1985, Series P-20, #437, pp. 13-45, table 1; pp. 107-111, table 22. C3.186/17:985

NOTES: 'All Races' includes other races not shown separately. 'Number of earners' excludes families with members in the armed forces.

UNITS: Number of households in thousands of family households.

Table 1.20 Selected Characteristics of Family Households, 1990

	Black	White	All Races
Type of family			
All families	7,470	56,590	66,090
married couple families	3,750	46,981	52,317
male householder, no wife present	446	2,303	2,884
female householder, no husband present	3,275	7,306	10,890
Size of family			
All family sizes	7,470	56,590	66,090
two persons	2,574	24,438	27,606
three persons	1,951	12,937	15,353
four persons	1,478	12,048	14,036
five persons	819	4,882	5,938
six persons	371	1,505	1,997
seven or more persons	276	781	1,170
average per family	3.46	3.11	3.17
Number of related children under 18 years old			
All families	7,470	56,590	66,090
no children	3,093	29,872	33,801
one child	1,894	11,186	13,530
two children	1,433	10,342	12,263
three children	635	3,853	4,650
four children	256	970	1,279
five children	107	247	379
six or more children	51	121	188
average per family	1.09	0.86	0.89
average per family with children	1.86	1.82	1.83

continued on the next page

Table 1.20 continued

	Black	White	All Races
Number of earners			
All families	7,470	56,590	66,090
no earner	1,396	7,816	9,439
one earner	2,601	14,970	18,146
two earners	2,609	25,737	29,235
three earners	659	5,832	6,724
four earners or more	259	2,236	2,546
Housing tenure			
All tenures	7,470	56,590	66,090
own housing unit	3,448	42,588	47,142
rent housing unit	4,023	14,003	18,948
Residence			
All residences	7,470	56,590	66,090
Northeast	1,279	11,837	13,494
Midwest	1,446	14,370	16,059
South	4,147	18,746	23,244
West	598	11,638	13,293
nonfarm	7,453	55,225	64,701
farm	17	1,365	1,390
inside metropolitan areas	6,256	42,592	50,619
outside metropolitan areas	1,215	13,999	15,471

SOURCE: U.S. Bureau of the Census, Current Population Reports: Money Income of Households, Families, and Persons in the United States: 1988 and 1989, Series P-60, #172, pp. 9-11, table 1; pp. 48-50, table 13; pp. 76-80, table 18. C3.186/2:989
U.S. Bureau of the Census, Current Population Reports: Household & Family Characteristics: March 1990 and 1989, Series P-20, #447, pp. 13-16, table 1; pp. 18-20, table 2. C3.186/17:989

NOTES: 'All Races' includes other races not shown separately. 'Number of earners' excludes families with members in the armed forces.

UNITS: Number of households in thousands of family households.

Table 1.21 Selected Characteristics of Family Households, 1997

	Black	White	All Races
Type of family			
All families	8,408	59,515	70,884
married couple families	3,921	48,070	54,321
male householder, no wife present	562	3,137	3,911
female householder, no husband present	3,926	8,308	12,652
Size of family			
All family sizes	8,408	59,515	70,884
two persons	3,022	26,380	30,287
three persons	2,184	13,312	16,231
four persons	1,789	12,078	14,633
five persons	866	5,366	6,555
six persons	317	1,598	2,047
seven or more persons	230	782	1,130

continued on the next page

Table 1.21 continued

	Black	White	All Races
Number of earners			
All families	8,408	59,515	70,884
no earner	1,202	8,367	9,835
one earner	3,396	16,239	20,494
two earners	2,973	27,467	31,752
three earners	676	5,618	6,638
four earners or more	160	1,824	2,165
Residence			
All residences	8,408	59,515	70,884
Northeast	1,501	11,390	13,338
Midwest	1,468	14,771	16,594
South	4,721	20,358	25,682
West	717	12,996	15,270
inside metropolitan areas	7,242	46,429	56,350
outside metropolitan areas	1,166	13,086	14,534

SOURCE: U.S. Bureau of the Census, Current Population Reports: Money Income in the United States: 1997, Series P-60, #200, pp 13-15, table 4. <www.census.gov/prod/3/98pubs/p60-200.pdf>, accessed 15 October 1998.

NOTES: 'All Races' includes other races not shown separately. 'Number of earners' excludes families with members in the armed forces.

UNITS: Number of households in thousands of family households.

Table 1.22 Families With Own Children Under 18 Years Old, 1985, 1990, 1997

	Black families	White families	All families
1985			
Total	6,778	54,400	62,706
all families with own children under 18 years old	3,890	26,232	31,112
- married couple families	1,822	21,565	24,210
- male householder families	126	744	896
- female householder families	1,942	3,922	6,006
all families with own children under 6 years old	1,784	11,937	14,202
- married couple families	882	10,410	11,715
- male householder families	50	211	276
- female householder families	853	1,315	2,210
all families with own children under 3 years old	918	7,290	8,503
- married couple families	485	6,550	7,295
- male householder families	24	101	136
- female householder families	410	639	1,073
1990			
Total	7,470	56,590	66,090
all families with own children under 18 years old	4,378	26,718	32,289
- married couple families	1,972	21,579	24,537
- male householder families	173	939	1,153
- female householder families	2,232	4,199	6,599
all families with own children under 6 years old	2,082	12,516	15,186
- married couple families	953	10,616	12,051
- male householder families	87	335	436
- female householder families	1,042	1,565	2,699
all families with own children under 3 years old	1,194	7,493	9,055
- married couple families	539	6,486	7,331
- male householder families	55	211	276
- female householder families	600	795	1,477

continued on the next page

Table 1.22 continued

	Black families	White families	All families
1997			
Total	8,455	58,934	70,241
all families with own children under 18 years old	4,886	28,236	34,665
- married couple families	1,974	21,914	25,083
- male householder families	319	1,325	1,709
- female householder families	2,594	4,997	7,874
all families with own children under 6 years old	2,178	12,551	15,394
- married couple families	876	10,169	11,585
- male householder families	146	545	715
- female householder families	1,155	1,837	3,095
all families with own children under 3 years old	1,158	7,217	8,761
- married couple families	457	6,066	6,838
- male householder families	93	304	411
- female householder families	608	848	1,511

SOURCE: U.S. Bureau of the Census, Current Population Reports: Household & Family Characteristics, March, 1985, Series P-20, #441, pp. 13-14, table 1; March, 1990 and 1989, Series P-20, #447, pp. 13-16, table 1 C3.186/17:(year); March, 1997 Series P-20, #509, pp. 1-4, table 1. <www.census.gov/prod/3/98pubs/p20-509u.pdf>, accessed 15 October 1998. C3.186/17:(year)

NOTES: 'All families' includes families of other races not shown separately.

UNITS: Thousands of family households.

Table 1.23 Living Arrangements of Children Under 18 Years of Age, by Selected Characteristic of the Parent 1985, 1990, 1997

	Black children	White children	All children
1985			
All children living with one or both parents	8,854	49,829	60,784
children living with both parents	3,741	40,690	46,149
- parents high school graduates	71.5%	82.2%	81.3%
- at least one parent employed	2,945	36,075	40,306
-- both parents employed	1,925	19,872	22,595
children living with mother only	4,837	7,929	13,081
- mother high school graduate	61.7%	66.4%	64.7%
- mother employed	1,959	4,553	6,675
-- mother employed full time	1,554	3,539	5,227
children living with father only	276	1,210	1,554
- father high school graduate	66.0%	77.6%	75.0%
- father employed	179	976	1,199
-- father employed full time	153	901	1,089
1990			
All children living with one or both parents	9,265	50,462	62,370
children living with both parents	3,781	40,593	46,503
- parents high school graduates	79.2%	84.5%	83.9%
- at least one parent employed	2,866	35,953	40,564
-- both parents employed	2,095	22,459	25,669
children living with mother only	5,132	8,321	13,874
- mother high school graduate	66.0%	72.2%	69.4%
- mother employed	2,421	5,050	7,646
-- mother employed full time	1,967	3,992	6,106
children living with father only	353	1,549	1,993
- father high school graduate	68.1%	74.6%	73.6%
- father employed	224	1,262	1,565
-- father employed full time	207	1,165	1,445

continued on the next page

Table 1.23 continued

	Black children	White children	All children
1997			
All children living with one or both parents	10,409	54,198	68,185
children living with both parents	3,940	41,654	48,386
- parents high school graduates	1,553	12,453	14,653
- at least one parent employed	3,194	35,553	41,027
-- both parents employed	2,415	25,004	28,936
children living with mother only	5,888	10,204	16,740
- mother high school graduate	2,215	3,830	6,228
- mother employed	3,323	6,840	10,505
-- mother employed full time	2,705	5,270	8,250
children living with father only	581	2,339	3,059
- father high school graduate	316	893	1,252
- father employed	436	1,929	2,456
-- father employed full time	416	1,793	2,297

SOURCE: U.S. Bureau of the Census, Current Population Reports: Marital Status and Living Arrangements: March, 1985 Series P-20, #410, pp. 51-62, table 9; March, 1990, Series P-20, #450, pp. 45-56, table 6; C3.186/6:(year); March, 1997(Update), Series P-20, #506, pp. 36-44, table 6. <www.census.gov/prod/3/98pubs/p20-506u.pdf>, accessed 15 October 1998.

NOTES: 'All children' includes children of other races not shown separately.

UNITS: Thousands of children living in family households.

Table 1.24 Primary Child Care Arrangements Used for Preschoolers by Families With Employed Mothers, Fall 1994

	Black children	White children	All children
All preschoolers	1,280	8,587	10,288
Care in child's home by:			
Father	146	1,663	1,898
Grandparent	93	460	604
Other relative	65	258	355
Non-relative	21	479	524
Care in another home by:			
Grandparent	203	834	1,068
Other relative	105	433	565
Non-relative	157	1,366	1,586
Organized facilities:			
Daycare center	291	1,879	2,218
Nursery/preschool	138	624	801
Mother cares for child	33	518	563

SOURCE: U.S. Bureau of the Census, Current Population Reports: Who's Minding our Preshcoolers? Fall 1994 (Update) Series P70-62, p. 1, table 1. C3.186/P70-62

NOTES: 'All children' includes children of other races not shown separately.

UNITS: Thousands of children living in family households.

Chapter 2: Vital Statistics & Health

Table 2.01 Births and Birth Rates, by Age of the Mother, 1997

	Black	White	All Races
Live births	601,998	3,094,579	3,903,260
Birth rate per 1,000 population	71.2	64.3	65.4
Birth rate per 1,000 women, by age group			
10-14 years old	3.4	0.7	1.1
15-19 years old	90.6	47.3	53.5
20-24 years old	138.9	107.4	110.9
25-29 years old	99.8	117.0	114.1
30-34 years old	64.2	87.3	84.8
35-39 years old	29.7	36.3	36.0
40-44 years old	6.4	6.8	7.0
45-49 years old	0.3	0.3	0.3

SOURCE: U.S. Department of Health and Human Services, Monthly Vital Statistics Report, Volume 46, No. 12 Supplement 2, September 4, 1998, p. 10, table 2, p. 11, table 3. HE 20.6217:998

NOTES: 'All Races' includes other races not shown separately. Data based on race of the mother.

UNITS: Live births in number of births; rates as shown.

Table 2.02 Birth Rates for Women 15-44 Years of Age, by Live Birth Order, 1997

	Black mothers	White mothers	mothers of All Races
All live births	71.2	64.3	65.4
first births	27.6	26.5	26.8
second births	20.8	21.3	21.2
third births	12.1	10.5	10.6
fourth births and higher	10.7	6.2	6.8

SOURCE: U.S. Department of Health and Human Services, Monthly Vital Statistics Report, Volume 46, No. 12 Supplement 2, Semtember 4, 1998, p. 11, table 3. HE 20.6217:998

NOTES: Data based on race of the mother..

UNITS: Live births per 1,000 women 15-44 years of age.

Table 2.03 Selected Characteristics of Live Births, 1975 - 1996

	Black births	White births	births of All Races
1975			
birth weight under 2,500 grams	13.09%	6.26%	7.39%
birth weight under 1,500 grams	2.37	0.92	1.16
mother under 18 years old	16.1	6.0	7.6
mother 18-19 years old	16.8	10.3	11.3
births to unmarried mothers	49.0	7.3	14.3
mother with less than 12 years of school	45.1	25.0	28.6
mother with 16 years or more of school	4.4	12.7	11.4
prenatal care began in 1st trimester	55.8	75.9	72.4
prenatal care began in 3rd trimester or no prenatal care	10.5	5.0	6.0
1980			
birth weight under 2,500 grams	12.49%	5.70%	6.84%
birth weight under 1,500 grams	2.44	0.90	1.15
mother under 18 years old	12.2	4.5	5.8
mother 18-19 years old	14.3	9.0	9.8
births to unmarried mothers	55.2	11.0	18.4
mother with less than 12 years of school	36.2	20.7	23.7
mother with 16 years or more of school	6.3	15.6	14.0
prenatal care began in 1st trimester	62.7	79.3	76.3
prenatal care began in 3rd trimester or no prenatal care	8.8	4.3	5.1

continued on the next page

Table 2.03 continued

	Black births	White births	births of All Races
1985			
birth weight under 2,500 grams	12.42%	5.64%	6.75%
birth weight under 1,500 grams	2.65	0.94	1.21
mother under 18 years old	10.3	3.7	4.7
mother 18-19 years old	12.7	7.1	8.0
births to unmarried mothers	60.1	14.5	22.0
mother with less than 12 years of school	32.3	17.8	20.6
mother with 16 years or more of school	7.1	18.7	16.7
prenatal care began in 1st trimester	61.8	79.4	76.2
prenatal care began in 3rd trimester or no prenatal care	10.0	4.7	5.7
1996			
birth weight under 2,500 grams	13.01%	6.34%	7.39%
birth weight under 1,500 grams	2.99	1.09	1.37
mother under 18 years old	10.3	4.2	5.1
mother 18-19 years old	12.5	7.2	7.9
births to unmarried mothers	69.8	25.7	32.4
mother with less than 12 years of school	28.2	21.6	22.4
mother with 16 years or more of school	10.0	23.9	22.1
prenatal care began in 1st trimester	71.4	84.0	81.9
prenatal care began in 3rd trimester or no prenatal care	7.3	3.3	4.0

SOURCE: U.S. Department of Health and Human Services, Health United States, 1998, p. 176, table 6, p. 177, table 7, p. 178, table 8, p. 179, table 9, p. 181, table 11. HE 20.6223:998

NOTES: Data based on race of the mother.

UNITS: Percent, as a percent of all live births, 100.0%.

Table 2.04 Lifetime Births Expected by Currently Married Women, Age 18-34 Years Old, by Age of the Woman, 1975 - 1992

	Black women	White women	women of All Races
Lifetime births expected by currently married women			
1975			
all women 18-34 years old	2.8	2.3	2.3
women 18-19 years old	na	2.2	2.2
women 20-21 years old	2.6	2.1	2.2
women 22-24 years old	2.5	2.1	2.2
women 25-29 years old	2.6	2.2	2.3
women 30-34 years old	3.2	2.6	2.6
1980			
all women 18-34 years old	2.4	2.2	2.2
women 18-19 years old	na	2.1	2.1
women 20-21 years old	2.2	2.2	2.2
women 22-24 years old	2.1	2.1	2.1
women 25-29 years old	2.4	2.1	2.2
women 30-34 years old	2.5	2.2	2.2
1985			
all women 18-34 years old	2.4	2.2	2.2
women 18-19 years old	na	2.0	2.1
women 20-21 years old	na	2.2	2.2
women 22-24 years old	2.3	2.2	2.2
women 25-29 years old	2.3	2.2	2.2
women 30-34 years old	2.5	2.1	2.2
1992			
all women 18-34 years old	2.4	2.2	2.2
women 18-19 years old	na	2.3	2.3
women 20-21 years old	na	2.3	2.3
women 22-24 years old	2.1	2.3	2.3
women 25-29 years old	2.4	2.3	2.3
women 30-34 years old	2.4	2.2	2.2

SOURCE: U.S. Department of Health and Human Services, Health United States, 1993, p. 67, table 6 (data from U.S. Bureau of the Census, *Current Population Reports*, series P-20). HE 20.6223:993

NOTES: 'Women of All Races' includes women of other races not shown separately.

UNITS: Expected births by currently married women in births expected per woman.

Table 2.05 Percent of Expected Lifetime Births Already Born to Currently Married Women 18-34 Years Old, by Age of the Woman, 1975 - 1992

	Black women	White women	women of All Races
Percent of expected lifetime births already born			
1975			
all women 18-34 years old	76.4%	68.2%	68.8%
women 18-19 years old	na	24.9	27.5
women 20-21 years old	43.3	29.4	30.7
women 22-24 years old	61.0	42.3	43.9
women 25-29 years old	78.2	70.5	70.9
women 30-34 years old	91.8	93.2	93.0
1980			
all women 18-34 years old	74.4%	66.3%	67.0%
women 18-19 years old	na	28.6	29.5
women 20-21 years old	46.1	31.8	32.9
women 22-24 years old	58.9	43.5	44.9
women 25-29 years old	73.8	64.0	64.7
women 30-34 years old	90.9	90.0	89.7
1985			
all women 18-34 years old	77.1%	63.3%	64.2%
women 18-19 years old	na	25.7	27.0
women 20-21 years old	na	30.6	30.9
women 22-24 years old	62.3	40.4	41.8
women 25-29 years old	72.8	59.4	60.2
women 30-34 years old	91.4	84.1	84.4
1992			
all women 18-34 years old	79.3%	65.4%	66.3%
women 18-19 years old	na	27.4	27.9
women 20-21 years old	na	33.6	36.1
women 22-24 years old	76.1	42.7	45.0
women 25-29 years old	73.3	58.1	59.4
women 30-34 years old	85.9	82.2	82.2

SOURCE: U.S. Department of Health and Human Services, Health United States, 1993, p. 67, table 6 (data from U.S. Bureau of the Census, *Current Population Reports*, series P-20). HE 20.6223:993

NOTES: 'Women of All Races' includes women of other races not shown separately.

UNITS: Percent of expected lifetime births already born to currently married woman.

Table 2.06 Projected Fertility Rates, Women 10-49 Years Old, 1997, 2010

	Black women	White women	women of All Races
1997			
Total fertility rate	2,428	1,992	2,063
birth rates			
10-14 years old	4.8	0.8	1.4
15-19 years old	110.1	50.9	59.6
20-24 years old	157.7	109.5	115.9
25-29 years old	112.6	119.0	118.1
30-34 years old	66.5	79.8	78.8
35-39 years old	27.7	31.5	31.6
40-44 years old	5.4	5.4	5.6
45-49 years old	0.3	0.2	0.3
2010			
Total fertility rate	2,438	2,046	2,108
birth rates			
10-14 years old	4.8	0.9	1.6
15-19 years old	111.5	56.0	63.6
20-24 years old	158.7	112.6	118.2
25-29 years old	113.1	120.7	119.5
30-34 years old	67.8	82.0	81.0
35-39 years old	27.7	31.7	32.1
40-44 years old	5.3	5.6	5.9
45-49 years old	0.2	0.2	0.3

SOURCE: U.S. Bureau of the Census, Statistical Abstract of the United States, 1998, p. 79, table 98. C 3.134:998

NOTES: 'All Races' includes women of other races not shown separately. The total fertility rate is the number of births that 1,000 women would have in their lifetime if, at each year of age they experienced the birth rates occurring in the specified year. A total fertility rate of 2,110 represents replacement level fertility for the total population under current mortality conditions (assuming no net immigration). Projections are based on middle fertility assumptions (1.8 births per woman)

UNITS: Total fertility rate and birth rate in births per 1,000 women.

Table 2.07 Abortions, 1973 - 1995

	Black	White	All Races
1973	42.0	32.6	19.6
1975	47.6	27.7	27.2
1980	54.3	33.2	35.9
1985	47.2	27.7	35.4
1987	50.0	26.7	35.6
1988	48.9	25.9	35.2
1989	49.6	25.2	34.6
1990	52.1	25.8	34.5
1991	50.2	24.6	33.9
1992	51.8	23.6	33.5
1993	55.2	23.1	33.4
1994	53.8	21.7	32.1
1995	53.4	20.4	31.1

SOURCE: U.S. Department of Health and Human Services, Health, United States, 1998, p. 185, table 15. HE 20.6223:998

NOTES: 'All Races' includes women of other races not shown separately. 1989 and later, "White" includes women of Hispanic ethnicity.

UNITS: Abortions per 100 live births.

Table 2.08 Contraceptive Usage for Women 15-44 Years of Age, by Method of Contraception, 1982 and 1995

	Black women	White women	women of All Races
1982			
all methods	52.0%	56.7%	55.7%
female sterilization	30.0	22.1	23.2
male sterilization	1.4*	12.2	10.9
birth control pill	38.0	26.7	28.0
intrauterine device	9.1	6.9	7.1
diaphragm	3.5	8.8	8.1
condom	6.2	12.7	12.0
1995			
all methods	61.5%	65.5%	64.2%
female sterilization	39.9	25.7	27.7
male sterilization	1.7	12.7	10.9
birth control pill	23.8	28.0	26.9
intrauterine device	0.8*	0.8	0.8
diaphragm	0.8*	2.1	1.9
condom	20.5	19.7	20.4

SOURCE: U.S. Department of Health and Human Services, Health United States, 1996-97, p. 96, table 18 (data from the National Survey of Family Growth). HE 20.6223:996

NOTES: 'Women of All Races' includes women of other races not shown separately. Data are based on household interviews of samples of women in the childbearing ages. * Relative standard error is greater than 30%.

UNITS: 'All methods' in percent of women using contraception; individual methods in percent, as a percent of all women using some form of contraception.

Table 2.09 Life Expectancy at Birth, by Sex, 1970 - 1996; Projections, 2000 - 2010

	Black		White		All Races	
	male	female	male	female	male	female
1970	60.0	68.3	68.0	75.6	67.1	74.7
1975	62.4	71.3	69.5	77.3	68.8	76.6
1980	63.8	72.5	70.7	78.1	70.0	77.4
1985	65.0	73.4	71.8	78.7	71.1	78.2
1990	64.5	73.6	72.7	79.4	71.8	78.8
1992	65.0	73.9	73.2	79.8	72.3	79.1
1994	64.9	74.1	73.2	79.6	72.3	79.0
1995	65.4	74.0	73.4	79.6	72.6	78.9
1996	66.1	74.2	73.8	79.6	73.0	79.0
2000	64.6	74.7	74.2	80.5	73.0	79.7
2005	64.5	75.0	74.7	81.0	73.5	80.2
2010	65.1	75.5	75.5	81.6	74.1	80.6

SOURCE: U.S. Bureau of the Census, Statistical Abstract of the United States, 1998, p. 94, table 128. C 3.134:998

NOTES: 'All Races' includes other races not shown separately. 1992 data, preliminary.

UNITS: Life expectancy in years.

Table 2.10 Life Expectancy, by Sex, by Age, 1995

	Black		White		All Races
	male	female	male	female	both sexes
at birth in 1990	65.2	73.9	73.4	79.6	75.8
age 10 in 1990	56.6	65.2	64.1	70.2	66.6
age 20 in 1990	47.2	55.4	54.5	60.4	56.9
age 30 in 1990	38.6	46.0	45.2	50.6	47.5
age 40 in 1990	30.5	36.9	36.1	41.0	38.3
age 50 in 1990	23.0	28.4	27.3	31.7	29.3
age 60 in 1990	16.4	20.6	19.3	23.0	21.1
age 70 in 1990	11.0	13.9	12.5	15.4	14.1
age 80 in 1990	6.8	8.4	7.2	8.9	8.3
age 85 and over in 1990	5.1	6.2	5.2	6.3	6.0

SOURCE: U.S. Bureau of the Census, Statistical Abstract of the United States, 1998, p. 95, table 130. C 3.134:998

NOTES: 'All Races' includes other races not shown separately.

UNITS: Life expectancy in years.

Table 2.11 Infant Mortality, Fetal Deaths, and Perinatal Mortality Rates, 1980, 1990 and 1996

	Black	White	All Races
1980			
infant mortality rate	22.2	10.9	12.6
neonatal mortality rates:			
- under 28 days	14.6	7.4	8.5
- under 7 days	12.3	6.1	7.1
post neonatal mortality rate	7.6	3.5	4.1
fetal death rate	14.7	8.1	9.1
late fetal death rate	9.1	5.7	6.2
perinatal mortality rate	21.3	11.8	13.2
1990			
infant mortality rate	18.0	7.6	9.2
neonatal mortality rates:			
- under 28 days	11.6	4.8	5.8
- under 7 days	9.7	3.9	4.8
post neonatal mortality rate	6.4	2.8	3.4
fetal death rate	13.3	6.4	7.5
late fetal death rate	6.7	3.8	4.3
perinatal mortality rate	16.4	7.7	9.1
1996			
infant mortality rate	14.7	6.1	7.3
neonatal mortality rates:			
- under 28 days	9.6	4.0	4.8
- under 7 days	7.8	3.2	3.8
post neonatal mortality rate	5.1	2.1	2.5
fetal death rate	12.5	5.9	6.9
late fetal death rate	5.5	3.3	3.6
perinatal mortality rate	13.3	6.4	7.4

SOURCE: U.S. Department of Health and Human Services, Health United States, 1998, p. 193, table 23. HE 20.6223:998

NOTES: 'All Races' includes other races not shown separately. Data based on race of the mother. Infant mortality rate is the number of deaths of infants under one year; neonatal deaths occur within 28 days of birth; post-neonatal deaths occur 28-365 days after birth; deaths within 7 days of birth are early neonatal deaths; fetal deaths are deaths of fetuses of more than 20 weeks gestation; late fetal deaths are deaths of fetuses of more than 28 weeks of gestation; perinatal mortality is the sum of late fetal deaths and infant deaths within the first 7 days of life.

UNITS: All rates per 1,000 live births, as shown.

Table 2.12 Death Rates, by Age and Sex, 1980 - 1996

	Black		White		All Races	
	male	female	male	female	male	female
1980						
All ages	1,034	733	983	806	977	785
under 1 year old	2,587	2,124	1,230	963	1,429	1,142
1-4 years old	111	84	66	49	73	55
5-14 years old	47	31	35	23	37	24
15-24 years old	209	71	167	56	172	58
25-34 years old	407	150	171	65	196	76
35-44 years old	690	324	257	138	299	159
45-54 years old	1,480	768	699	373	767	413
55-64 years old	2,873	1,561	1,729	876	1,815	934
65-74 years old	5,131	3,057	4,036	2,067	4,105	2,145
75-84 years old	9,232	6,212	8,830	5,402	8,817	5,440
85 years old and over	16,099	12,367	19,097	14,980	18,801	14,747
1985						
All ages	989	734	964	840	949	809
under 1 year old	2,220	1,821	1,057	799	1,220	951
1-4 years old	90	71	53	40	59	45
5-14 years old	42	29	30	20	32	21
15-24 years old	174	60	134	48	139	50
25-34 years old	352	138	159	59	180	69
35-44 years old	630	277	243	122	279	139
45-54 years old	1,293	668	612	342	672	375
55-64 years old	2,780	1,533	1,626	869	1,711	926
65-74 years old	5,172	2,968	3,771	2,027	3,856	2,097
75-84 years old	9,262	6,078	8,486	5,112	8,502	5,162
85 years old and over	15,774	12,703	18,980	14,745	18,614	14,554

continued on the next page

Table 2.12 continued

	Black male	Black female	White male	White female	All Races male	All Races female
1996						
All ages	940	752	923	899	900	852
under 1 year old	1,698	1,407	683	557	821	673
1-4 years old	73	63	37	28	43	34
5-14 years old	39	26	24	16	26	18
15-24 years old	235	67	115	43	132	46
25-34 years old	363	155	156	63	180	75
35-44 years old	632	317	263	123	301	146
45-54 years old	1,190	611	519	292	577	325
55-64 years old	2,397	1,311	1,314	784	1,397	831
65-74 years old	4,423	2,790	3,176	1,930	3,248	1,989
75-84 years old	8,588	5,766	7,230	4,840	7,271	4,879
85 years old and over	16,017	13,315	17,903	14,647	17,580	14,441

SOURCE: U.S. Bureau of the Census, Statistical Abstract of the United States, 1993, p. 87, table 119; 1998, p. 96, table 132. C 3.134:9(year)

NOTES: 'All Races' includes other races not shown separately. Rates are crude rates (**not** age adjusted). 1993 data based on a 10-percent sample of deaths.

UNITS: Rates per 100,000 of population in specified age groups, as shown.

Table 2.13 Deaths, by Selected Cause of Death, 1995

	Black	White	All Races
1995			
All causes	286.4	1,987.4	2,312.1
diseases of the heart	78.6	649.1	737.6
cancer	60.6	468.9	538.5
accidents and adverse effects	12.7	77.7	93.3
cerebrovascular diseases	18.5	136.5	158.0
chronic obstructive pulmonary diseases	6.7	95.1	102.9
pneumonia, flu	7.8	73.6	82.9
suicide	2.2	28.2	31.3
chronic liver disease, cirrhosis	3.1	21.4	25.2
diabetes mellitus	10.4	47.5	59.3
homicide and legal intervention	10.8	11.4	22.9

SOURCE: U.S. Bureau of the Census, Statistical Abstract of the United States, 1998, p. 102, table 140. C 3.134:998

NOTES: 'All Races' includes other races not shown separately.

UNITS: Deaths in thousands of persons.

Table 2.14 Maternal Mortality Rates, by Age of the Mother, 1970 - 1996

	Black mothers	White mothers	mothers of All Races
1970			
All ages, age adjusted rate	64.2	14.5	21.5
All ages, crude rate	59.8	14.4	21.5
women under 20 years old	31.8	13.9	18.9
women 20-24 years old	41.0	8.4	13.0
women 25-29 years old	63.8	11.2	17.0
women 30-34 years old	115.6	18.8	31.6
women 35 years old and over	204.7	59.6	81.9
1980			
All ages, age adjusted rate	24.0	7.0	9.6
All ages, crude rate	21.5	6.7	9.2
women under 20 years old	12.8	5.9	7.6
women 20-24 years old	13.4	4.3	5.8
women 25-29 years old	21.4	5.5	7.7
women 30-34 years old	41.9	9.4	13.6
women 35 years old and over	96.5	25.8	36.3
1985			
All ages, age adjusted rate	22.2	5.1	7.9
All ages, crude rate	20.4	5.2	7.8
women under 20 years old	12.1*	4.3*	6.9
women 20-24 years old	14.0	3.4	5.4
women 25-29 years old	18.4	4.7	6.4
women 30-34 years old	35.8	5.2	8.9
women 35 years old and over	72.6	17.8	25.0

continued on the next page

Table 2.14 continued

	Black mothers	White mothers	mothers of All Races
1989			
All ages, age adjusted rate	18.6	5.4	7.3
All ages, crude rate	18.4	5.6	7.9
women under 20 years old	7.0*	5.2*	5.8
women 20-24 years old	13.5	4.9	6.4
women 25-29 years old	17.9	4.8	6.7
women 30-34 years old	33.8	6.4	10.0
women 35 years old and over	57.5*	9.7	15.3
1990			
All ages, age adjusted rate	21.7	5.1	7.6
All ages, crude rate	22.4	5.4	8.2
women under 20 years old	12.0*	5.3*	7.5
women 20-24 years old	14.7	3.9	6.1
women 25-29 years old	14.9	4.8	6.0
women 30-34 years old	44.2	5.0	9.5
women 35 years old and over	79.7	12.6	20.7
1996			
All ages, age adjusted rate	19.9	4.1	6.4
All ages, crude rate	20.3	5.1	7.6
women under 20 years old	*	*	*
women 20-24 years old	15.1	*	5.0
women 25-29 years old	25.5	4.0	6.6
women 30-34 years old	28.6	5.0	7.6
women 35 years old and over	49.9	14.9	19.0

SOURCE: U.S. Department of Health and Human Services, Health United States, 1998, p. 245, table 45. HE 20.6223:998

NOTES: 'Mothers of All Races' include mothers of other races not show separately. Data for maternal mortality for complications of pregnancy, childbirth and the puerperium. Rates for women 35 years old and over computed by relating deaths to live births to women in this age group. *Indicates data based on fewer than 20 deaths.

UNITS: Rate is the number of deaths of mothers per 100,000 live births.

Table 2.15 Death Rates for Malignant Neoplasms of the Breast, for Females, by Age, 1970 - 1996

	Black women	White women	women of All Races
1970			
All ages, age adjusted rate	21.5	23.4	23.1
All ages, crude rate	19.7	29.9	28.4
under 25 years old	0.1*	0.0*	0.0*
25-34 years old	5.9	3.7	3.9
35-44 years old	24.4	20.2	20.4
45-54 years old	52.0	53.0	52.6
55-64 years old	64.7	79.3	77.6
65-74 years old	77.3	95.9	93.8
75-84 years old	101.8	129.6	127.4
85 years old and over	112.1	161.9	157.1
1980			
All ages, age adjusted rate	23.3	22.8	22.7
All ages, crude rate	22.9	32.3	30.6
under 25 years old	0.0*	0.0*	0.0*
25-34 years old	5.3	3.0	3.3
35-44 years old	24.1	17.3	17.9
45-54 years old	52.7	48.1	48.1
55-64 years old	79.9	81.3	80.5
65-74 years old	84.3	103.7	101.1
75-84 years old	114.1	128.4	126.4
85 years old and over	149.9	171.7	169.3

continued on the next page

Table 2.15 continued

	Black women	White women	women of All Races
1985			
All ages, age adjusted rate	25.3	23.3	23.2
All ages, crude rate	25.6	34.6	32.7
under 25 years old	0.1*	0.0*	0.0
25-34 years old	4.4	2.8	3.0
35-44 years old	26.3	16.7	17.5
45-54 years old	54.4	46.5	46.7
55-64 years old	88.5	84.2	83.6
65-74 years old	99.3	110.0	107.7
75-84 years old	121.0	140.4	137.7
85 years old and over	152.5	178.9	175.9
1996			
All ages, age adjusted rate	26.5	19.8	20.2
All ages, crude rate	29.9	33.3	31.8
35-44 years old	24.6	12.9	14.2
45-54 years old	59.1	36.9	38.8
55-64 years old	82.9	67.2	67.4
65-74 years old	109.9	99.8	99.1
75-84 years old	152.9	140.6	139.8
85 years old and over	206.9	207.1	204.9

SOURCE: U.S. Department of Health and Human Services, Health United States, 1995, p. 138, table 41; 1998, p. 238, table 42. HE 20.6223:(year)

NOTES: 'Women of All Races' includes women of other races not shown separately. Data excludes deaths of nonresidents of the United States. *Indicates data based on fewer than 20 deaths.

UNITS: Rate is the number of deaths per 100,000 resident female population, by age group.

Table 2.16 Death Rates for Motor Vehicle Accidents, by Sex and Age, 1993, 1996

	Black		White		All Races	
	male	female	male	female	both sexes	
1993						
All ages, age adjusted	25.3	8.5	22.5	9.7	16.0	
All ages, crude	24.6	8.7	22.7	10.3	16.3	
under 1 year	7.2	*	4.4	4.5	4.9	
1-4 years old	9.6	7.3	5.4	4.8	5.6	
5-14 years old	7.7	5.6	6.2	4.0	5.3	
15-24 years old	34.3	10.6	43.8	17.1	29.1	
25-34 years old	30.9	9.5	29.3	10.2	19.6	
35-44 years old	28.6	9.1	20.9	8.2	14.9	
45-54 years old	28.6	7.2	17.8	7.9	13.3	
55-64 years old	28.1	8.5	18.0	9.3	13.9	
65-74 years old	32.3	9.6	20.5	13.2	16.7	
75-84 years old	39.9	15.4	41.9	22.8	29.8	
85 years old and over	72.6	11.0	61.5	17.2	29.7	
	male	female	male	female	male	female
1996						
All ages, age adjusted	24.9	9.4	22.2	10.4	22.3	10.2
All ages, crude	24.3	9.5	22.4	11.0	22.4	10.7
under 1 year	7.6	7.8	5.2	5.7	5.7	5.8
1-14 years old	7.6	4.8	5.7	4.3	5.9	4.4
15-24 years old	35.2	13.3	42.2	18.1	40.7	17.1
25-34 years old	32.5	10.9	27.0	10.8	27.5	10.7
35-44 years old	26.6	9.6	21.4	9.3	21.8	9.4
45-64 years old	26.8	8.9	19.2	9.3	19.8	9.4
65 years old and over	35.6	13.1	31.1	17.4	31.4	17.2

SOURCE: U.S. Department of Health and Human Services, Health United States, 1998, pp. 246-248, table 46. HE 20.6223:998

NOTES: 'All Races' includes other races not shown separately. Excludes deaths of nonresidents of the United States. *Indicates data based on fewer than 20 deaths.

UNITS: Rate is the number of deaths per 100,000 resident population.

Table 2.17 Death Rates for Homicide and Legal Intervention, by Sex and Age, 1993, 1996

	Black		White		All Races	
	male	female	male	female	both sexes	
1993						
All ages, age adjusted	70.7	13.4	8.9	3.0	10.7	
All ages, crude	69.7	13.6	8.6	3.0	10.1	
under 1 year	23.9	18.1	7.0	5.9	8.8	
1-4 years old	9.6	7.7	2.2	1.4	2.9	
5-14 years old	6.6	3.6	1.3	1.0	1.8	
15-24 years old	167.0	22.0	17.1	4.2	23.4	
25-34 years old	116.5	25.2	14.4	4.7	17.4	
35-44 years old	72.6	15.5	10.1	3.7	11.1	
45-54 years old	45.4	7.3	7.8	2.5	7.2	
55-64 years old	27.9	4.9	5.2	1.9	4.7	
65-74 years old	24.5	6.9	3.6	2.1	3.7	
75-84 years old	22.9	10.3	3.1	2.4	3.5	
85 years old and over	26.9	11.5	4.0	2.8	4.1	
	male	female	male	female	male	female
1996						
All ages, age adjusted	52.6	10.2	7.3	2.5	13.3	3.6
All ages, crude	51.5	10.2	7.0	2.5	12.5	3.5
under 1 year	23.1	21.1	6.5	6.8	8.7	8.9
1-14 years old	4.8	3.9	1.4	1.1	1.9	1.6
15-24 years old	123.1	14.7	14.0	3.3	30.4	5.1
25-44 years old	71.0	15.8	9.9	3.3	17.3	5.0
45-64 years old	30.5	6.0	5.5	2.1	8.0	2.5
65 years old and over	15.6	5.2	3.2	1.8	4.1	2.1

SOURCE: U.S. Department of Health and Human Services, Health United States, 1998, pp. 250-252, table 47. HE 20.6223:998

NOTES: 'All Races' includes other races not shown separately. Excludes deaths of nonresidents of the United States. *Based on fewer than 20 deaths.

UNITS: Rate is the number of deaths per 100,000 resident population

Table 2.18 Death Rates for Suicide, by Sex and Age, 1993, 1996

	Black		White		All Races	
	male	female	male	female	both sexes	
1993						
All ages, age adjusted	12.9	2.1	19.7	4.6	11.3	
All ages, crude	12.5	2.1	21.4	5.0	12.1	
under 1 year	-	-	-	-	-	
1-4 years old	-	-	-	-	-	
5-14 years old	1.1	*	1.2	0.5	0.9	
15-24 years old	20.1	2.7	23.1	4.3	13.5	
25-34 years old	21.5	3.1	25.9	5.5	15.1	
35-44 years old	16.2	3.0	25.5	7.1	15.1	
45-54 years old	14.1	2.2	23.9	7.8	14.5	
55-64 years old	9.7	2.6	25.7	6.8	14.6	
65-74 years old	11.7	2.2	31.4	6.2	16.3	
75-84 years old	16.3	*	52.1	6.1	22.3	
85 years old and over	*	*	73.6	5.4	22.8	
	male	female	male	female	male	female
1996						
All ages, age adjusted	11.8	2.0	19.1	4.4	18.0	4.0
All ages, crude	11.4	2.0	20.9	4.8	19.3	4.4
15-24 years old	16.7	2.3	20.9	3.8	20.0	3.6
25-44 years old	17.8	2.9	25.7	6.4	24.3	5.8
45-64 years old	11.8	2.3	24.9	7.0	23.0	6.4
65 years old and over	12.6	2.1	37.8	5.0	35.2	4.8

SOURCE: U.S. Department of Health and Human Services, Health United States, 1998, pp. 253-255, table 48. HE 20.6223:998

NOTES: 'All Races' includes other races not shown separately. Excludes deaths of nonresidents of the United States. *Indicates data based on fewer than 20 deaths.

UNITS: Rate is the number of deaths per 100,000 resident population.

Table 2.19 AIDS (Acquired Immunodeficiency Syndrome) Cases, by Sex and Age, 1985 - 1997

	Black	White	All Races
All years*			
children under 13 years old	4,579	1,399	7,526
persons over 13 years old			
male	160,859	256,246	496,642
female	51,352	21,311	87,976
1985			
children under 13 years old	84	26	128
persons over 13 years old			
male	1,707	4,756	7,509
female	280	141	524
1990			
children under 13 years old	387	159	723
persons over 13 years old			
male	10,276	20,894	36,314
female	2,542	1,225	4,532
1992			
children under 13 years old	485	128	749
persons over 13 years old			
male	12,158	20,832	39,069
female	3,408	1,468	5,953
1993			
children under 13 years old	535	151	871
persons over 13 years old			
male	28,368	43,346	85,393
female	9,104	4,048	15,947

continued on the next page

Table 2.19 continued

	Black	White	All Races
1994			
children under 13 years old	633	143	972
persons over 13 years old			
male	22,471	29,556	62,935
female	7,861	3,090	13,330
1995			
children under 13 years old	483	117	747
persons over 13 years old			
male	21,027	26,260	57,231
female	7,637	3,067	13,061
1996			
children under 13 years old	427	96	656
persons over 13 years old			
male	20,144	23,270	52,781
female	8,119	2,875	13,222
1997 (January-June)			
children under 13 years old	178	35	266
persons over 13 years old			
male	9,656	9,164	23,336
female	4,083	1,327	6,551

SOURCE: U.S. Department of Health and Human Services, Health United States, 1998, p. 265, table 55 (data from Centers for Disease Control, Center for Infectious Diseases, Division of HIV/AIDS. HE 20.6223:998

NOTES: 'All Races' includes other races not shown separately. 'Black' excludes Black hispanics, 'White' excludes white hispanics. Data excludes residents of U.S. Territories. Historic data is revised continually on an ongoing basis. Data for all years have been updated through June 30, 1997. *'All years' includes cases prior to 1985.

UNITS: Number of cases known to the Centers for Disease Control, by year of report.

Table 2.20 Death rates for Human Immunodeficiency Virus (HIV) infection, 1987 - 1996

	Black		White		All Races	
	male	female	male	female	male	female
1987	25.4	4.7	8.4	0.6	10.0	1.1
1988	31.6	6.2	10.0	0.7	12.1	1.4
1989	40.3	8.1	13.2	0.9	15.8	1.8
1990	44.2	9.9	15.0	1.1	17.7	2.1
1991	52.9	12.0	16.7	1.3	20.1	2.7
1992	61.8	14.3	18.1	1.6	22.3	3.2
1993	70.0	17.3	19.0	1.9	24.1	3.8
1994	81.7	21.8	20.1	2.3	26.4	4.8
1995	84.3	24.0	19.6	2.5	26.2	5.2
1996	66.4	20.2	12.5	1.8	18.1	4.2

SOURCE: U.S. Department of Health and Human Services, Health United States, 1998, p. 243, table 44 (data from Centers for Disease Control and Prevention, National Center for Health Statistics. HE 20.6223:998

NOTES: 'All Races' includes other races not shown separately. 'Black' excludes Black hispanics, 'White' excludes white hispanics. Data excludes residents of U.S. Territories.

UNITS: Number of deaths known to the Centers for Disease Control, by year of report.

Table 2.21 AIDS (Acquired Immunodeficiency Syndrome) Cases, by Transmission Category, 1985 - 1996

	Black	White	All Races
All years*, all transmission categories	212,211	277,557	584,618
men who have sex with men	61,844	193,985	295,355
injecting drug use	81,025	32,092	144,567
men who have sex with men and injecting drug use	12,239	20,377	37,514
hemophilia/coagulation disorder	529	3,531	4,508
heterosexual contact	28,931	12,206	50,356
heterosexual contact with injecting drug user	11,979	5,068	21,114
transfusion	2,054	4,774	7,860
undetermined	25,589	10,592	44,458
1985, all transmission categories	1,987	4,897	8,033
men who have sex with men	785	3,983	5,357
injecting drug use	740	246	1,387
men who have sex with men and injecting drug use	161	409	655
hemophilia/coagulation disorder	5	59	71
heterosexual contact	91	33	151
heterosexual contact with injecting drug user	65	18	107
transfusion	30	125	166
undetermined	175	42	246

continued on the next page

Table 2.21 continued

	Black	White	All Races
1990, all transmission categories	12,818	22,119	40,846
men who have sex with men	4,481	16,589	23,826
injecting drug use	5,172	2,059	9,280
men who have sex with men and injecting drug use	900	1,562	2,804
hemophilia/coagulation disorder	34	280	348
heterosexual contact	1,224	650	2,261
heterosexual contact with injecting drug user	857	352	1,495
transfusion	170	512	788
undetermined	837	467	1,539
1996, all transmission categories	28,263	26,145	66,003
men who have sex with men	6,846	16,349	27,316
injecting drug use	9,312	3,692	16,405
men who have sex with men and injecting drug use	1,085	1,517	3,044
hemophilia/coagulation disorder	66	211	321
heterosexual contact	5,226	1,856	8,609
heterosexual contact with injecting drug user	1,522	633	2,647
transfusion	225	221	548
undetermined	5,503	2,245	9,760

SOURCE: U.S. Department of Health and Human Services, Health United States, 1998, p. 266, table 56 (data from Centers for Disease Control, Center for Infectious Diseases, Division of HIV/AIDS.Prevention) HE 20.6223:998

NOTES: 'All Races' includes other races not shown separately. 'Black' excludes Black hispanics, 'White' excludes White hispanics. Data excludes cases of residents of U.S. Territories. 'Heterosexual' includes persons who have had heterosexual contact with a person with HIV infection or at risk of HIV infection. Data are updated through June 30, 1997. *'All years' includes cases prior to 1985.

UNITS: Number of cases for persons 13 years of age and over at diagnosis known to the Centers for Disease Control, by year of report.

Table 2.22 Vaccinations of children 19-35 Months of Age for Selected Diseases, 1996

	Black	White	All Races
1996			
combined series (4:3:1:3)	74%	79%	77%
DTP (4 doses or more)	79	83	81
Polio (3 doses or more)	90	92	91
Measles-containing	89	92	91
Hib (3 doses or more)	90	93	92
Hepatitus B (3 doses or more)	82	82	82

SOURCE: U.S. Department of Health and Human Services, Health United States, 1998, p. 261, table 52 (Centers for Disease Control and Prevention, National Center for Health Statistics and National Immunization Program. Data from the National Immunization Survey) HE 20.6223:993

NOTES: 'All Races' includes other races not shown separately. 'Black' excludes Black hispanics, 'White' excludes White hispanics. Data excludes cases of residents of U.S. Territories.
The 4:3:1:3 combined series consists of 4 doses of diphtheria-tetanus-pertussis (DTP) vaccine, 3 doses of polio vaccine, 1 dose of a measles-containing vaccine, and 3 doses of Haemophilus influenzae type b (Hib) vaccine.
DTP is the Diphtheria-tetanus-pertussis vaccine.
Hib is the Haemophilus influenzae type b (Hib) vaccine.

UNITS: Percent of children 19-35 months of age.

Table 2.23 Five Year Relative Cancer Survival Rates for Selected Cancer Sites, 1989 - 1994

	Black		White	
	male	female	male	female
1989 - 1994				
All cancer sites	45.1%	48.8%	60.0%	63.1%
prostrate gland	81.2	-	95.1	-
lung and bronchus	9.7	13.9	13.0	16.5
breast	-	70.6	-	86.7
colon	51.4	53.1	64.6	63.1
rectum	53.3	53.2	61.0	61.6
corpus uteri	-	54.4	-	86.5
ovary	-	46.3	-	50.1
cervix uteri	-	59.0	-	71.5
urinary bladder	66.5	-	86.3	-
oral cavity and pharynx	27.4	-	52.0	-
stomach	20.5	-	16.1	-
esophagus	8.2	-	12.5	-
leukemia	27.5	-	45.3	-
non-Hodgkin's lymphoma	37.3	46.9	48.5	57.3
pancreas	3.3	4.0	3.7	4.2
melanoma of skin	-	77.3	-	91.2

SOURCE: U.S. Department of Health and Human Services, Health United States, 1998, p. 270, table 59; (data from National Cancer Institute, National Institutes of Health, Cancer Statistics Branch.) HE 20.6223:998

NOTES: 'All Races' includes other races not shown separately. Data are based on the Surveillance, Epidemiology, and End Results program's population-based registries in Atlanta, Detroit, Seattle-Puget Sound, San Francisco-Oakland, Connecticut, Iowa, New Mexico, Utah, and Hawaii. Rates are based on follow-up of patients through 1995.

UNITS: The five year cancer relative survival rate is the ratio of the observed survival rate for the patient group to the expected survival rate for persons in the general population similar to the patient group with respect to age, sex, race, and calendar year of observation. It estimates the chance of surviving cancer. Percent of patients surviving is shown.

Table 2.24 Current Cigarette Smoking by Persons 18 Years Old and Older, by Sex and Age, 1995

	Black		White		All Races	
	male	female	male	female	male	female
1995						
18 years old and over, age adjusted	28.5%	22.8%	26.4%	23.6%	26.7%	22.8%
18 years old and over, crude	28.5	23.5	26.6	23.1	27.0	22.6
18-24 years old	14.6	8.8	28.4	24.9	27.8	21.8
25-34 years old	25.1	26.7	29.9	27.3	29.5	26.4
35-44 years old	36.3	31.9	31.2	27.0	31.5	27.1
45-64 years old	33.9	27.5	26.3	24.3	27.1	24.0
65 years old and over	28.5	13.3	14.1	11.7	14.9	11.5

SOURCE: U.S. Department of Health and Human Services, Health United States, 1998, p. 273, table 62 (data from the National Health Interview Survey). HE 20.6223:998

NOTES: 'All Races' includes other races not shown separately.

UNITS: Percent as a percent of total U.S. civilian non-institutionalized population, 100.0%.

Table 2.25 Current Cigarette Smoking by Persons 25 Years Old and Older, by Sex and Education, 1995

	Black	White	All Races
1995			
All males	31.4%	26.0%	26.4%
less than 12 years	41.4	38.8	39.7
12 years	36.4	32.7	32.6
13-15 years	26.4	23.6	24.0
16 or more years	16.9*	13.4	13.9
All females	25.7%	23.3%	23.0%
less than 12 years	31.6	33.1	32.1
12 years	27.9	26.7	26.3
13-15 years	21.0	22.5	22.0
16 or more years	18.0*	13.5	13.3

SOURCE: U.S. Department of Health and Human Services, Health United States, 1998, p. 274, table 63 (data from the National Health Interview Survey). HE 20.6223:998

NOTES: 'All Races' includes other races not shown separately. *Small sample size--data may be unreliable

UNITS: Percent as a percent of total U.S. civilian non-institutionalized population, 100.0%.

Table 2.26 Current Users of Cigarettes, Alcohol, Marijuana, and Cocaine, by Age, 1996

	Black	White	All Races
1996			
Cigarettes			
persons 12-17 years old	12%	21%	18%
Alcohol			
persons 12-17 years old	15	20	19
persons 18-25 years old	50	65	60
Marijuana			
persons 12-17 years old	7	7	7
persons 18-25 years old	14	14	13
Cocaine			
persons 12-17 years old	0.1	0.5	0.6
persons 18-25 years old	1.1	2.3	2.0

SOURCE: U.S. Department of Health and Human Services, Health United States, 1998, pp. 275-276, table 64 HE 20.6223:998

NOTES: 'All Races' includes other races not shown separately. Both 'Black' and 'White"exclude hispanic persons.

UNITS: Percent as a percent of population by age.

Table 2.27 Limitation of Activity Caused by Chronic Health Conditions, 1983, 1987, 1990 and 1995

	Black	White	All Races
1983			
Total with any limitation of activity	17.5%	13.4%	13.8%
persons limited, but not in a major activity	3.8	4.2	4.1
persons limited in amount or kind of major activity	7.5	5.9	6.0
persons unable to carry on an activity	6.2	3.3	3.6
1987			
Total with any limitation of activity	16.0%	12.7%	12.9%
persons limited, but not in a major activity	3.5	4.1	4.0
persons limited in amount or kind of major activity	6.2	5.2	5.2
persons unable to carry on an activity	6.2	3.4	3.7

continued on the next page

Table 2.27 continued

	Black	White	All Races
1990			
Total with any limitation of activity	15.5%	12.8%	12.9%
persons limited, but not in a major activity	3.8	4.2	4.1
persons limited in amount or kind of major activity	5.3	5.0	5.0
persons unable to carry on an activity	6.5	3.6	3.9
1995			
Total with any limitation of activity	15.9%	14.8%	14.7%
persons limited, but not in a major activity	3.7	4.9	4.6
persons limited in amount or kind of major activity	5.8	5.5	5.5
persons unable to carry on an activity	6.3	4.4	4.6

SOURCE: U.S. Department of Health and Human Services, Health United States, 1988, p. 93, table 48 (data from the National Health Interview Survey). HE 20.6223:988

U.S. Department of Health and Human Services, Vital and Health Statistics, Series 10, #173, p. 108, table 67 (data from the National Health Interview Survey). HE 20.6209/4:988

U.S. Department of Health and Human Services, Vital and Health Statistics, Series 10, #176, p. 200, table 59 (data from the National Health Interview Survey). HE 20.6209/4:990

U.S. Department of Health and Human Services, Vital and Health Statistics, Series 10, #199, p. 101, table 67 (data from the National Health Interview Survey). HE 20.6209/4:998

NOTES: 'All Races' includes other races not shown separately. Each person identified by the National Health Interview Survey as having a chronic condition (a chronic condition is one lasting three months or more: a health condition is a departure from a state of physical or mental well being) is classified to the extent according to which his or her activities are limited because of the condition. A major activity is the principal activity of a person or of his or her sex-age group. For persons 1-5 years of age, it refers to ordinary play with other children; for persons 6-16 years of age it refers to school attendance; for persons 17 years of age and over, it usually refers to a job, housework, or school attendance.

UNITS: Percent as a percent of the civilian non-institutionalized population.

Table 2.28 Selected Characteristics of Persons With a Work Disability, 1997

	Black	White	All Races
Persons with a work disability by age			
Total	3,456	13,293	17,439
persons 16-24 years old	341	955	1,390
persons 25-34 years old	612	1,916	2,622
persons 35-44 years old	907	3,024	4,075
persons 45-54 years old	785	3,419	4,368
persons 55-64 years old	811	3,980	4,983
Work disabled as a percent of total population, by age			
Total	16.2%	9.4%	10.2%
persons 16-24 years old	6.9	3.6	4.2
persons 25-34 years old	11.4	5.9	6.5
persons 35-44 years old	16.8	8.3	9.3
persons 45-54 years old	22.3	12.2	13.2
persons 55-64 years old	37.4	21.6	23.1
Percent of work disabled:			
receiving Social Security Income	26.5%	31.6%	30.3%
receiving Food Stamps	36.9	19.9	23.6
covered by Medicaid	49.0	30.4	34.7
residing in public housing	14.4	4.9	7.0
residing in subsidized housing	6.6	2.5	3.4

SOURCE: U.S. Bureau of the Census, Statistical Abstract of the United States, 1998, p. 388, table 622 (data from the Current Population Survey). C 3.134:998

NOTES: 'All Races' includes other races not shown separately. Covers the civilian noninstitutional population and members of the armed forces living off post or with members of their families on post. Persons are classified as having a work disability if they (1) have a health problem or disability which prevents them from or which limits the kind or amount of work they can do; (2) have a service disability or ever retired or left a job for health reasons; (3) did not work in survey reference week or previous year because of long-term illness or disability; or, (4) are under age 65 and are covered by Medicare or receive Supplemental Security Income.

UNITS: Persons with a work disability in thousands of persons; work disabled as a percent of total population in percent; percent of the work disabled by characteristic as a percent of the work disabled.

Table 2.29 Work-Loss Days Associated With an Acute Condition, by Type of Condition, 1985, 1989 and 1995

	Black	White	All Races
1985			
All acute conditions	426.5	297.3	309.6
infective and parasitic diseases	16.3*	26.3	24.7
respiratory conditions	135.8	106.3	108.0
digestive system conditions	31.1*	16.8	18.4
injuries	166.1	98.0	104.4
all other acute conditions	77.2*	49.8	54.1
1989			
All acute conditions	480.8	316.1	336.5
infective and parasitic diseases	24.6	19.0	20.0
respiratory conditions	130.2	125.5	126.3
digestive system conditions	18.8*	8.2	10.5
injuries	210.0	94.4	106.5
all other acute conditions	97.3*	58.6	73.2
1995			
All acute conditions	308.0	279.1	284.5
infective and parasitic diseases	31.4*	19.1	21.3
respiratory conditions	107.0	107.6	107.8
digestive system conditions	31.4*	15.1	16.8
injuries	71.9	77.8	78.8
all other acute conditions	17.3*	20.6	19.9

SOURCE: U.S. Department of Health and Human Services, Vital and Health Statistics, Series 10, #160, p. 55, table 36; p. 57, table 38 (data from the National Health Interview Survey). HE 20.6209/4:985
U.S. Department of Health and Human Services, Vital and Health Statistics, Series 10, #176, p. 56, table 58 (data from the National Health Interview Survey). HE 20.6209/4:990
U.S. Department of Health and Human Services, Vital and Health Statistics, Series 10, #199, p. 50, table 36, and p. 52, table 38 (data from the National Health Interview Survey). HE 20.6209/4:998

NOTES: 'All Races' includes other races not shown separately. Covers the civilian noninstitutional population. *Figure does not meet standard of reliability or precision.

UNITS: Number of work-loss days per 100 persons 18 years old and over, currently employed.

Table 2.30 School-Loss Days Associated With an Acute Condition, by Type of Condition, 1985, 1989 and 1995

	Black	White	All Races
1985			
All acute conditions	339.8	399.7	386.9
infective and parasitic diseases	125.7	91.3	93.9
respiratory conditions	143.7	229.2	215.6
digestive system conditions	16.6*	12.1*	12.9*
injuries	27.6*	22.9	23.6
all other acute conditions	26.3*	44.0*	40.8*
1989			
All acute conditions	373.5	489.4	463.5
infective and parasitic diseases	71.3	102.6	95.7
respiratory conditions	198.6	305.6	280.9
digestive system conditions	19.3*	10.6	12.3
injuries	27.8*	21.9	22.0
all other acute conditions	56.5*	48.8*	52.6*
1995			
All acute conditions	273.4	338.2	323.2
infective and parasitic diseases	39.2*	66.0	59.5
respiratory conditions	179.6	195.5	191.7
digestive system conditions	12.6*	9.4*	9.8*
injuries	24.4*	28.1	26.6
all other acute conditions	1.0*	8.4*	6.9*

SOURCE: U.S. Department of Health and Human Services, Vital and Health Statistics, Series 10, #160, p. 65, table 46 (data from the National Health Interview Survey). HE 20.6209/4:985
U.S. Department of Health and Human Services, Vital and Health Statistics, Series 10, #176, p. 66, table 61 (data from the National Health Interview Survey). HE 20.6209/4:990
U.S. Department of Health and Human Services, Vital and Health Statistics, Series 10, #199, p. 60, table 46 (data from the National Health Interview Survey). HE 20.6209/4:998

NOTES: 'All Races' includes other races not shown separately. Covers the civilian noninstitutional population and members of the armed forces living off post or with members of their families on post. * Figure does not meet standard of reliability or precision.

UNITS: Number of school-loss days per 100 persons 5-17 years old.

Table 2.31 Injuries, by Selected Characteristic, 1989 and 1995

	Black	White	All Races
1989			
All episodes of injury	23.2	24.3	23.8
involving a motor vehicle	3.4	2.1	2.2
happened while at work	6.3	6.2	6.1
by place of occurrence			
- at home	6.1	7.5	7.2
- on a street or highway	4.8	3.2	3.4
- at an industrial place	4.0	3.4	3.4
- other	4.3	6.2	5.9
1995			
All episodes of injury	17.7	24.6	23.4
involving a motor vehicle	1.4*	1.5	1.4
happened while at work	3.1*	4.2	4.1
by place of occurrence			
- at home	4.2	7.4	6.9
- on a street or highway	1.7*	2.7	2.6
- at an industrial place	1.8*	1.9	1.8
- other	5.2	6.6	6.4

SOURCE: U.S. Department of Health and Human Services, Vital and Health Statistics, Series 10, #176, p. 71, table 63 (data from the National Health Interview Survey). HE 20.6209/4:990
U.S. Department of Health and Human Services, Vital and Health Statistics, Series 10, #199, p. 65, table 51 (data from the National Health Interview Survey). HE 20.6209/4:998

NOTES: 'All Races' includes other races not shown separately. Covers the civilian noninstitutional population and members of the armed forces living off post or with members of their families on post. Figure does not meet standard of reliability or precision.

UNITS: Number of episodes of injuries per 100 persons per year.

Table 2.32 Restricted Activity Days, 1970 - 1995

	total number of days			days per person		
	Black	White	All Races	Black	White	All Races
1970	365	2,526	2,913	16.2	14.4	14.6
1980	580	3,518	4,165	22.7	18.7	19.1
1985	489	2,899	3,453	17.4	14.5	14.8
1988	487	2,969	3,536	16.6	14.6	14.7
1989	511	3,087	6,693	17.1	15.0	15.2
1992	586	3,384	4,096	18.6	16.2	16.3
1994	608	3,375	4,143	18.4	15.7	16.0
1995	558	3,392	4,097	17.0	15.6	15.6

SOURCE: U.S. Bureau of the Census, Statistical Abstract of the United States, 1988, p. 105, table 166 (data from the National Health Interview Survey). C 3.134:988

U.S. Department of Health and Human Services, Vital and Health Statistics, Series 10, #173, p. 112, table 69 (data from the National Health Interview Survey). HE 20.6209/4:988

U.S. Department of Health and Human Services, Vital and Health Statistics, Series 10, #176, p. 111, table 69 (data from the National Health Interview Survey). HE 20.6209/4:990

U.S. Department of Health and Human Services, Vital and Health Statistics, Series 10, #179, p. 111, table 69 (data from the National Health Interview Survey). HE 20.6209/4:992

U.S. Department of Health and Human Services, Vital and Health Statistics, Series 10, #193, p. 109, table 69 (data from the National Health Interview Survey). HE 20.6209/4:995

U.S. Department of Health and Human Services, Vital and Health Statistics, Series 10, #199, p. 105, table 69 (data from the National Health Interview Survey). HE 20.6209/4:998

NOTES: 'All Races' includes other races not shown separately. A restricted activity day is a day when a person cuts down on his or her usual activities for the whole day because of illness or injury. Restricted activity days include bed disability days, work-loss days, and school loss days.

UNITS: Total number of days in thousands of days; days per person.

Table 2.33 Personal Health Practices, 1990

	Black	White	All Races
Persons who:			
eat breakfast	46.9%	57.8%	56.4%
rarely snacks	22.7	25.8	25.5
exercised regularly	34.3	41.5	40.7
had 2 or more drinks on any day during the past 2 weeks	4.3	5.8	5.5
are current smokers	26.2	25.6	25.5
are 20% or more above their desireable weight	38.0	26.7	27.5

SOURCE: U.S. Bureau of the Census, Statistical Abstract of the United States, 1993, p. 139, table 213 (data from the National Health Interview Survey). C 3.134:993

NOTES: 'All Races' includes other races not shown separately. Includes persons whose health practices are unknown. Weight data are self-reported.

UNITS: Percent of persons 18 years of age and over.

Table 2.34 Characteristics of Physicians Visits, 1984 and 1995

	Black	White	All Races
Physician visits by site of visit			
1984			
all physicians visits (per person)	4.8	5.1	5.0
- at doctor's offices	43.9%	57.6%	56.0%
- at hospital outpatient department	25.4	12.8	14.3
- by telephone	10.2	15.8	15.1
- home	2.2	1.5	1.6
- other	18.4	12.3	13.1
1995			
all physicians visits (per person)	100.0%	100.0%	100.0%
- at doctor's offices	48.3%	58.0%	56.6%
- at hospital outpatient department	19.5	11.5	12.6
- by telephone	10.1	14.0	13.5
- home	3.3	3.2	3.2
- other	18.8	13.2	14.1
Interval since last physician visit			
1984			
less than one year	75.2%	76.1%	75.7%
1 year to 2 years	12.3	10.6	10.9
2 years or more	12.6	13.3	13.3
1995			
less than one year	80.6	79.6	79.5
1 year to 2 years	9.7	9.4	9.5
2 years or more	9.6	10.9	11.0

SOURCE: U.S. Department of Health and Human Services, Health United States, 1990, pp. 137-138, tables 67-68; 1998, p. 288, table 75, p. 290, table 77 (data from the National Health Interview Survey). HE 20.6223:(year)

NOTES: 'All Races' includes other races not shown separately. 'Hospital outpatient department' includes outpatient clinics and emergency rooms; 'other' includes clinics and places outside a hospital. '2 years or more' includes persons who never visited a physician.

UNITS: Physicians visits in visits per person; data by place of visit as a percent of all visits to physicians; interval since last physician visit as a percent of the population. All visits per person, are age-adjusted.

Table 2.35 Dental Visits by Persons 25 Years Old and Older, by Education, 1990 and 1993

	Black	White	All Races
1990			
Total	49.1	64.9	62.3
Education:			
less than 12 years	37.9	41.8	41.2
12 years	51.1	62.8	61.3
13 years or more	64.4	77.3	75.7
1993			
Total	47.3	64.0	60.8
Education:			
less than 12 years	33.1	41.2	38.0
12 years	48.2	60.4	58.7
13 years or more	61.3	75.8	73.8

SOURCE: U.S. Department of Health and Human Services, Health United States, 1995, p. 196, table 81 (data from the National Health Interview Survey). HE 20.6223:95

NOTES: 'All Races' includes other races not shown separately. 'Black' excludes Black hispanics, 'White' excludes white hispanics. Data excludes residents of U.S. Territories.

UNITS: Percent of the civilian noninstitutionalized population with a dental visit within the past year.

Table 2.36 Short Stay Hospitals: Discharges, Days of Care, Average Length of Stay, 1981, 1987, 1989, 1995

	Black	White	All Races
1981			
discharges	137.7	120.0	121.7
days of care	1,302.4	912.5	952.1
average length of stay	9.5	7.6	7.8
1987			
discharges	117.4	94.8	96.5
days of care	942.8	621.5	649.7
average length of stay	8.0	6.6	6.7
1989			
discharges	112.0	89.5	91.0
days of care	875.9	580.9	607.1
average length of stay	7.8	6.5	6.7
1995			
discharges	108.0	84.2	86.2
days of care	730.9	458.5	486.3
average length of stay	6.8	5.4	5.6

SOURCE: U.S. Department of Health and Human Services, Health United States, 1988, p. 111, table 66; 1991, p. 224, table 81; 1998, p. 302, table 87 (data from the National Health Interview Survey). HE 20.6223:(year)

NOTES: 'All Races' includes other races not shown separately. Data **are** age adjusted.

UNITS: Discharges and days of care in number per 1,000 population; average length of stay, in average number of days.

Table 2.37 Self-Assessment of Health, 1983, 1987, 1990, 1995

	Black	White	All Races
Self-assessment of health			
1983			
excellent	28.5%	42.6%	40.7%
very good	21.8	25.8	25.4
good	30.0	22.1	23.2
fair or poor	19.7	9.6	10.7
1987			
excellent	29.5%	42.1%	40.3%
very good	24.4	28.2	27.8
good	29.4	21.1	22.4
fair or poor	16.7	8.5	9.5
1990			
excellent	31.1%	42.1%	40.5%
very good	25.3	29.0	28.5
good	28.5	20.8	22.0
fair or poor	15.1	8.1	8.9
1995			
fair or poor	15.4%	8.7%	9.4%

SOURCE: U.S. Department of Health and Human Services, Health United States, 1988, p. 95, table 50; 1991, p. 202, table 61; 1992, p. 101, table 63, 1998, p. 272, table 61 (data from the National Health Interview Survey). HE 20.6223:(year)

U.S. Department of Health and Human Services, Vital and Health Statistics, Series 10, #173, p. 114, table 70 (data from the National Health Interview Survey). HE 20.6209/4:988

NOTES: 'All Races' includes other races not shown separately. Data **are** age-adjusted.

UNITS: Percent of the population.

Table 2.38 Nursing Home and Personal Care Home Residency, by Age, 1977, 1985 and 1995

	residents			residency rate		
	Black	White	All Races	Black	White	All Races
1977						
persons of all ages	61	1,060	1,126	30.7	48.9	47.1
persons 65-74 years old	22	188	211	17.6	14.2	14.4
persons 75-84 years old	20	443	465	33.4	67.0	64.0
persons 85 years old and older	19	429	450	133.6	234.2	225.9
1985						
persons of all ages	82	1,227	1,318	35.0	47.7	46.2
persons 65-74 years old	23	188	212	15.4	12.3	12.5
persons 75-84 years old	31	474	509	45.3	59.1	57.7
persons 85 years old and older	29	566	597	141.5	228.7	220.3
1995						
persons 65-74 years old	30	154	190	18.4	9.3	10.1
persons 75-84 years old	47	454	512	57.2	44.9	45.9
persons 85 years old and older	46	663	720	167.1	200.7	198.6

SOURCE: U.S. Department of Health and Human Services, Health United States, 1987, p. 119, table 69; 1996-97, p. 223, table 93. HE 20.6223:(year)

NOTES: 'All Races' includes other races not shown separately. 1977 data includes domiciliary care homes. A nursing home is an establishment with three or more beds that provides nursing or personal care to the aged, infirm, or chronically ill. A personal care home without nursing has no residents receiving nursing care. These homes provide administration of medications and treatments in accordance with physicians' orders, supervision of self-administered medications or three or more personal services. A domiciliary care home provides supervisory care and one or two personal services.

UNITS: Residents in thousands of persons; residency rate, residents per 1,000 population.

Table 2.39 Health Care Coverage for Persons Under 65 Years of Age, by Type of Coverage, 1984 - 1996

	Black	White	All Races
1984			
Private insurance	58.3%	79.7%	76.6%
Private insurance obtained through workplace	52.4	71.9	68.9
Medicaid or other public assistance	20.5	5.0	7.3
not covered	19.5	13.3	14.2
1993			
private insurance	51.0%	75.1%	71.3%
private insurance obtained through workplace	48.0	68.8	65.3
Medicaid or public assistance	26.4	8.1	11.1
not covered	21.1	15.6	16.5
1996			
private insurance	54.9%	74.2%	76.6%
private insurance obtained through workplace	51.8	67.6	64.8
Medicaid or other public assistance	24.5	9.3	11.7
not covered	19.0	15.4	16.1

SOURCE: U.S. Department of Health and Human Services, Health United States, 1998, pp. 361-362, table 133 (data from the National Health Interview Survey). HE 20.6223:98

NOTES: 'All Races' includes other races not shown separately. Medicaid includes persons receiving AFDC (Aid to Families with Dependent Children) or SSI (Supplemental Security Income), or those with a current medicaid card. Not covered includes those persons not covered by private insurance, Medicaid, Medicare, and military plans. Data are age-adjusted.

UNITS: Percent of the population.

Table 2.40 Health Care Coverage for Persons 65 Years of Age and Over, by Type of Coverage, 1984 - 1996

	Black	White	All Races
1984			
Private insurance	42.3%	76.8%	73.5%
Private insurance obtained through workplace	24.0	40.9	39.1
Medicaid or other public assistance	24.9	5.0	6.9
Medicare only	30.7	16.5	17.7
1993			
Private insurance	45.0%	80.9	77.3%
Private insurance obtained through workplace	25.7	42.7	40.9
Medicaid or other public assistance	20.5	5.6	7.4
Medicare only	29.9	12.4	14.0
1996			
Private insurance	44.0%	75.3%	72.0%
Private insurance obtained through worplace	30.1	39.8	38.6
Medicaid or other public assistance	21.8	6.6	8.3
Medicare only	30.1	16.9	18.1

SOURCE: U.S. Department of Health and Human Services, Health United States, 1998, pp. 363-364, table 134 (data from the National Health Interview Survey). HE 20.6223:98

NOTES: 'All Races' includes other races not shown separately. Medicaid includes persons receiving AFDC (Aid to Families with Dependent Children) or SSI (Supplemental Security Income), or those with a current medicaid card. Not covered includes those persons not covered by private insurance, Medicaid, Medicare, and military plans. Data are age-adjusted.

UNITS: Percent of the population.

Chapter 3: Education

Table 3.01 School Enrollment, by Age, 1985, 1991, 1996

	enrollment			enrollment rate		
	Black	White	All Races	Black	White	All Races
1985						
all persons 3-34 years old	8.4	47.5	58.0	50.9%	47.8%	48.3%
persons 3 and 4 years old	0.5	2.3	2.8	42.7	38.6	38.9
persons 5 and 6 years old	1.0	5.4	6.7	95.7	96.4	96.1
persons 7-13 years old	3.5	18.5	22.8	99.1	99.3	99.2
persons 14 and 15 years old	1.1	6.0	7.4	97.9	98.1	98.1
persons 16 and 17 years old	1.0	5.4	6.7	91.7	91.6	91.7
persons 18 and 19 years old	0.5	3.1	3.7	44.1	52.4	51.6
persons 20 and 21 years old	0.3	2.3	2.7	27.7	36.1	35.3
persons 22-24 years old	0.2	1.7	2.1	13.7	17.0	16.9
persons 25-29 years old	0.2	1.6	1.9	7.4	9.2	9.2
persons 30-34 years old	0.1	1.0	1.2	5.1	6.2	6.1
persons 35 years old and older	0.2	1.5	1.8	1.9	1.7	1.7
1991						
all persons 3-34 years old	9,031	49,156	61,276	52.5%	50.0%	50.7%
persons 3 and 4 years old	428	2,502	3,068	37.2	41.3	40.5
persons 5 and 6 years old	1,108	5,727	7,178	95.8	95.3	95.4
persons 7-9 years old	1,664	8,825	11,022	99.6	99.6	99.6
persons 10-13 years old	2,277	11,500	14,423	100.0	99.7	99.7
persons 14 and 15 years old	1,032	5,311	6,634	99.1	98.7	98.8
persons 16 and 17 years old	959	4,902	6,155	91.7	93.3	93.3
persons 18 and 19 years old	578	3,197	3,969	55.6	59.7	59.6
persons 20 and 21 years old	329	2,517	3,041	30.0	43.2	42.0
persons 22-24 years old	249	1,910	2,365	18.2	21.7	22.2
persons 25-29 years old	229	1,646	2,045	8.7	9.9	10.2
persons 30-34 years old	177	1,119	1,377	6.5	6.0	6.2
persons 35 years old and over	289	2,219	2,620	2.5	2.2	2.2

continued on the next page

Table 3.01 continued

	enrollment			enrollment rate		
	Black	White	All Races	Black	White	All Races
1996						
all persons 3-34 years old	10,443	52,987	67,317	56.2%	53.4%	54.1%
persons 3 and 4 years old	687	3,052	3,959	49.9	47.9	48.3
persons 5 and 6 years old	1,233	6,215	7,893	90.5	94.8	94.0
persons 7-9 years old	1,895	9,042	11,577	97.4	97.1	97.2
persons 10-13 years old	2,431	12,133	15,359	97.4	98.2	98.1
persons 14 and 15 years old	1,197	5,997	7,598	98.9	98.0	98.0
persons 16 and 17 years old	1,151	5,680	7,220	92.1	92.8	92.8
persons 18 and 19 years old	613	3,645	4,539	52.8	62.5	61.5
persons 20 and 21 years old	389	2,428	3,017	37.0	44.9	44.4
persons 22-24 years old	300	2,070	2,605	21.0	24.6	24.8
persons 25-29 years old	349	1,741	2,265	13.7	11.3	11.9
persons 30-34 years old	197	984	1,286	7.1	5.7	6.1
persons 35 years old and over	408	2,392	2,979	3.0	2.2	2.3

SOURCE: U.S. Bureau of the Census, Statistical Abstract of the United States, 1988, p. 122, table 196 (data from *Current Population Reports*, Series P-20). C 3.134:(year)
U.S. Bureau of the Census, Current Population Reports: School Enrollment-Social and Economic Characteristics of Students: October 1991, Series P-20, #469, pp. 1-2, table 1; C3.186/12:99(year) October, 1996(Update), #500, pp. 1-2, table 1, <ww.census.gov/prod/3/98pubs/p20-500u.pdf>, accessed 15 October 1998.

NOTES: 'All Races' includes other races not shown separately.

UNITS: 1985 data: Enrollment in millions of persons enrolled; 1991 & 1996 data: enrollment in thousands of persons enrolled. All years: rate as a percent of the civilian non-institutionalized population, by age group.

Table 3.02 School Enrollment, by Level and Control of School, 1985, 1991, 1996

	Black	White	All Races
1985			
Total enrolled	8,444	47,452	58,014
nursery school	332	2,087	2,491
public	212	617	854
private	120	1,470	1,637
kindergarten	625	3,060	3,815
public	562	2,545	3,221
private	63	515	594
elementary school	4,307	21,593	26,866
public	4,131	18,817	23,803
private	175	2,776	3,063
high school	2,131	11,378	13,979
public	2,068	10,258	12,764
private	63	1,120	1,215
college	1,049	9,334	10,863
public	860	7,131	8,379
private	190	2,203	2,483
1991			
Total enrolled	9,031	49,156	61,276
nursery school	360	2,447	2,933
public	244	810	1,094
private	177	1,637	1,839
kindergarten	676	3,274	4,152
public	598	2,766	3,531
private	79	508	621
elementary school	4,672	23,547	29,591
public	4,445	20,948	26,632
private	229	2,599	2,958
high school	2,100	10,309	13,010
public	2,044	9,467	12,069
private	56	841	945
college	1,220	9,579	11,589
public	1,004	7,464	9,078
private	217	2,118	2,511
college full time	900	6,919	8,461

continued on the next page

Table 3.02 continued

	Black	White	All Races
1996			
Total enrolled	8,870	42,971	54,762
public	8,123	36,483	47,203
private	746	6,489	7,559
nursery school	702	3,284	4,212
public	459	1,314	1,868
private	243	1,969	2,344
kindergarten	634	3,163	4,034
public	545	2,596	3,353
private	89	567	680
elementary school	5,156	24,667	31,467
public	4,839	21,763	28,116
private	317	2,905	3,351
high school	2,378	11,857	15,049
public	2,281	10,809	13,865
private	97	1,048	1,184

SOURCE: U.S. Bureau of the Census, Current Population Reports: School Enrollment-Social and Economic Characteristics of Students: October 1988 and 1987, Series P-20, #443, pp. 166-167, table A2; October 1991, Series P-20, #469, pp. A2-A5, Table A-1; October, 1996(Update), #500, p. 21, table 5. C3.186/12:(year)

NOTES: 'All Races' includes other races not shown separately.

UNITS: Enrollment in thousands of persons enrolled; civilian non-institutionalized population.

Table 3.03 Preprimary School Enrollment of Children 3 - 5 Years Old, by Selected Characteristic of the Mother, 1996

	Black	White	All Races
1996			
All children 3 and 4 years old enrolled in nursery school	615	2,847	3,655
with mother in labor force	438	1,828	2,385
- mother employed	376	1,745	2,236
- employed full time	302	1,091	1,465
with mother with 0-8 years of school	3	95	99
with mother high school graduate	172	734	956
with mother with bachelor's degree	90	856	1,031
All children 3 and 4 years old enrolled in kindergarten	72	205	304
with mother in labor force	48	106	170
- mother employed	34	102	151
- employed full time	26	67	108
with mother with 0-8 years of school	-	24	24
with mother high school graduate	18	49	75
with mother with bachelor's degree	2	34	39

continued on the next page

Table 3.03 continued

	Black	White	All Races
All children 5 years old enrolled in nursery school	76	382	492
with mother in labor force	49	225	303
- mother employed	35	212	275
- employed full time	27	149	199
with mother with 0-8 years of school	3	26	33
with mother high school graduate	19	117	150
with mother with bachelor's degree	6	78	90
All children 5 years old enrolled in kindergarten	481	2,469	3,129
with mother in labor force	318	1,526	1,964
- mother employed	277	1,451	1,835
- employed full time	236	937	1,245
with mother with 0-8 years of school	9	127	142
with mother high school graduate	148	710	889
with mother with bachelor's degree	32	525	612

SOURCE: U.S. Bureau of the Census, Current Population Reports: School Enrollment-Social and Economic Characteristics of Students: October 1996(Update), Series P-20, #500, pp. 15-18, table 4. <ww.census.gov/prod/3/98pubs/p20-500u.pdf>, accessed 15 October 1998.

NOTES: 'All Races' includes other races not shown separately. Includes children enrolled in public and non-public nursery school and kindergarten programs. Excludes five year olds enrolled in elementary school. 'All children' includes children whose mothers' labor force status is unknown and children with no mother present in the household.

UNITS: Enrollment in thousands of children enrolled.

Table 3.04 Estimates of the School Age Population, 1975 - 1996

	Black	White	All Races
1975			
Total	7,199	42,950	51,044
male	3,611	21,956	26,022
female	3,588	20,994	25,022
1980			
Total	6,989	39,002	47,232
male	3,520	19,982	24,135
female	3,469	19,020	23,097
1985			
Total	6,729	36,393	44,782
male	3,400	18,679	22,927
female	3,329	17,714	21,855
1990			
Total	6,916	36,320	45,307
male	3,501	18,667	23,225
female	3,415	17,653	22,082
1996			
Total	7,770	39,431	49,762
male	3,949	20,276	25,534
female	3,820	19,154	24,229

SOURCE: U.S. Department of Education, Center for Education Statistics, Digest of Education Statistics, 1997, p. 23 table 16 (data from U.S. Bureau of the Census, *Current Population Reports*, Series P-25). ED 1.113\997

NOTES: 'All Races' includes other races not shown separately. Some data have been revised from previously published figures.

UNITS: Estimates of the civilian non-institutionalized population, 5-17 years old as of July 1, in thousands of persons.

Table 3.05 Enrollment in Public Elementary and Secondary Schools, by State, Fall, 1996

	Black	White	All Races
Alabama	36.4%	61.5%	100.0%
Alaska	4.7	63.1	"
Arizona	4.3	56.6	"
Arkansas	23.5	73.5	"
California	8.7	39.5	"
Colorado	5.5	72.0	"
Connecticut	13.6	71.7	"
Delaware	29.9	63.9	"
District of Columbia	87.3	4.0	"
Florida	25.4	56.7	"
Georgia	37.6	57.9	"
Hawaii	3.3	25.0	"
Idaho	0.7	88.0	"
Illinois	21.2	62.8	"
Indiana	11.2	85.4	"
Iowa	3.4	92.2	"
Kansas	8.6	81.9	"
Kentucky	9.9	88.9	"
Louisiana	46.4	50.6	"
Maine	0.9	97.2	"
Maryland	35.6	56.7	"
Massachusetts	8.4	77.9	"
Michigan	18.8	75.8	"
Minnesota	5.2	86.5	"
Mississippi	51.0	47.9	"
Missouri	16.5	81.1	"
Montana	0.6	87.2	"
Nebraska	6.0	86.4	"
Nevada	9.6	65.1	"
New Hampshire	1.0	96.4	"
New Jersey	na	na	"

continued on the next page

Table 3.05 continued

	Black	White	All Races
New Mexico	2.4%	38.8%	100.0%
New York	20.3	56.3	"
North Carolina	30.8	63.9	"
North Dakota	0.9	89.1	"
Ohio	15.4	82.0	"
Oklahoma	10.5	68.8	"
Oregon	2.6	84.6	"
Pennsylvania	14.2	80.2	"
Rhode Island	7.3	78.3	"
South Carolina	42.2	56.0	"
South Dakota	1.0	83.7	"
Tennessee	23.4	74.6	"
Texas	14.3	45.6	"
Utah	0.7	89.5	"
Vermont	0.8	97.3	"
Virginia	25.5	67.7	"
Washington	4.8	77.5	"
West Virginia	4.0	95.2	"
Wisconsin	9.6	82.6	"
Wyoming	1.2	89.0	"

SOURCE: U.S. Department of Education, Center for Education Statistics, Digest of Education Statistics, 1998, p. 11, table 45. ED 1.113\998

NOTES: 'All Races' includes other races not shown separately. Both 'Black' and 'White' exclude persons of Hispanic origin.

UNITS: Enrollment as a percent of total enrollment, 100.0%.

Table 3.06 Public Elementary and Secondary School Teachers, by Selected Characteristic, 1993-94

	Black	White	All Races
Total number of teachers	188,371	2,216,605	2,561,294
Percent of teachers, by highest degree earned			
no degree	0.5%	0.5%	0.6%
associate degree	0.2	0.1	0.2
bachelor's degree	48.4	51.8	52.0
master's degree	44.6	42.5	42.0
education specialist	5.4	4.4	4.6
doctor's	0.9	0.7	0.7
Percent of teachers, by years of full-time teaching experience			
less than 3 years	8.5%	9.4%	9.7%
3-9 years	20.9	25.5	25.5
10-20 years	35.6	35.2	35.0
over 20 years	35.3	30.0	29.8

SOURCE: U.S. Department of Education, Center for Education Statistics, Digest of Education Statistics, 1995, p. 77, table 66 (data from U.S. Department of Educations, National Center for Education Statististics, *Schools and Staffing Survey, 1993-94*). ED 1.113\995

NOTES: 'All Races' includes other races not shown separately. Both 'Black' and 'White' exclude persons of Hispanic origin.

UNITS: Percent, as a percent of all public elementary and secondary school teachers, 100.0%.

Table 3.07 Private Elementary and Secondary School Teachers, by Selected Characteristic, 1993-94

	Black	White	All Races
Total number of teachers	11,664	347,811	378,365
Percent of teachers, by highest degree earned			
no degree	8.3%	4.8%	5.2%
associate degree	3.7	1.3	1.5
bachelor's degree	55.8	59.4	59.0
master's degree	26.4	30.2	29.8
education specialist	4.8	2.6	2.9
doctor's	1.0	1.6	1.7
Percent of teachers, by years of full-time teaching experience			
less than 3 years	26.9%	20.4%	20.9%
3-9 years	34.9	33.6	33.9
10-20 years	27.9	30.0	29.6
over 20 years	10.3	16.0	15.6

SOURCE: U.S. Department of Education, Center for Education Statistics, Digest of Education Statistics, 1995, p. 77, table 66 (data from U.S. Department of Educations, National Center for Education Statististics, *Schools and Staffing Survey, 1993-94*). ED 1.113\995

NOTES: 'All Races' includes other races not shown separately. Both 'Black' and 'White' exclude persons of Hispanic origin.

UNITS: Percent, as a percent of all private elementary and secondary school teachers, 100.0%.

Table 3.08 Student Achievement: Reading and Writing Performance on Standardized Tests, 1984, 1990 and 1996

	Black	White	All Races
Reading			
1984			
students age 9	185.7	218.2	210.9
students age 13	236.3	262.6	257.1
students age 17	264.3	295.2	288.8
1990			
students age 9	181.8	217.0	209.2
students age 13	241.5	262.3	256.8
students age 17	267.3	296.6	290.2
1996			
students age 9	190.0	219.9	212.4
students age 13	235.6	267.0	259.1
students age 17	265.4	294.4	286.9
Writing			
1984			
students grade 4	181.6	210.7	203.8
students grade 8	247.1	271.7	266.7
students grade 11	270.3	296.8	289.7
1990			
students grade 4	171.4	211.0	201.7
students grade 8	239.0	262.1	256.6
students grade 11	268.2	292.8	287.1
1996			
students grade 4	182	216	207
students grade 8	242	271	264
students grade 11	267	289	283

SOURCE: U.S. Department of Education, Center for Education Statistics, Digest of Education Statistics, 1997, table 107, p. 114; table 113, p. 120. ED 1.113:997

NOTES: 'All Races' includes other races not shown separately.

UNITS: Reading level shown as scale score on scale: 150=rudimentary, 200=basic, 250=intermediate, 300=adept, 350=advanced. Writing level shown as score on scale: 100=unsatisfactory, 200=minimal, 300=adequate, 400=elaborate.

Table 3.09 Student Achievement: Math and Science Proficiency, 1986, 1990 and 1996

	Black	White	All Races
Average mathematics proficiency			
1986			
students age 9	201.6	226.9	221.7
students age 13	249.2	273.6	269.0
students age 17	278.6	307.5	302.0
1990			
students age 9	208.4	235.2	229.6
students age 13	249.1	276.3	270.4
students age 17	288.5	309.5	304.6
1996			
students age 9	212	237	231
students age 13	252	281	274
students age 17	286	313	307
Average science proficiency			
1986			
students age 9	196.2	231.9	224.3
students age 13	221.6	259.2	251.4
students age 17	252.8	297.5	288.5
1990			
students age 9	196.4	237.5	228.7
students age 13	225.7	264.1	255.2
students age 17	253.0	300.9	290.4
1996			
students age 9	201	239	230
students age 13	226	266	256
students age 17	260	307	296

SOURCE: U.S. Department of Education, Center for Education Statistics, Digest of Education Statistics, 1997, table 118, p. 123; table 126, p. 131. ED 1.113:997

NOTES: 'All Races' includes other races not shown separately.

UNITS: Math proficiency scale: 150=performs simple addition and subtraction, 200= use basic operations to solve simple problems, 250=uses intermediate level mathematics skills to solve two-step problems, 300=understands measurement and geometry and solves more complex problems, 350= understands and applies more advanced mathematical concepts. Percent, percentage of students taking this level of mathematics course.

Table 3.10 Expected Occupations of 12th Graders at Age 30, 1992

	Black	White	All Races
Expected occupation at age 30			
craftsperson or operator	3.4%	3.7%	3.5%
farmer or farm manager	0.6	1.0	0.9
housewife/homemaker	0.4	1.2	1.0
laborer or farm worker	0.3	0.7	0.7
military, police or security officer	7.7	6.4	6.6
professional, business or managerial	55.1	50.0	50.8
teacher	3.7	8.4	7.5
business owner	6.8	5.6	6.0
technical	5.5	5.0	5.4
salesperson, clerical or office worker	5.3	4.6	4.8
service worker	3.1	2.3	2.4
other employment	8.0	10.8	10.2
don't know	0.2	0.2	0.2

SOURCE: U.S. Department of Education, Center for Education Statistics, Digest of Education Statistics, 1994, p. 136, table 140 (data from the National Educational Longitudinal Study 1988, Second Followup). ED 1.113:994

NOTES: 'All Races' includes other races not shown separately.

UNITS: Percent of 10th graders as a percent of all 10th graders, by race.

Table 3.11 Testing: Students Taking the SAT (Scholastic Aptitude Test), and the ACT (American College Testing Program), 1975 - 1997

	Black	White	All Races
1975			
SAT	7.9%	86.0%	100.0%
ACT	7.0	77.0	100.0
1980			
SAT	9.1%	82.1%	100.0%
ACT	8.0	83.0	100.0
1985			
SAT	7.5%	81.0%	100.0%
ACT	8.0	82.0	100.0
1990			
SAT	10.0%	73.4%	100.0%
ACT	9.0	79.0	100.0
1993			
SAT	10.8%	70.4%	100.0%
ACT	9.0	80.0	100.0
1994			
SAT	10.8%	69.4%	100.0%
ACT	9.0	79.0	100.0
1995			
SAT	10.7%	69.2%	100.0%
ACT	9.0	80.0	100.0
1996			
SAT	10.8%	68.7%	100.0%
ACT	9.0	80.0	100.0
1997			
SAT	10.8%	68.0%	100.0%
ACT	10.0	74.0	100.0

SOURCE: U.S. Bureau of the Census, Statistical Abstract of the United States, 1998, p. 183, tables 290 and 291 (data from College Entrance Examination Board, and American College Testing Program, *High School Profile Report*). C 3.134:998

NOTES: 'All Races' includes other races not shown separately. Beginning 1985, ACT data is for seniors who graduated in the year shown and had taken the ACT in their junior or senior years.

UNITS: Percent, as a percent of all students taking the respective tests, 100.0%.

Table 3.12 SAT (Scholastic Aptitude Test) Scores, 1975 - 1995

	Black	White	All Races
1975-1976			
SAT-Scholastic Aptitude Test			
verbal score	332	451	431
math score	354	493	472
1980-1981			
SAT-Scholastic Aptitude Test			
verbal score	332	442	424
math score	362	483	466
1989-1990			
SAT-Scholastic Aptitude Test			
verbal score	352	442	424
math score	385	491	476
1990-1991			
SAT-Scholastic Aptitude Test			
verbal score	351	441	422
math score	385	489	474
1991-1992			
SAT-Scholastic Aptitude Test			
verbal score	352	442	423
math score	385	491	476
1993-1994			
SAT-Scholastic Aptitude Test			
verbal score	352	443	423
math score	388	495	479
1994-1995			
SAT-Scholastic Aptitude Test			
verbal score	356	448	428
math score	388	498	482

SOURCE: U.S. Department of Education, Center for Education Statistics, Digest of Education Statistics, 1996, p. 127, table 126. ED 1.113:996

NOTES: 'All races' includes other races not shown separately.

UNITS: Average scores, (minimum score, 200; maximum score 800).

Table 3.13 Labor Force Status of 1997 High School Graduates and 1996-97 High School Dropouts, October 1997

	Black	White	Total
1997 high school graduates			
total	193	1,337	1,590
employed	140	1,168	1,362
unemployed	53	169	228
not in labor force	201	891	1,179
1996-97 high school dropouts			
total	41	250	302
employed	18	199	225
unemployed	22	51	77
not in labor force	49	136	200

SOURCE: U.S. Department Labor, Bureau Labor Statistics; "Employment Characteristics of Families, 1997 (Table) 1. Labor force status of 1997 high school graduates and 1996-97 high school dropouts 16 to 24 years old by school enrollment, sex, race, and Hispanic origin"; (accessed: 19 November 1998); <http://stats.bls.gov/news.release/hsgec.t01.htm>

NOTES: 'High school dropouts' refers to persons who dopped out of school between October 1995 and October 1996.

UNITS: Number of persons in thousands of persons.

Table 3.14 High School Dropout Rates, Grades 10-12, by Sex, 1975 - 1994

	Black		White		All Races	
	male	female	male	female	male	female
1975	8.3%	9.0%	5.0%	5.8%	5.4%	6.2%
1980	8.0	8.5	6.4	4.9	6.6	5.4
1981	9.4	10.2	5.6	4.9	6.0	5.8
1982	9.0	6.5	5.3	4.9	5.7	5.1
1983	7.0	6.8	5.4	4.2	5.7	4.6
1984	6.2	5.3	5.3	4.6	5.4	4.7
1985	8.3	7.2	3.0	4.5	5.4	5.0
1986	4.8	4.6	4.2	4.1	4.3	4.2
1987	6.2	6.4	4.1	3.4	4.4	3.8
1988	6.7	6.0	5.1	4.3	5.2	4.5
1989	6.9	8.6	4.1	3.8	4.5	4.5
1990	4.1	6.0	4.1	3.5	4.1	3.9
1991	5.5	7.0	3.6	3.8	3.8	4.3
1992	3.3	6.7	3.8	4.4	3.8	4.8
1993	5.8	4.9	4.1	4.1	4.4	4.1
1994	6.5	5.7	4.6	4.9	4.9	5.1

SOURCE: U.S. Bureau of the Census, Current Population Reports: School Enrollment-Social and Economic Characteristics of Students: October 1994, Series P-20, #487, pp. A25-27, table A-4. C3.186/12:994

NOTES: 'All Races' includes other races not shown separately.

UNITS: Dropout rate as a percent of all persons enrolled in grades 10-12.

Table 3.15 College Enrollment This Year, by Enrollment Status Last Year, by Age, October 1996

	Black	White	All Races
All persons 15 years old and over			
Not enrolled in college in 1996			
total	15,179	123,402	144,450
not enrolled in 1994	14,428	118,462	138,469
enrolled in 1994	752	4,941	5,981
Enrolled in college in 1996			
total	1,869	12,109	15,098
not enrolled in 1994	499	2,540	3,212
enrolled in 1994	1,369	9,569	11,886
enrolled full time in 1996			
total	1,159	7,805	9,761
not enrolled in 1994	212	1,000	1,302
enrolled in 1994	947	6,805	8,459
Persons 15-19 years old			
Not enrolled in college in 1996			
total	395	1,523	1,994
not enrolled in 1994	202	784	1,020
enrolled in 1994	193	739	974
Enrolled in college in 1996			
total	379	2,855	3,483
not enrolled in 1994	52	272	332
enrolled in 1994	327	2,583	3,151
enrolled full time in 1996			
total	327	2,551	3,101
not enrolled in 1994	37	204	248
enrolled in 1994	290	2,347	2,853

continued on the next page

Table 3.15 continued

	Black	White	All Races
Persons 20-24 years old			
Not enrolled in college in 1996			
total	1,382	7,623	9,467
not enrolled in 1994	1,199	6,234	7,798
enrolled in 1994	183	1,389	1,669
Enrolled in college in 1996			
total	629	4,384	5,440
not enrolled in 1994	137	664	850
enrolled in 1994	492	3,719	4,591
enrolled full time in 1996			
total	516	3,571	4,433
not enrolled in 1994	104	405	539
enrolled in 1994	411	3,166	3,894
Persons 25 years old and over			
Not enrolled in college in 1996			
total	13,402	114,257	132,990
not enrolled in 1994	13,027	111,444	129,652
enrolled in 1994	376	2,813	3,338
Enrolled in college in 1996			
total	860	4,870	6,174
not enrolled in 1994	310	1,603	2,030
enrolled in 1994	551	3,267	4,144
enrolled full time in 1996			
total	316	1,683	2,227
not enrolled in 1994	71	391	515
enrolled in 1994	246	1,292	1,712

SOURCE: U.S. Bureau of the Census, Current Population Reports: School Enrollment-Social and Economic Characteristics of Students: October 1996(Update), Series P-20, #500u, pp. 73-75, table 18. <www.census.gov/prod/3/98pubs/p20-500u.pdf>, accessed 15 October 1998.

NOTES: 'All Races' includes other races not shown separately. College in enrollment at the undergraduate level in two and four year institutions.

UNITS: College enrollment in thousands of students.

Table 3.16 Enrollment in Institutions of Higher Education, by Type of Institution, 1980 - 1995

	Black	White	All Races
1980			
All institutions	1,107	9,883	12,087
4-year institutions	634	6,275	7,565
2-year institutions	472	3,558	4,521
1986			
All institutions	1,081	9,915	12,501
4-year institutions	615	6,340	7,826
2-year institutions	466	3,575	4,675
1988			
All institutions	1,130	10,283	13,043
4-year institutions	656	6,582	8,175
2-year institutions	473	3,702	4,868
1990			
All institutions	1,223	10,675	13,710
4-year institutions	715	6,757	8,529
2-year institutions	509	3,918	5,181
1992			
All institutions	1,392.9	10,875.4	14,487.4
4-year institutions	791.2	6,744.3	8,765.0
2-year institutions	601.6	4,131.2	5,722.4
1995 (preliminary)			
All institutions	3,496.2	10,311.2	14,261.8
4-year institutions	1,885.8	6,517.2	8,769.3
2-year institutions	1,610.4	3,794.0	5,492.5

SOURCE: U.S. Department of Education, Center for Education Statistics, Condition of Education, 1993, p. 345, table 44-1. ED 1.109:993
U.S. Department of Education, Center for Education Statistics, Digest of Education Statistics, 1997, p. 214, table 206. ED 1.113:997

NOTES: 'All Races' includes other races not shown separately. Both 'Black' and 'White' exclude persons of Hispanic origin.

UNITS: Enrollment in thousands of students enrolled.

Table 3.17 Enrollment in Institutions of Higher Education, by State, Fall, 1996

	Black	White	All Races
UNITED STATES	1,499,439	10,226,034	14,300,255
Alabama	52,334	157,161	219,846
Alaska	1,058	22,369	28,499
Arizona	9,243	200,429	276,832
Arkansas	15,287	80,089	100,688
California	143,885	922,781	1,882,634
Colorado	8,311	193,944	242,949
Connecticut	11,864	123,344	155,361
Delaware	6,357	35,287	44,838
District of Columbia	22,420	35,897	74,239
Florida	87,889	418,043	641,173
Georgia	80,696	214,549	317,999
Hawaii	1,285	16,394	61,383
Idaho	383	54,827	59,904
Illinois	92,070	504,144	720,987
Indiana	17,799	246,370	286,326
Iowa	4,996	156,705	177,021
Kansas	8,155	145,757	172,350
Kentucky	12,416	158,077	177,749
Louisiana	53,664	133,455	203,517
Maine	402	52,887	55,645
Maryland	58,514	170,259	260,757
Massachusetts	23,372	316,804	410,327
Michigan	60,497	436,671	546,974
Minnesota	7,624	243,962	275,262
Mississippi	38,396	83,659	126,234
Missouri	25,930	243,600	290,533
Montana	144	37,389	43,145
Nebraska	3,458	107,274	119,300
Nevada	4,396	55,008	73,467
New Hampshire	915	60,068	64,463

continued on the next page

Table 3.17 continued

	Black	White	All Races
New Jersey	38,804	223,256	328,188
New Mexico	2,568	57,323	103,546
New York	137,124	672,311	1,027,870
North Carolina	74,808	275,630	373,168
North Dakota	339	35,916	40,554
Ohio	51,225	448,218	537,535
Oklahoma	12,848	133,516	177,255
Oregon	2,784	138,104	165,168
Pennsylvania	52,118	518,526	621,994
Rhode Island	3,185	60,722	72,432
South Carolina	40,371	126,593	174,303
South Dakota	288	31,431	35,373
Tennessee	36,841	198,139	247,043
Texas	94,758	582,317	955,439
Utah	912	136,543	151,637
Vermont	366	32,762	35,090
Virginia	58,191	260,077	353,788
Washington	10,735	231,505	292,180
West Virginia	3,572	78,727	85,689
Wisconsin	12,863	264,203	299,127
Wyoming	276	27,976	30,805

SOURCE: U.S. Department of Education, Center for Education Statistics, Digest of Education Statistics, 1998, p. 259, table 210. ED 1.113\998

NOTES: 'All Races' includes other races not shown separately. Both 'White' and 'Black' exclude Hispanic.

UNITS: Enrollment in number of students enrolled.

Table 3.18 Enrollment Rates of 18 - 24 Year Olds in Institutions of Higher Education, 1975 - 1996

	Black	White	All Races
Enrollment as a percent of 18-24 year olds			
1975	20.4%	27.4%	26.3%
1980	19.4	27.3	25.7
1981	19.9	27.7	26.2
1983	19.2	28.0	26.2
1984	20.3	28.9	27.1
1986	21.9	29.7	27.9
1987	23.0	31.9	29.7
1988	21.1	33.1	30.2
1990	25.3	35.2	32.1
1991	23.4	36.8	33.3
1992	25.2	37.3	34.4
1993	24.5	36.8	34.0
1994	27.7	38.1	34.6
1995	27.5	37.9	34.3
1996	27.4	39.5	35.5
Enrollment as a percent of high school graduates			
1975	31.5%	32.3%	32.5%
1980	27.6	32.1	31.8
1981	28.0	32.7	32.5
1983	27.0	33.0	32.5
1984	27.2	34.0	33.2
1985	26.0	34.9	33.7
1986	28.6	34.5	34.0
1987	30.0	37.5	36.4
1988	28.0	38.6	37.2
1990	30.4	39.2	37.7
1991	28.2	41.0	39.3
1992	33.9	42.8	42.0
1993	32.8	42.6	41.6
1994	35.6	43.7	42.3
1995	35.4	44.0	42.3
1996	35.9	45.1	43.4

Source: U.S. Department of Education, Center for Education Statistics, Digest of Education Statistics, 1997 p. 196, table 186. ED 1.113\997

NOTES: 'All Races' includes other races not shown separately. Both 'White' and 'Black' exclude Hispanic.

UNITS: Percent as a percent of 18-24 year olds, and high school graduates as shown, 100.0%.

Table 3.19 Enrollment of Persons 14 - 34 Years Old in Institutions of Higher Education, by Sex, 1975 - 1996

	enrollment			percent distribution		
	Black	White	All Races	Black	White	All Races
1975						
Total	927	8,141	9,697	9.6%	84.0%	100.0%
men	433	4,566	5,342	4.5	47.1	55.1
women	494	3,576	4,355	5.1	36.9	44.9
1980						
Total	996	8,453	10,181	9.8%	83.0%	100.0%
men	431	4,225	5,193	4.2	41.5	51.0
women	565	4,228	5,244	5.5	41.5	49.0
1985						
Total	1,036	8,781	10,863	9.5%	80.0%	100.0%
men	458	4,361	5,345	4.2	40.1	49.2
women	578	4,420	5,518	5.3	40.7	50.8
1990						
Total	1,167	8,892	11,303	10.3%	78.7%	100.0%
men	508	4,289	na	4.5	38.0	na
women	659	4,594	na	5.8	40.6	na
1993						
Total	1,227	8,592	11,409	10.8%	75.3%	100.0%
men	515	4,168	na	4.5	36.5	na
women	713	4,424	na	6.2	38.8	na
1996						
Total	1,513	8,943	12,448	12.2%	71.8%	100.0%
men	633	4,222	na	5.1	33.9	na
women	879	4,721	na	7.1	37.9	na

SOURCE: U.S. Department of Education, Center for Education Statistics, Digest of Education Statistics, 1997, p. 221, table 212. ED 1.113\997

NOTES: 'All Races' includes other races not shown separately. Both 'White' and 'Black' exclude Hispanic.

UNITS: Enrollment in thousands of students enrolled; percent as a percentage of 14-34 year olds, by sex as shown, 100.0%.

Table 3.20 Enrollment in Institutions of Higher Education, by Control of the Institution, Fall, 1980 - 1996

	Black	White	All Races
1980			
both public and private control	1,052	9,033	10,473
public control	815	6,677	7,781
private control	237	2,356	2,692
1986			
both public and private control	1,161	9,098	10,784
public control	924	6,951	8,312
private control	233	2,148	2,472
1990			
both public and private control	1,187	9,465	11,303
public control	961	7,410	8,887
private control	226	2,055	2,416
1991			
both public and private control	1,220	9,579	11,589
public control	1,004	7,464	9,078
private control	217	2,118	2,511
1996			
both public and private control	1,901	12,189	15,226
public control	1,519	9,566	12,014
private control	381	2,622	3,212

SOURCE: U.S. Bureau of the Census, Current Population Reports: School Enrollment-Social and Economic Characteristics of Students: October 1994, Series P-20, #487, pp. A2-A4, Table A-1; 1996(Update), #500, pp. 33-36, Table 9. C3.186/12:(year)

NOTES: 'All Races' includes other races not shown separately. Both 'White' and 'Black' exclude Hispanic.

UNITS: Enrollment in thousands of students.

Table 3.21 Traditionally Black Institutions of Higher Education: Enrollment, Fall, 1995, and Earned Degrees Conferred, 1995-96

	Traditionally Black Institutions				
	public		private		
	4 year	2 year	4 year	2 year	Total
Enrollment, Fall 1996					
Total	182,063	18,506	72,383	979	273,931
men	72,929	7,763	28,900	464	110,056
women	109,134	10,743	43,483	515	163,875
full-time enrollment					
total	136,341	9,927	64,959	713	211,940
men	56,756	4,016	25,959	311	87,042
women	79,585	5,911	39,000	402	124,898
part-time enrollment					
total	45,722	8,579	7,424	266	61,991
men	16,173	3,747	2,941	153	23,014
women	29,549	4,832	4,483	113	38,977
Earned degrees conferred, 1995-96					
Associate degrees					
total	1,285	1,496	137	135	3,053
men	481	535	43	52	1,111
women	804	961	94	83	1,942
Bachelors's degrees					
total	20,187	-	9,541	-	29,728
men	7,584	-	3,300	-	10,884
women	12,603	-	6,241	-	18,844
Master's degrees					
total	4,777	-	1,071	-	5,848
men	1,545	-	336	-	1,881
women	3,232	-	735	-	3,967

continued on the next page

Table 3.21 continued

	Traditionally Black Institutions				
	public		private		
	4 year	2 year	4 year	2 year	Total
Earned degrees conferred, 1994-95 - continued					
Doctor's degrees					
total	105	-	131	-	236
men	50	-	77	-	127
women	55	-	54	-	109
First professional degrees					
total	442	-	736	-	1,178
men	212	-	314	-	526
women	230	-	422	-	652

SOURCE: U.S. Department of Education, Center for Education Statistics, Digest of Education Statistics, 1998, p. 274, table 219. ED 1.113\998

NOTES: Historically black colleges and universities are accreditied institutions of higher education established prior to 1964 with the principal mission of educating black Americans. There are some exceptions to the founding date. Most institutions are in the southern and border States.

UNITS: Enrollment in number of students; Earned degrees conferred, number.

Table 3.22 Employment Status of Students 16 - 24 Years of Age, Enrolled in School, 1996

	Black	White	All Races
All students 16-24 years of age enrolled in school	2,209	11,708	14,904
in the civilian labor force			
number	764	6,164	7,286
percent	34.6%	52.6%	48.9%
employed	589	5,546	6,448
unemployed	175	618	838
All high school students 16-24 years of age enrolled in school	1,324	5,960	7,687
in the civilian labor force			
number	356	2,628	3,087
percent	26.9%	44.1%	40.2%
employed	245	2,234	2,559
unemployed	111	394	528
All college students 16-24 years of age enrolled in school	885	5,748	7,217
in the civilian labor force			
number	407	3,536	4,199
percent	46.0%	61.5%	58.2%
employed	344	3,312	3,889
unemployed	63	224	310

SOURCE: U.S. Department of Labor, Bureau of Labor Statistics, *Employment and Earnings*, January, 1997, p. 166, table 7, (data from the Current Population Survey). L 2.41/2:37/1:997

NOTES: 'All Races' includes other races not shown separately.

UNITS: Number of students in thousands; percent as a percent of the civilian noninstitutional population 16-24 years of age.

Table 3.23 Enrollment in Schools of Medicine, Dentistry and Related Fields, 1980-81 and 1995-96

	Black	White	All Races
1980-81			
allopathic medicine	5.7%	85.0%	100.0%
osteopathic medicine	1.9	94.9	"
podiatry	4.3	91.3	"
dentistry	4.5	88.5	"
optometry	1.3	91.4	"
pharmacy	4.4	88.6	"
veterinary medicine	2.3	95.2	"
registered nursing	na	na	"
1995-96			
allopathic medicine	8.0%	66.6%	100.0%
osteopathic medicine	3.8	80.3	"
podiatry	4.8	77.2	"
dentistry	5.8	68.0	"
optometry	2.3	75.4	"
pharmacy	7.7	71.9	"
registered nursing	9.4	82.4	"

SOURCE: U.S. Department of Health and Human Services, Health United States, 1992, p. 150, table 105; 1998, pp. 331-332, table 107 (data from the Association of American Medical Colleges, American Association of Colleges of Osteopathic Medicine, National League for Nursing, American Association of Colleges of Podiatric Medicine, American Dental Association American Optometric Association, American Association of Colleges of Pharmacy, Association of American Veterinary Medical Colleges). HE 20.6223:(year)

NOTES: 'All Races' includes other races not shown separately. Both 'White' and 'Black' exclude Hispanic.

UNITS: Enrollment as a percentage of all students enrolled, 100.0%.

Table 3.24 Earned Degrees Conferred, by Type of Degree, 1979 - 1996

	Black	White	All Races
1979			
Bachelor's degrees	60,130	799,617	916,347
Master's degrees	19,393	249,051	299,887
Doctor's degrees	1,267	26,128	32,664
First Professional degrees	2,836	62,430	68,611
1981			
Bachelor's degrees	60,673	807,319	934,800
Master's degrees	17,133	241,216	294,183
Doctor's degrees	1,265	25,908	32,839
First Professional degrees	2,931	64,551	71,340
1985			
Bachelor's degrees	57,473	826,106	968,311
Master's degrees	13,939	223,628	280,421
Doctor's degrees	1,154	23,934	32,307
First Professional degrees	3,029	63,219	71,057
1991-92			
Bachelor's degrees	72,326	936,771	1,129,833
Master's degrees	18,116	268,371	348,682
Doctor's degrees	1,223	25,813	40,090
First Professional degrees	3,560	59,800	72,129
1995-96			
Bachelor's degrees	91,166	904,709	1,163,036
Master's degrees	25,801	297,558	405,521
Doctor's degrees	1,636	27,756	44,645
First Professional degrees	5,016	59,456	76,641

SOURCE: U.S. Department of Education, Center for Education Statistics, 1989 Education Indicators, pp. 228-229, table 2:5-1. ED 1.109:989
U.S. Department of Education, Center for Education Statistics, Digest of Education Statistics, 1994, pp. 276-288, tables 252-264; 1998, p. 337, table 266, p. 340, table 269, p. 343, table 272, p. 346, table 275. ED 1.113\9(year)

NOTES: 'All Races' includes other races not shown separately. Both 'White'and 'Black' exclude Hispanic. 'First professional Degrees' include degrees awarded in chiropractic, dentistry, law, medicine,optometry, osteopathy, pharmacy, podiatry, theology, and veterinary medicine.

UNITS: Earned degrees conferred in number of degrees.

Table 3.25 Associate Degrees Conferred, by Major Field of Study, 1994-95

	Black	White	All Races
All Fields, Total	47,142	419,323	538,545
agriculture and natural resources	57	5,380	5,730
architecture and related programs	4	243	277
area, ethnic and cultural studies	9	19	68
biological sciences/life sciences	150	1,225	1,879
business and management	11,366	76,068	101,926
communications	216	2,687	3,160
communications technologies	194	1,512	1,984
computer and information sciences	1,037	6,470	9,152
construction trades	81	1,456	1,728
education	915	7,350	9,658
engineering	153	1,703	2,232
engineering technologies	2,866	27,453	34,732
English language and literature/letters	103	756	1,548
foreign languages and literatures	10	466	616
health professions and related sciences	7,211	83,473	98,474
home economics	1,005	5,580	7,821
law and legal studies	986	7,278	9,140
liberal/general studies	14,545	130,736	170,817
library science	4	91	101
mathematics	46	488	782
mechanics and repairers	745	9,089	11,497
multi/interdisciplinary studies	884	6,863	8,692
parks, recreation, and fitness studies	81	680	864
philosophy and religion	3	66	81
physical sciences	173	1,840	2,456
precision production trades	373	7,605	9,344
protective services	1,601	15,395	19,709
psychology	128	1,163	1,600
public administration and services	859	2,484	3,882
military technologies	36	279	364
social sciences and history	425	2,418	3,634
theological studies/religious vocations	34	521	607
transportation	88	1,154	1,446
visual and performing arts	754	9,332	12,544

SOURCE: U.S. Department of Education, Center for Education Statistics, Digest of Education Statistics, 1997, p. 293, table 263. ED 1.113\997

NOTES: 'All Races' includes other races not shown separately. Both 'White' and 'Black' exclude Hispanic.

UNITS: Earned Associate degrees conferred in number of degrees.

Table 3.26 Bachelor's Degrees Conferred, by Major Field of Study, 1995-96

	Black	White	All Races
All Fields, Total	91,166	904,709	1,163,036
agriculture and natural resources	606	19,286	21,431
architecture and related programs	317	6,293	8,352
area, ethnic and cultural studies	690	3,583	5,786
biological sciences/life sciences	3,874	44,676	60,994
business and management	20,190	168,220	227,102
communications	4,220	38,144	47,320
communications technologies	74	564	683
computer and information sciences	2,471	15,827	24,098
construction trades	2	73	80
education	7,149	91,259	105,509
engineering	3,073	44,185	62,114
engineering technologies	1,326	11,719	15,189
English language and literature/letters	3,499	42,166	50,698
foreign languages and literatures	488	10,137	13,952
health professions and related sciences	6,317	69,156	84,036
home economics	1,101	13,351	15,803
law and legal studies	214	1,634	2,052
liberal/general studies	3,474	26,053	33,997
library science	3	52	58
mathematics	986	10,033	13,143
mechanics and repairers	3	39	54
multi/interdisciplinary studies	2,115	20,043	26,515
parks, recreation, and fitness studies	790	12,146	13,983
philosophy and religion	346	6,182	7,388
physical sciences	1,130	15,551	19,647
precision production trades	32	345	401
protective services	3,710	18,386	24,810
psychology	6,157	57,254	73,291
public administration and services	3,433	14,205	19,849
military technologies	0	7	7
social sciences and history	10,977	96,637	126,479
theological studies/religious vocations	205	4,740	5,358
transportation	192	3,020	3,561
visual and performing arts	2,002	39,743	49,296

SOURCE: U.S. Department of Education, Center for Education Statistics, Digest of Education Statistics, 1998, p. 337, table 266. ED 1.113\998

NOTES: 'All Races' includes other races not shown separately. Both 'White' and 'Black' exclude Hispanic.

UNITS: Earned Bachelor's degrees conferred in number of degrees.

Table 3.27 Master's Degrees Conferred, by Major Field of Study, 1995-96

	Black	White	All Races
All Fields, Total	25,801	297,558	405,521
agriculture and natural resources	116	3,334	4,569
architecture and related programs	142	2,664	3,993
area, ethnic and cultural studies	115	1,198	1,713
biological sciences/life sciences	207	4,262	6,157
business and management	5,753	65,685	93,982
communications	406	3,471	5,080
communications technologies	26	297	524
computer and information sciences	406	4,382	10,151
construction trades	0	0	0
education	8,557	87,310	106,253
engineering	704	14,250	27,441
engineering technologies	62	843	1,125
English language and literature/letters	292	6,736	7,893
foreign languages and literatures	55	2,054	3,124
health professions and related sciences	1,875	27,008	33,398
home economics	192	2,293	2,917
law and legal studies	119	1,245	2,751
liberal/general studies	136	2,347	2,778
library science	211	4,411	5,099
mathematics	165	2,430	4,031
multi/interdisciplinary studies	119	1,865	2,347
parks, recreation, and fitness studies	124	1,483	1,751
philosophy and religion	37	1,067	1,302
physical sciences	123	3,548	5,847
precision production trades	1	6	8
protective services	240	1,437	1,812
psychology	992	11,249	13,792
public administration and services	3,004	17,968	24,229
military technologies	5	127	136
social sciences and history	911	10,339	15,012
theological studies/religious vocations	298	3,858	5,107
transportation	26	830	919
visual and performing arts	382	7,561	10,280

SOURCE: U.S. Department of Education, Center for Education Statistics, Digest of Education Statistics, 1998, p. 340, table 269. ED 1.113\998

NOTES: 'All Races' includes other races not shown separately. Both 'White' and 'Black' exclude Hispanic.

UNITS: Earned Master's degrees conferred in number of degrees.

Table 3.28 Doctor's Degrees Conferred, by Major Field of Study, 1995-96

	Black	White	All Races
All Fields, Total	1,636	27,756	44,645
agriculture and natural resources	23	575	1,271
architecture and related programs	5	67	141
area, ethnic and cultural studies	22	117	184
biological sciences/life sciences	79	2,838	4,780
business and management	45	817	1,368
communications	19	232	338
communications technologies	1	0	7
computer and information sciences	10	367	867
education	564	5,128	6,676
engineering	74	2,507	6,369
engineering technologies	0	3	11
English language and literature/letters	50	1,240	1,535
foreign languages and literatures	8	499	876
health professions and related sciences	64	1,342	2,119
home economics	33	289	414
law and legal studies	2	40	91
liberal/general studies	6	61	75
library science	2	39	53
mathematics	9	547	1,209
multi/interdisciplinary studies	38	301	441
parks, recreation, and fitness studies	7	71	104
philosophy and religion	15	436	549
physical sciences	56	2,446	4,571
precision production trades	0	0	0
protective services	2	32	38
psychology	159	3,087	3,711
public administration and services	44	340	499
military technologies	0	0	0
social sciences and history	121	2,471	3,760
theological studies/religious vocations	147	1,062	1,521
transportation	0	0	0
visual and performing arts	31	802	1,067

SOURCE: U.S. Department of Education, Center for Education Statistics, Digest of Education Statistics, 1998, p. 343, table 272. ED 1.113\998

NOTES: 'All Races' includes other races not shown separately. Both 'White' and 'Black' exclude Hispanic.

UNITS: Earned Doctor's degrees conferred in number of degrees.

Table 3.29 First Professional Degrees Conferred, by Field of Study, 1995-96

	Black	White	All Races
All Fields, Total	5,016	59,456	76,641
Dentistry	175	2,516	3,697
Medicine	988	10,956	15,341
Optometry	35	911	1,231
Osteopathic medicine	45	1,529	1,895
Pharmacy	275	1,570	2,555
Podiatry	56	462	650
Veterinary medicine	33	1,935	2,109
Chiropractic medicine	65	2,777	3,379
Law	2,842	32,085	39,828
Theological professions	501	4,657	5,879

SOURCE: U.S. Department of Education, Center for Education Statistics, Digest of Education Statistics, 1998, p. 45, table 275. ED 1.113\998

NOTES: 'All Races' includes other races not shown separately. Both 'White' and 'Black' exclude Hispanic.

UNITS: Earned first professional degrees conferred, in number of degrees.

Table 3.30 Educational Attainment: Years of School Completed by Persons 25 Years Old and Older, 1997

	Black	White	All Races
All persons 25 years old and over	19,072	144,058	170,581
percent of the population:			
not a high school graduate	25.1%	17.0%	17.9%
high school graduate	35.8	33.9	33.8
with some college, no degree	19.1	17.2	17.2
with associate's degree	6.7	7.4	7.3
with bachelor's degree	9.5	16.5	16.0
with advanced degree	3.8	8.1	7.8

SOURCE: U.S. Bureau of the Census, Statistical Abstract of the United States, 1998, p. 168, table 262. C 3.134:998

NOTES: 'All Races' includes other races not shown separately. Data as of March.

UNITS: Percent as a percent of the population 25 years old and older; number in thousands of persons 25 years old and older.

Table 3.31 Highest Educational Level and Degree Earned, Persons 18 Years Old and Older, 1997

	Black	White	All Races
Total civilian noninstitutional population	22,186	145,855	195,568
less than 7 years of elementary school	789	1,834	6,799
7 or 8 years of elementary school	830	4,860	7,250
1 to 3 years of high school	3,395	12,372	19,393
4 years of high school	581	1,584	2,868
high school graduate	8,060	50,200	65,370
some college	4,604	29,052	38,041
Associate degree	1,312	10,595	13,336
Bachelor's degree	1,904	24,072	29,089
Master's degree	564	7,731	9,205
First professional degree	84	2,076	2,455
Doctorate degree	62	1,477	1,761

SOURCE: U.S. Department of Education, Center for Education Statistics, Digest of Education Statistics, 1998, p. 4, table 9 (data from U.S. Bureau of the Census, *Current Population Reports*, unpublished data.) ED 1.113\998

NOTES: 'All Races' includes other races not shown separately. Both 'White' and 'Black' exclude Hispanic.

UNITS: Persons in thousands, by highest educational level attained.

Table 3.32 College Completion, Persons 25 Years Old and Older, 1970 - 1995

	Black	White	All Races
1970			
total	4.5%	11.6%	11.0%
men	4.6	15.0	14.1
women	4.4	8.6	8.2
1975			
total	6.4	14.5	13.9
men	6.7	18.4	17.6
women	6.2	11.0	10.6
1980			
total	7.9	17.8	17.0
men	7.7	22.1	20.9
women	8.1	14.0	13.6
1985			
total	11.1	16.0	19.4
men	11.2	20.0	23.1
women	11.0	24.0	16.0
1990			
total	11.3	22.0	21.3
men	11.9	25.3	24.4
women	10.8	19.0	18.4
1995			
total	13.2	24.0	23.0
men	13.6	27.2	26.0
women	12.9	21.0	20.2

SOURCE: U.S. Bureau of the Census, Current Population Reports: Educational Attainment in the United States: March 1995, Series P-20, #489, p. 91, table 18. C3.186/23:995 http://www.census.gov

NOTES: 'All Races' includes other races not shown separately.

UNITS: Percent as a percent of all persons 25 years old and older completing four or more years of college (1970-1991) or Bachelor's degree or more (1992 and later).

Table 3.33 Employment of 12th Graders, 1992

	Black	White	All Races
Most recent type of work for employed students, total	100.0%	100.0%	100.0%
lawn work or odd jobs	0.8	2.5	2.2
food service	34.8	22.8	24.0
delivery person	1.9	1.5	1.6
babysitter or child care	2.4	4.8	4.3
camp counselor/life guard	0.0	0.9	0.7
farm worker	0.0	2.7	2.2
mechanic	0.7	1.5	1.4
grocery clerk or cashier	15.9	14.8	14.5
beautician	1.1	0.1	0.2
house cleaning	0.8	0.8	0.9
construction	1.0	2.1	2.0
office or clerical	9.2	6.3	6.9
health services	2.1	1.6	1.6
salesperson	8.7	12.0	11.8
warehouse worker	1.3	2.2	2.1
other	19.3	23.5	23.5

SOURCE: U.S. Department of Education, Center for Education Statistics, Digest of Education Statistics, 1994, p. 403, table 373. Data from U.S. Department of Education, National Center for Education Statistics, "National Education Longitudianl Study of 1988,"Second Followup. ED 1.113\994

NOTES: 'All Races' includes other races not shown separately.

UNITS: Percent as a percent of all high school seniors of a given race/ethnicity who were employed in 1992.

Chapter 4: Government, Elections & Public Opinion

Table 4.01 Black Elected Public Officials, by Type of Office Held, 1970 - 1993

	education	law enforcement	city & county offices	US & state legislatures	total
1970 (February)	368	213	719	179	1,479
1976 (April)	1,008	387	2,284	299	4,006
1977 (July)	1,066	415	2,509	316	4,342
1978 (July)	1,154	451	2,616	316	4,544
1979 (July)	1,155	458	2,675	315	4,636
1980 (July)	1,232	491	2,871	326	4,963
1981 (July)	1,293	534	2,914	343	5,109
1982 (July)	1,309	573	3,017	342	5,241
1983 (July)	1,430	620	3,283	386	5,719
1984 (January)	1,445	657	3,367	396	5,865
1985 (January)	1,531	685	3,689	407	6,312
1986 (January)	1,498	676	3,800	410	6,384
1987 (January)	1,542	727	3,949	428	6,646
1988 (January)	1,542	738	4,089	424	6,793
1989 (January)	1,602	759	4,388	441	7,190
1990 (January)	1,645	769	4,481	440	7,335
1991 (January)	1,629	847	4,493	476	7,445
1992 (January)	1,614	847	4,557	499	7,517
1993 (January)	1,682	922	4,819	561	7,984

SOURCE: U.S. Bureau of the Census, Statistical Abstract of the United States, 1994, p. 284, table 443 (data from Joint Center for Political Studies, *Black Elected Officials: A National Roster*). C 3.134:994

NOTES: 'U.S. and state legislatures' includes elected state administrators; 'city & county officials' includes county commissioners and mayors, councilmen, vice-mayors, aldermen, regional officials and others; 'law enforcement' includes judges, magistrates, sheriffs, justices of the peace, and others; 'education' includes members of state education agencies, college boards, school boards, and others.

UNITS: Number of Black elected public officials.

Table 4.02 Members of Congress, 1981 - 1995

	Black	White	All Races
House of Representatives			
97th Congress, 1981	17	415	435
98th Congress, 1983	21	411	"
99th Congress, 1985	20	412	"
100th Congress, 1987	23	408	"
101st Congress, 1989	24	406	"
102nd Congress, 1991	25	407	"
103rd Congress, 1993	38	393	"
104th Congress, 1995	40	391	"
Senate			
97th Congress, 1981	0	97	100
98th Congress, 1983	0	98	"
99th Congress, 1985	0	98	"
100th Congress, 1987	0	98	"
101st Congress, 1989	0	98	"
102nd Congress, 1991	0	98	"
103rd Congress, 1993	1	97	"
104th Congress, 1995	1	97	"

SOURCE: U.S. Bureau of the Census, Statistical Abstract of the United States, 1995, p. 281, table 444 (data from Congressional Quarterly, Inc.). C 3.134:995

NOTES: 'All Races' includes other races not shown separately.

UNITS: Number of members of the House and Senate respectively, as shown.

Table 4.03 Voting Age Population, Registration, and Voting, 1972 - 1996

	Black	White	All Races
Voting age population			
1972	13.5	121.2	136.2
1974	14.2	125.1	141.3
1976	14.9	129.3	146.5
1978	15.6	133.4	151.6
1980	16.4	137.7	157.1
1982	17.6	143.6	165.5
1984	18.4	146.8	170.0
1986	19.0	149.9	173.9
1988	19.7	152.8	178.1
1990	20.4	155.6	182.1
1992	21.0	157.8	185.7
1994	21.8	160.3	190.3
1996	22.5	162.8	193.7
Presidential election years			
percent reporting registration			
1972	65.5%	73.4%	72.3%
1976	58.5	68.3	66.7
1980	60.0	68.4	66.9
1984	66.3	69.6	68.3
1988	64.5	67.9	66.6
1992	63.9	70.1	68.2
1996	63.5	67.7	65.9
percent reporting voting			
1972	52.1%	64.5%	63.0%
1976	48.7	60.9	59.2
1980	50.5	60.9	59.2
1984	55.8	61.4	59.9
1988	51.5	59.1	57.4
1992	54.0	63.6	61.3
1996	50.6	56.0	54.2

continued on the next page

Table 4.03 continued

	Black	White	All Races
Congressional election years			
percent reporting registration			
1974	54.9%	63.5%	62.6%
1978	57.1	63.8	62.6
1982	59.1	65.6	64.1
1986	64.0	65.3	64.3
1990	58.8	63.8	62.2
1994	58.5	64.6	62.5
percent reporting voting			
1974	33.8%	46.3%	44.7%
1978	37.2	47.3	45.9
1982	43.0	49.9	48.5
1986	43.2	47.0	46.0
1990	39.2	46.7	45.0
1994	37.1	47.3	45.0

SOURCE: U.S. Bureau of the Census, Statistical Abstract of the United States, 1989, p. 257, table 432 (data from U.S. Bureau of the Census, *Current Population Reports*, Series P-20). C 3.134:989
U.S. Bureau of the Census, Current Population Reports: Voting and Registration in the Election of November, 1988, Series P-20, #440, pp. 48-49, table 8. C 3.186/3-2:989
U.S. Bureau of the Census, Current Population Reports: Voting and Registration in the Election of November, 1990, Series P-20, #453, pp. 16-17, table 2. C 3.186/3-2:990
U.S. Bureau of the Census, Current Population Reports: Voting and Registration in the Election of November, 1992, Series P-20, #466, pp. 4-5, table 2. C 3.186/3-2:992
Voting and Registration Data from the November 1994 Current Population Survey, Table 1, Table VI. http://www.census.gov
U.S. Bureau of the Census, Current Population Reports: Voting and Registration in the Election of November, 1996, Series P-20, #504, tabl 23. C 3.186/3-2:996

NOTES: 'All Races' includes other races not shown separately.

UNITS: Voting age population in millions of persons; percent reporting registration and percent reporting voting as a percent of the voting age population.

Table 4.04 Voting Age Population, Selected Characteristics, 1990

	Black	White	All Races
Voting age population, 1990			
by age			
total 18 years and over	20,371	155,587	182,118
18-20 years old	1,671	8,722	10,800
21-24 years old	1,854	11,635	14,031
25-34 years old	5,352	35,682	45,652
35-44 years old	4,153	32,281	37,889
45-54 years old	2,669	21,983	25,648
55-64 years old	2,144	18,477	21,223
65-74 years old	1,609	16,180	18,126
75 years and over	919	10,627	11,748
by sex			
male	9,093	74,625	86,621
female	11,277	80,962	95,496
by years of school completed			
elementary			
0-4 years of school	712	2,617	3,669
5-7 years of school	1,038	5,096	6,445
8 years of school	832	6,564	7,617
high school			
1-3 years high school	3,729	16,733	20,956
4 years high school	8,241	61,342	71,492
college			
1-3 years college	3,714	31,481	36,300
4 years college	1,331	18,900	21,350
5 or more years college	774	12,855	14,288

continued on the next page

Table 4.04 continued

	Black	White	All Races
by family income			
under $5,000	1,981	4,503	6,799
$5,000-$9,999	2,395	6,978	9,808
$10,000-$14,999	2,173	11,049	13,759
$15,000-$19,999	1,439	8,677	10,496
$20,000-$24,999	1,284	10,619	12,304
$25,000-$34,999	2,120	20,827	23,627
$35,000-$49,999	1,852	22,698	25,367
$50,000 and over	1,348	30,330	32,818
income not reported	1,547	9,555	11,576

SOURCE: U.S. Bureau of the Census, Current Population Reports: Voting and Registration in the Election of November, 1990, Series P-20, #453, pp. 16-17, table 2; pp. 47-48, table 8; p. 64, table 13. C 3.186/3-2:990

NOTES: 'All Races' includes other races not shown separately.

UNITS: Voting age population in thousands of persons.

Table 4.05 Selected Characteristics of Persons Registered to Vote, 1990

	Black	White	All Races
Persons registered to vote, 1990			
by age			
total 18 years and over	58.8%	63.8%	62.2%
18-20 years old	30.4	37.0	35.4
21-24 years old	49.1	43.1	43.3
25-34 years old	52.1	53.2	52.0
35-44 years old	63.6	67.2	65.5
45-54 years old	67.0	71.3	69.8
55-64 years old	71.4	74.9	73.5
65-74 years old	72.5	79.7	78.3
75 years and over	68.9	74.8	73.7
by sex			
male	56.0%	63.0%	61.2%
female	60.9	64.6	63.1
by years of school completed			
elementary			
0-4 years of school	50.7%	26.4%	29.5%
5-7 years of school	58.2	38.7	41.1
8 years of school	53.2	54.3	53.3
high school			
1-3 years high school	49.5	48.2	47.9
4 years high school	57.1	61.2	60.0
college			
1-3 years college	65.4	70.2	68.7
4 years college	72.2	77.1	74.5
5 or more years college	80.4	83.5	81.5

continued on the next page

Table 4.05 continued

	Black	White	All Races
by households income			
under $5,000	47.5%	53.1%	50.7%
$5,000-$9,999	53.5	47.6	48.3
$10,000-$14,999	58.6	55.4	54.8
$15,000-$19,999	61.4	57.5	56.8
$20,000-$24,999	58.8	59.0	58.0
$25,000-$34,999	62.3	65.0	63.9
$35,000-$49,999	67.9	69.4	68.3
$50,000 and over	74.4	77.8	76.4
income not reported	55.0	59.7	57.6

SOURCE: U.S. Bureau of the Census, Current Population Reports: Voting and Registration in the Election of November, 1990, Series P-20, #453, pp. 16-17, table 2; pp. 47-48, table 8; p. 64, table 13. C 3.186/3-2:990

NOTES: 'All Races' includes other races not shown separately.

UNITS: Person reporting registration to vote as a percent of the voting age population, 100.0%.

Table 4.06 Selected Characteristics of Persons Voting, 1990

	Black	White	All Races
Persons voting, 1990			
by age			
total 18 years and over	39.2%	46.7%	45.0%
18-20 years old	15.0	19.4	18.4
21-24 years old	24.9	21.8	22.0
25-34 years old	32.4	34.9	33.8
35-44 years old	44.7	50.0	48.4
45-54 years old	45.7	54.9	53.2
55-64 years old	54.0	60.4	58.9
65-74 years old	54.6	65.7	64.1
75 years and over	45.4	55.8	54.5
by sex			
male	37.3%	46.4%	44.6%
female	40.6	46.9	45.4
by years of school completed			
elementary			
0-4 years of school	27.4%	14.8%	16.5%
5-7 years of school	37.9	23.7	25.7
8 years of school	33.3	35.7	34.8
high school			
1-3 years high school	30.7	31.3	30.9
4 years high school	36.2	43.6	42.2
college			
1-3 years college	45.8	51.4	50.0
4 years college	58.1	61.6	59.0
5 or more years college	65.9	69.6	67.8

continued on the next page

Table 4.06 continued

	Black	White	All Races
by household income			
under $5,000	26.8%	35.1%	32.2%
$5,000-$9,999	31.9	31.3	30.9
$10,000-$14,999	38.2	38.5	37.7
$15,000-$19,999	39.2	39.9	38.8
$20,000-$24,999	38.2	42.5	41.3
$25,000-$34,999	42.6	47.5	46.4
$35,000-$49,999	51.2	51.8	51.0
$50,000 and over	54.3	60.5	59.2
income not reported	39.1	45.1	43.3

SOURCE: U.S. Bureau of the Census, Current Population Reports: Voting and Registration in the Election of November, 1990, Series P-20, #453, pp. 16-17, table 2; pp. 47-48, table 8; p. 64, table 13. C 3.186/3-2:990

NOTES: 'All Races' includes other races not shown separately.

UNITS: Persons reporting voting as a percent of the voting age population, 100.0%.

Table 4.07 Voting Age Population, Selected Characteristics, 1996

	Black	White	All Races
Voting age population, 1996			
by age			
total 18 years and over	22,483	162,779	193,651
18-20 years old	1,621	8,641	10,785
21-24 years old	1,992	11,028	13,865
25-34 years old	5,315	32,632	40,066
35-44 years old	5,338	36,000	43,327
45-54 years old	3,472	27,793	32,684
55-64 years old	2,122	18,228	21,037
65-74 years old	1,568	16,080	18,176
75 years and over	1,055	12,376	13,712
by sex			
male	9,993	78,654	92,632
female	12,490	84,125	101,020
by years of school completed			
less than 5th grade	485	2,194	3,069
5th to 8th grade	1,318	9,142	10,917
9th to 12th grade, no diploma	3,821	16,508	21,002
high school graduate	8,179	54,924	65,208
some college or associate degree	5,884	42,983	50,939
bachelor's degree	1,964	25,064	28,829
advanced degree	832	11,965	13,688
by labor force status			
in civilian labor force	15,009	111,332	132,043
employed	13,560	106,660	125,634
unemployed	1,449	4,672	6,409

continued on the next page

Table 4.07 continued

	Black	White	All Races
by occupation			
managerial and professional	2,791	32,947	37,462
technical, sales, and administrative support	3,875	31,504	36,973
service occupations	2,905	12,576	16,238
farming, forestry, fishing	131	2,960	3,171
precision production, craft and repair	1,059	12,077	13,647
operators, fabricators, laborers	2,800	14,596	18,143
by family income			
under $5,000	1,285	2,169	3,590
$5,000-$9,999	1,793	4,163	6,302
$10,000-$14,999	1,865	7,861	10,281
$15,000-$24,999	2,726	15,551	19,135
$25,000-$34,999	2,263	17,067	20,187
$35,000-$49,999	2,255	22,013	25,319
$50,000-$74.999	1,834	24,490	27,451
$75,000 and over	937	21,170	23,348
income not reported	1,640	11,727	13,875

SOURCE: U.S. Bureau of the Census, Current Population Reports: Voting and Registration in the Election of November, 1996, Series P-20, #504, pp. 4-5, table 2; pp. 39-40, table 8; pp. 47-53, tables 10, 11; p. 56, table 13. <www.census.gov/prod/3/98pubs/p20-504u.pdf>, accessed 15 October 1998.

NOTES: 'All Races' includes other races not shown separately.

UNITS: Voting age population in thousands of persons.

Table 4.08 Selected Characteristics of Persons Registered to Vote, 1996

	Black	White	All Races
Persons registered to vote, 1996			
by age			
total 18 years and over	14,267	110,259	127,651
18-20 years old	689	4,078	4,919
21-24 years old	1,094	5,722	7,099
25-34 years old	3,106	18,997	22,778
35-44 years old	3,432	24,675	28,828
45-54 years old	2,408	20,530	23,559
55-64 years old	1,567	14,043	15,930
65-74 years old	1,220	12,745	14,218
75 years and over	752	9,470	10,329
by sex			
male	6,001	52,218	59,672
female	8,266	58,041	67,989
by years of school completed			
less than 5th grade	258	582	872
5th to 8th grade	744	3,974	4,825
9th to 12th grade, no diploma	2,080	7,809	10,059
high school graduate	4,849	34,999	40,542
some college or associate degree	4,119	32,099	37,160
bachelor's degree	1,534	20,424	22,752
advanced degree	684	10,373	11,451
by labor force status			
in civilian labor force	9,800	75,428	87,532
employed	8,986	72,998	84,166
unemployed	814	2,430	3,365

continued on the next page

Table 4.08 continued

	Black	White	All Races
by occupation			
managerial and professional	2,156	26,852	29,889
technical, sales, and administrative support	2,628	22,772	26,068
service occupations	1,785	7,075	9,083
farming, forestry, fishing	76	1,787	1,893
precision production, craft and repair	682	6,937	7,811
operators, fabricators, laborers	1,659	7,575	9,423
by family income			
under $5,000	725	964	1,719
$5,000-$9,999	1,047	1,876	3,025
$10,000-$14,999	1,207	4,156	5,494
$15,000-$24,999	1,680	9,235	11,169
$25,000-$34,999	1,480	11,263	13,059
$35,000-$49,999	1,507	16,090	18,008
$50,000-$74,999	1,430	19,230	21,169
$75,000 and over	789	17,778	19,243
income not reported	830	6,748	7,712

SOURCE: U.S. Bureau of the Census, Current Population Reports: Voting and Registration in the Election of November, 1996, Series P-20, #504, pp. 4-5, table 2; pp. 39-40, table 8; pp. 47-53, tables 10, 11; p. 56, table 13. <www.census.gov/prod/3/98pubs/p20-504u.pdf>, accessed 15 October 1998.

NOTES: 'All Races' includes other races not shown separately.

UNITS: Voting age population in thousands of persons.

Table 4.09 Selected Characteristics of Persons Voting, 1996

	Black	White	All Races
Persons voting, 1996			
by age			
total 18 years and over	11,386	91,208	105,017
18-20 years old	461	2,808	3,366
21-24 years old	709	3,748	4,630
25-34 years old	2,338	14,426	17,265
35-44 years old	2,757	20,432	23,785
45-54 years old	2,098	17,786	20,360
55-64 years old	1,351	12,629	14,255
65-74 years old	1,062	11,477	12,748
75 years and over	610	7,903	8,608
by sex			
male	4,658	43,111	48,909
female	6,728	48,097	56,108
by years of school completed			
less than 5th grade	184	408	618
5th to 8th grade	568	2,928	3,570
9th to 12th grade, no diploma	1,459	5,535	7,099
high school graduate	3,700	27,802	32,019
some college or associate degree	3,462	26,643	30,835
bachelor's degree	1,364	18,257	20,256
advanced degree	649	9,637	10,621
by labor force status			
in civilian labor force	7,834	62,059	71,682
employed	7,295	60,303	69,300
unemployed	538	1,755	2,383

continued on the next page

Table 4.09 continued

	Black	White	All Races
by occupation			
managerial and professional	1,956	23,606	26,309
technical, sales, and administrative support	2,146	18,870	21,530
service occupations	1,383	5,465	6,992
farming, forestry, fishing	56	1,479	1,557
precision production, craft and repair	533	5,320	5,988
operators, fabricators, laborers	1,221	5,563	6,923
by family income			
under $5,000	529	631	1,179
$5,000-$9,999	719	1,269	2,064
$10,000-$14,999	894	3,078	4,057
$15,000-$19,999	1,368	7,234	8,778
$20,000-$24,999	1,179	9,095	10,499
$25,000-$34,999	1,248	13,466	15,037
$35,000-$49,999	1,254	16,694	18,347
$50,000 and over	722	15,883	17,177
income not reported	661	5,835	6,598

SOURCE: U.S. Bureau of the Census, Current Population Reports: Voting and Registration in the Election of November, 1996, Series P-20, #504, pp. 4-5, table 2; pp. 39-40, table 8; pp. 47-53, tables 10, 11; p. 56, table 13. <www.census.gov/prod/3/98pubs/p20-504u.pdf>, accessed 15 October 1998.

NOTES: 'All Races' includes other races not shown separately.

UNITS: Voting age population in thousands of persons.

Chapter 5: Crime, Law Enforcement & Corrections

Table 5.01 Victimization Rates for Personal Crimes, 1997

	Black victims	White victims	Victims of All Races
1997			
crimes of violence	49.0	38.3	39.2
rape/sexual assault	1.6	1.4	1.4
robbery	7.4	3.8	4.3
assault	39.9	33.1	33.5
personal theft	3.3	1.4	1.6

SOURCE: U.S. Department of Justice, Bureau of Justice Statistics, Criminal Victimization in the United States, 1997, p. 3, table 1, p. 4, table 2. (data from the *National Crime Victimization Survey*). J29.9/2:997

NOTES: 'Victims of All Races' includes victims of other races not shown separately. Personal crimes include completed and attempted rape, robbery, assault, and larceny, but exclude homicide. *Based on 10 or fewer sample cases.
The National Crime Victimization Survey has been redesigned. Comparisons of estimates of crime based on previous survey procedures (before 1993) are not recommended.

UNITS: Rates per 1,000 persons, 12 years old and over.

Table 5.02 Victimization Rates for Personal Crimes, by Type of Crime, 1994

	Black	White	All Races
All personal crimes	**65.4**	**51.5**	**53.1**
Crimes of violence	61.8	49.4	50.8
completed	24.6	13.6	15.0
attempted/threatened	37.2	35.8	35.8
rape/sexual assault	2.7	1.9	2.0
rape/attempted rape	2.4	1.3	1.5
- rape	1.4	0.7	0.8
- attempted rape	1.0	0.7	0.7
sexual assault	0.3*	0.6	0.5
robbery	14.0	4.8	6.1
completed/property taken	11.0	2.6	3.7
- with injury	3.5	1.0	1.3
- without injury	7.5	1.6	2.4
attempted to take property	3.1	2.2	2.4
- with injury	0.7*	0.5	0.6
- without injury	2.4	1.6	1.8
assault	45.1	42.7	42.7
aggravated	16.6	10.9	11.6
- with injury	5.7	2.8	3.2
- threatened with weapon	11.0	8.1	8.4
simple	28.4	31.8	31.1
- with minor injury	6.4	7.0	6.9
- without injury	22.0	24.8	24.3
purse snatching/pocket picking	3.6	2.1	2.3

SOURCE: U.S. Department of Justice, Bureau of Justice Statistics, Criminal Victimization in the United States, 1994, p. 7, table 2; p. 10, table 5 (data from the *National Crime Victimization Survey*). J 29.9/2:994

NOTES: 'All Races' includes other races not shown separately. *10 or fewer sample cases. The National Crime Victimization Survey has been redesigned. Comparisons of estimates of crime based on previous survey procedures (before 1993) are not recommended.

UNITS: Rates per 1,000 persons, 12 years old and over.

Table 5.03 Victimization Rates for Personal Crimes, by Sex of the Victim, 1994

	Black		White		All Races	
	male	female	male	female	male	female
All personal crimes	**71.7**	**60.1**	**60.4**	**43.1**	**61.7**	**45.1**
Crimes of violence	68.5	56.2	58.6	40.7	59.7	42.5
completed	29.3	20.7	14.2	13.0	16.0	14.1
attempted/threatened	39.2	35.4	44.4	27.6	43.7	28.4
rape/sexual assault	0.5	4.5	0.2	3.5	0.2	3.7
robbery	18.5	10.3	6.5	3.2	8.1	4.1
completed/property taken	14.8	7.7	3.3	2.0	4.7	2.8
- with injury	5.6	1.7	1.2	0.9	1.7	1.0
- without injury	9.3	6.0	2.1	1.1	3.0	1.8
attempted to take property	3.6	2.6	3.3	1.2	3.4	1.3
- with injury	0.6	0.8	0.8	0.4	0.7	0.4
- without injury	3.0	1.9	2.5	0.8	2.7	0.9
assault	49.6	41.3	51.8	34.0	51.3	34.7
aggravated	20.6	13.3	14.6	7.4	15.3	8.1
- with injury	7.9	3.8	3.3	2.3	3.9	2.5
- threatened with weapon	12.6	9.6	11.2	5.1	11.4	5.6
simple	29.0	28.0	37.2	26.6	36.0	26.6
- with minor injury	6.2	6.5	7.5	6.5	7.2	6.5
- without injury	22.8	21.4	29.7	20.1	28.7	20.1
purse snatching/pocket picking	3.2	3.9	1.8	2.4	2.0	2.5

SOURCE: U.S. Department of Justice, Bureau of Justice Statistics, Criminal Victimization in the United States, 1994, p. 7, table 2; p. 11, table 6 (data from the *National Crime Victimization Survey*). J 29.9/2:994

NOTES: 'All Races' includes other races not shown separately. *Based on 10 or fewer sample cases.
The National Crime Victimization Survey has been redesigned. Comparisons of estimates of crime based on previous surveyprocedures (before 1993) are not recommended

UNITS: Rates per 1,000 persons, 12 years old and over.

Table 5.04 Victimization Rates for Personal Crimes, by Age of the Victim, 1994

	Black	White	All Races
Persons 12-15 years old			
crimes of violence	135.7	112.5	114.8
completed	37.7	33.5	34.3
attempted	97.9	78.9	80.5
purse snatching/pocket picking	2.1*	2.7	2.6
Persons 16-19 years old			
crimes of violence	117.2	124.7	121.7
completed	56.4	36.3	38.4
attempted	60.8	88.4	83.3
purse snatching/pocket picking	2.8*	4.7	4.2
Persons 20-24 years old			
crimes of violence	85.9	100.9	99.2
completed	34.2	27.6	29.0
attempted	51.8	73.3	70.2
purse snatching/pocket picking	5.4*	2.9	3.3
Persons 25-34 years old			
crimes of violence	62.7	61.5	60.9
completed	26.1	18.9	19.5
attempted	36.5	42.6	41.4
purse snatching/pocket picking	4.4	2.0	2.3
Persons 35-49 years old			
crimes of violence	44.8	39.0	39.5
completed	19.1	8.8	10.3
attempted	25.8	30.2	29.3
purse snatching/pocket picking	1.9*	1.9	1.9

continued on the next page

Table 5.04 continued

	Black	White	All Races
Persons 50-64 years old			
crimes of violence	20.2	14.8	15.1
completed	8.9	2.9	3.5
attempted	11.4	11.9	11.6
purse snatching/pocket picking	6.9	1.2	1.7
Persons 65 years old and over			
crimes of violence	17.0	4.0	5.1
completed	7.5*	1.5	2.0
attempted	9.5	2.5	3.1
purse snatching/pocket picking	2.6*	2.1	2.1

SOURCE: U.S. Department of Justice, Bureau of Justice Statistics, Criminal Victimization in the United States, 1994, p. 8, table 3; p. 14, table 9 (data from the *National Crime Victimization Survey*). J 29.9/2:994

NOTES: 'All Races' includes other races not shown separately. *Based on 10 or fewer sample cases. The National Crime Vicitimization Survey has been redesigned. Comparisons of estimates of crime baesd on previous survey procedures (before 1993) are not recommended.

UNITS: Rates per 1,000 persons.

Table 5.05 Victimization Rates for Personal Crimes, by Age and Sex of the Victim, 1994

	Black		White		All Races	
	male	female	male	female	male	female
Crimes of violence						
persons 12-15 years old	141.6	129.8	135.6	88.2	134.6	94.2
persons 16-19 years old	124.8	109.3	146.0	102.4	141.3	101.2
persons 20-24 years old	71.1	97.5	123.3	78.1	116.9	81.8
persons 25-34 years old	66.9	59.0	65.0	57.9	64.8	57.2
persons 35-49 years old	49.9	40.5	44.5	33.6	45.0	34.2
persons 50-64 years old	28.5	13.5	15.2	14.3	16.3	14.1
persons 65 years old and over	33.7	6.7*	5.7	2.8	7.9	3.0

SOURCE: U.S. Department of Justice, Bureau of Justice Statistics, Criminal Victimization in the United States, 1994, p. 9, table 4; p. 15, table 10 (data from the *National Crime Victimization Survey*). J 29.9/2:994

NOTES: 'All Races' includes other races not shown separately. *Based on 10 or fewer sample cases.
The National Crime Victimization Survey has been redesigned. Comparisons of estimates of crime based on previous survey procedures (before 1993) are not recommended.

UNITS: Rates per 1,000 persons, 12 years old and over.

Table 5.06 Victimization Rates for Personal Crimes, by Annual Household Income of the Victim, 1994

	Black	White	All Races
With household incomes of:			
Less than $7,500.			
crimes of violence	68.2	90.2	83.6
completed	33.6	29.3	30.0
attempted	34.6	60.9	53.6
purse snatching/pocket picking	6.0	4.5	4.7
$7,500.-$14,999.			
crimes of violence	61.5	56.7	58.6
completed	21.9	17.4	19.0
attempted	39.5	39.2	39.5
purse snatching/pocket picking	2.8*	2.0	2.2
$15,000.-$24,999.			
crimes of violence	70.6	46.8	49.9
completed	28.4	13.7	15.7
attempted	42.2	33.1	34.2
purse snatching/pocket picking	2.7*	1.6	1.8
$25,000.-$34,999.			
crimes of violence	55.7	48.2	49.3
completed	17.7	12.2	12.9
attempted	38.0	36.0	36.4
purse snatching/pocket picking	3.4*	1.9	2.0

continued on the next page

Table 5.06 continued

	Black	White	All Races
$35,000.-$49,999.			
crimes of violence	52.1	46.8	46.8
completed	15.8	12.1	12.4
attempted	36.3	34.7	34.4
purse snatching/pocket picking	2.6*	2.6	2.6
$50,000.-$74,000.			
crimes of violence	51.0	46.2	46.1
completed	20.6	10.3	10.9
attempted	30.4	35.9	35.2
purse snatching/pocket picking	5.8*	1.2	1.5
$75,000. or more			
crimes of violence	42.5	41.0	40.0
completed	14.1*	7.8	7.9
attempted	28.4	33.2	32.1
purse snatching/pocket picking	0.0*	2.7	2.7

SOURCE: U.S. Department of Justice, Bureau of Justice Statistics, Criminal Victimization in the United States, 1994, pp. 19-20, tables 14, 15 (data from the *National Crime Victimization Survey*). J 29.9/2:993

NOTES: 'All Races' includes other races not shown separately. *Based on 10 or fewer sample cases.
The National Crime Victimization Survey has been redesigned. Comparisons of estimates of crime based on previous survey procedures (before 1993) are not recommended.

UNITS: Rates per 1,000 persons, 12 years old and over.

Table 5.07 Personal Crimes Involving Strangers, by Sex of the Victim, 1994

	Black		White		All Races	
	male	female	male	female	male	female
Crimes of violence	64.3%	39.8%	65.2%	41.8%	65.6%	41.8%
rape/sexual asault	61.7*	29.4*	10.6*	37.4	21.5	36.8
robbery	84.3	60.3	85.3	64.4	85.9	63.5
assault	56.8	35.8	63.0	40.2	62.6	39.7
aggravated assault	61.2	49.1	70.3	50.2	68.7	51.0
simple assault	53.8	29.4	60.1	37.4	60.0	36.3

SOURCE: U.S. Department of Justice, Bureau of Justice Statistics, Criminal Victimization in the United States, 1994, p. 31, tables 29-30 (data from the *National Crime Victimization Survey*). J 29.9/2:994

NOTES: 'All Races' includes other races not shown separately. *Based on 10 or fewer sample cases.
The National Crime Victimization Survey has been redesigned. Comparisons of estimates of crime based on previous survey procedures (before 1993) are not recommended.

UNITS: Percent as a percent of all personal crimes, 100.0%.

Table 5.08 Victimization Rates for Crimes Against Households, 1993 - 1994

	Black households	White households	All households
Burglary			
1993	85.6	56.6	59.9
1994	70.8	51.7	54.4
Theft			
1993	249.6	241.0	242.6
1994	70.8	51.7	54.4
Motor vehicle theft			
1993	33.7	17.2	19.6
1994	70.8	51.7	54.4

SOURCE: U.S. Department of Justice, Bureau of Justice Statistics, Criminal Victimization in the United States,1993, p. 24, table 16; 1994, p. 21, table 16 (data from the *National Crime Victimization Survey*). J 29.9/2(year)

NOTES: 'All households' includes households of other races not shown separately.
The National Crime Victimization Survey has been redesigned. Comparisons of estimates of crime based on previous survey procedures (before 1993) are not recommended.

UNITS: Rates per 1,000 households.

Table 5.09 Chances of Going to State or Federal Prison

	Black	White	All Races
For the first time, by age			
20	4.1%	0.4%	1.1%
25	8.4	0.9	2.4
30	11.6	1.4	3.3
35	13.6	1.7	4.0
40	14.9	2.0	4.4
45	15.4	2.1	4.7
50	15.7	2.3	4.9
55	15.8	2.4	5.0
65	16.0	2.5	5.1
Lifetime	16.2	2.5	5.1
At some time during the rest of life, by age			
birth	16.2%	2.5%	5.1%
20	14.1	2.3	4.5
25	9.6	1.7	3.1
30	6.0	1.2	2.1
35	3.6	0.9	1.4
40	2.0	0.6	0.9
45	1.2	0.4	0.6

SOURCE: U.S. Department of Justice, Bureau of Justice Statistics, Lifetime Likelihood of Going to State or Federal Prision,March 1997, pp. 2-3, tables 1, 2 J 29.11/8:997

NOTES: Chances of going to State or Federal Prison for the first time are cumulative percents. These estimates were obtained by sequentially applying age-specific first-incarceration rates and mortality rates for each group to a hypothetical population of 100,000 births. Changes of going to State or Federal Prison at some time are for persons not previously incarcerated. These estimates were obtained by subtracting the cumulative percent first incarcerated for each age from the lifetime likelihood of incarceration. 'White' and 'Black' exclude persons of Hispanic origin.

UNITS: Percent of all resident population.

Table 5.10 Victimization Rates for Property Crimes, by Type of Crime, 1994

	Black households	White households	All households
All property crimes	341.3	302.0	307.6
Household burglary	70.8	51.7	54.4
completed	57.1	43.4	45.4
- forcible entry	31.3	15.1	17.1
- unlawful entry without force	25.8	28.4	28.2
attempted forcible entry	13.7	8.3	9.0
Theft	243.8	234.6	235.8
completed	235.3	224.2	225.6
- less than $50.	74.4	95.7	93.0
- $50-$249	89.9	76.4	78.1
- $250 or more	52.8	40.6	42.2
- amount not available	18.2	11.5	12.3
attempted	8.6	10.4	10.1
Motor vehicle theft	26.6	15.6	17.5
completed	19.8	10.1	11.6
attempted	6.8	5.5	5.9

SOURCE: U.S. Department of Justice, Bureau of Justice Statistics, Criminal Victimization in the United States, 1994, p. 21, table 16 (data from the *National Crime Victimization Survey*). J 29.9/2:994

NOTES: 'All households' includes households of other races not shown separately.
The National Crime Victimization Survey has been redesigned. Comparisons of estimates of crime based on previous survey procedures (before 1993) are not recommended.

UNITS: Rates per 1,000 households.

Table 5.11 Victimization Rates for Property Crimes, by Annual Household Income, 1994

Household with incomes of:	Black	White	All Races
Less than $7,500.			
household burglary	93.7	74.0	78.7
theft	158.7	218.1	203.2
motor vehicle theft	11.8	14.9	13.9
$7,500.-$14,999.			
household burglary	74.9	63.5	65.5
theft	238.3	212.9	216.0
motor vehicle theft	25.6	11.8	15.2
$15,000.-$24,999.			
household burglary	69.5	58.4	60.5
theft	294.9	220.9	230.2
motor vehicle theft	32.7	13.1	16.3
$25,000.-$34,999.			
household burglary	87.2	46.7	50.9
theft	251.8	233.7	236.3
motor vehicle theft	28.5	19.3	20.0
$35,000.-$49,999.			
household burglary	65.6	50.0	51.6
theft	291.5	253.5	257.2
motor vehicle theft	29.8	15.5	17.0
$50,000.-$74,999.			
household burglary	47.3	38.6	39.6
theft	459.4	286.5	296.0
motor vehicle theft	28.3*	19.2	20.7
$75,000. or more			
household burglary	8.1*	42.3	40.9
theft	362.7	297.1	297.9
motor vehicle theft	34.1*	16.4	17.7

SOURCE: U.S. Department of Justice, Bureau of Justice Statistics, Criminal Victimization in the United States, 1994, pp. 23-47, tables 20-23, (data from the *National Crime Victimization Survey*). J 29.9/2:994

NOTES: 'All Races' includes other races not shown separately. *Based on 10 or fewer sample cases. The National Crime Victimization Survey has been redesigned. Comparisons of estimates of crime based on previous survey procedures (before 1993) are not recommended.

UNITS: Rates per 1,000 households.

Table 5.12 Victimization Rates for Property Crimes: Type of Crime, by Housing Tenure, 1994

	Black households	White households	All households
Owner households			
All property crimes	342.4	264.8	272.2
Household burglary	58.3	43.7	45.5
completed	48.1	37.8	39.1
- forcible entry	26.8	12.2	13.4
- unlawful entry without force	21.3	25.6	25.6
attempted forcible entry	10.2	5.9	6.5
Theft	253.9	208.3	212.2
completed	246.7	199.4	203.4
- less than $50.	80.7	89.9	89.0
- $50. - $249	88.6	63.3	65.7
- $250. or more	55.7	34.5	36.3
- amount not available	21.6	11.6	12.5
attempted	7.3	8.9	8.7
Motor vehicle theft	30.2	12.8	14.5
completed	24.4	8.1	9.7
attempted	5.8	4.7	4.9
Renter households			
All property crimes	340.4	379.6	371.2
Household burglary	80.5	68.5	70.3
completed	64.0	55.3	56.7
- forcible entry	34.8	21.1	23.7
- unlawful entry without force	29.3	34.2	32.9
attempted forcible entry	16.5	13.2	13.6

continued on the next page

Table 5.12 continued

	Black households	White households	All households
Renter households - continued			
Theft	236.1	289.5	278.1
completed	226.5	275.9	265.4
- less than $50.	69.5	107.8	100.3
- $50. - $249.	90.9	103.8	100.3
- $250. or more	50.5	53.1	52.8
- amount not available	15.6	11.3	12.0
attempted	9.6	13.5	12.6
Motor vehicle theft	23.9	21.5	22.8
completed	16.2	14.5	15.2
attempted	7.6	7.0	7.7

SOURCE: U.S. Department of Justice, Bureau of Justice Statistics, Criminal Victimization in the United States, 1994, p. 54, table 56, (data from the *National Crime Victimization Survey*). J 29.9/2:994

NOTES: 'All households' includes households of other races not shown separately. *Based on 10 or fewer sample cases.
The National Crime Victimization Survey has been redesigned. Comparisons of estimates crime based on previous survey procedures (before 1993) are not recommended.

UNITS: Rates per 1,000 households.

Table 5.13 Lifetime Likelihood of Victimization by Crime, by Type of Crime and Number of Likely Victimizations

	Black	White	All Races
All violent crimes			
both sexes			
one or more victimizations	87%	82%	83%
one victimization	26	31	30
two victimization	27	26	27
three or more victimizations	34	24	25
male			
one or more victimizations	92	88	89
one victimization	21	25	24
two victimization	26	27	27
three or more victimizations	45	37	38
female			
one or more victimizations	81	71	73
one victimization	31	36	35
two victimization	26	22	23
three or more victimizations	24	13	14
All completed violent crimes			
both sexes			
one or more victimizations	53	41	42
one victimization	35	31	32
two victimization	13	8	9
three or more victimizations	4	2	2

continued on the next page

Table 5.13 continued

	Black	White	All Races
rape (female victimization)			
one or more victimizations	11%	8%	8%
one victimization	10	7	8
two victimization	1	*	*
three or more victimizations	*	*	*
robbery			
one or more victimizations	51	27	30
one victimization	35	23	25
two victimization	12	4	5
three or more victimizations	4	*	1
assault			
one or more victimizations	73	74	74
one victimization	35	35	35
two victimization	25	24	24
three or more victimizations	12	16	15
Personal theft			
both sexes			
one or more victimizations	99	99	99
one victimization	5	9	4
two victimization	12	9	8
three or more victimizations	81	87	87
male			
one or more victimizations	99	99	99
one victimization	5	3	3
two victimization	10	8	8
three or more victimizations	84	88	88
female			
one or more victimizations	98	99	99
one victimization	7	4	4
two victimization	15	10	10
three or more victimizations	76	86	84

SOURCE: U.S. Department of Justice, Bureau of Justice Statistics, Technical Report: Lifetime Likelihood of Victimization, p. 2, table 1, (data from the *National Crime Survey*). J.29.15:v66

NOTES: 'All Races' includes other races not shown separately.

UNITS: Percent of persons who will be victimized by crime, starting at 12 years of age. *less than 0.5%.

Table 5.14 Death Rates for Injury by Firearms, Ages 5-24, 1995

	Black		White		All Races
	male	female	male	female	both sexes
5 to 14 years old					
Total firearm mortality	5.5	1.4	2.5	0.8	na
Accidents	0.8	na	0.7	0.1	na
Suicide	na	na	0.8	0.3	na
Homicide	4.1	1.2	0.9	0.4	na
15 to 24 years old					
Total firearm mortality	140.2	13.5	31.4	4.6	na
Accidents	4.3	na	1.8	0.2	na
Suicide	13.2	1.5	15.4	2.0	na
Homicide	121.0	11.8	13.6	2.2	na

SOURCE: U.S. Bureau of the Census, Statistical Abstract of the United States, 1998, p. 108, table 149 (data from U.S. National Center for Health Statistics). C 3.134:998

NOTES: 'All Races' includes other races not shown separately.

UNITS: Death rate per 100,000 population.

Table 5.15 Selected Characteristics of Murders and Nonnegligent Homicides, 1997

	Black	White	All Races
All murders and nonnegligent homicides, 1997	7,394	7,261	15,289
by age of the victim			
under 1 year old	73	128	219
1-4 years old	138	160	313
5-8 years old	44	59	111
9-12 years old	29	59	95
13-16 years old	289	240	568
17-19 years old	920	597	1,579
20-24 years old	1,674	1,084	2,831
25-29 years old	1,132	883	2,095
30-34 years old	895	839	1,785
35-39 years old	713	736	1,507
40-44 years old	514	619	1,178
45-49 years old	319	490	855
50-54 years old	167	333	519
55-59 years old	103	231	352
60-64 years old	101	154	268
65-69 years old	64	132	203
70-74 years old	50	136	191
75 years old and older	74	259	339
age unknown	95	122	281
race of the victim,			
*race of the offender**			
white victims	520	3,184	3,787
black victims	3,388	209	3,646
victims of all races	3,958	3,454	7,721

SOURCE: U.S. Federal Bureau of Investigation, Crime in the United States, 1997, pp. 18-19, tables 2.5, 2.8 (data from the Uniform Crime Reporting program). J 1.14/7:997

NOTES: 'All Races' includes other races not shown separately. *Data covers only those murders and nonnegligent homicides in which there was a single offender and single victim.

UNITS: Number of murders and nonnegligent homicides known to police.

Table 5.16 Law Enforcement Officers Killed, 1978 - 1996

	Black	White	All Races	
1978	9%	91%	100%	(93)
1979	9	88	"	(106)
1980	13	86	"	(104)
1981	14	85	"	(91)
1982	15	84	"	(92)
1983	13	84	"	(80)
1984	14	85	"	(72)
1985	10	88	"	(78)
1986	11	89	"	(66)
1987	10	90	"	(73)
1988	9	91	"	(78)
1989	11	89	"	(66)
1990	18	80	"	(65)
1991	13	87	"	(71)
1992	16	82	"	(62)
1993	14	86	"	(70)
1994	14	84	"	(76)
1995	12	84	"	(74)
1996	15	80	"	(55)

SOURCE: U.S. Department of Justice, Bureau of Justice Statistics, Sourcebook of Criminal Justice Statistics, 1997, p. 311, table 3.162, (data from Federal Bureau of Investigation, *Law Enforcement Officers Killed and Assaulted, {annual}*). J.29.9/6:997

NOTES: 'All Races' includes other races not shown separately. Data have been revised since last publication.

UNITS: Percent distribution of law enforcement officers killed as a percent of total, 100.0% (total number of law enforcement officers killed shown in parenthesis).

Table 5.17 Arrests, by Offense Charged, 1985

	number of arrests			percent distribution		
	Black	White	All Races	Black	White	All Races
All arrests	2,721	7,338	10,239	26.6%	71.7%	100.0%
Arrests for crime index crimes	713.3	1,365.6	2,118.5	33.7	64.5	"
arrests for violent crimes	202.1	221.3	429.3	47.1	51.5	"
arrests for property crimes	511.2	1,144.3	1,689.2	30.3	67.7	"
arrests for violent crimes:						
murder and nonnegligent homicide	7.6	7.8	15.6	48.4	50.1	"
forcible rape	14.7	16.5	31.6	46.5	52.2	"
robbery	73.9	44.8	119.9	61.7	37.4	"
aggravated assault	105.9	152.2	262.2	40.4	58.0	"
arrests for property crimes:						
burglary	110.1	265.1	380.6	28.9	69.7	"
larceny-theft	360.1	790.9	1,177.0	30.6	67.2	"
motor vehicle theft	37.2	75.6	114.9	32.4	65.8	"
arson	3.8	12.6	16.7	22.8	75.7	"

SOURCE: U.S. Department of Justice, Bureau of Justice Statistics, Sourcebook of Criminal Justice Statistics, 1986, p. 300, table 4.8, (data from the Uniform Crime Reporting program). J 29.9/6:986

NOTES: 'All Races' includes other races not shown separately. Crime index crimes are made up of the four violent crimes (murder and nonnegligent homicide, rape, robbery, and aggravated assault), and four property crimes (burglary, larceny-theft, motor vehicle theft, and arson) which are tracked by the FBI.

UNITS: Arrests in thousands of arrests; percent distribution as a percent of total, 100.0%

Table 5.18 Arrests, by Offense Charged, 1997

	number of arrests			percent distribution		
	Black	White	All Races	Black	White	All Races
All arrests	3,201,014	7,061,803	10,516,707	30.4%	67.1%	100.0%
Arrests for crime index crimes	661,292	1,196,581	1,908,414	34.7	62.7	"
arrests for violent crimes	205,823	284,523	500,621	41.1	56.8	"
arrests for property crimes	455,469	912,058	1,407,793	32.4	64.8	"
arrests for violent crimes:						
murder and nonnegligent manslaughter	7,194	5,345	12,759	56.4	41.9	"
forcible rape	8,788	12,867	22,115	39.7	58.2	"
robbery	53,657	38,679	93,979	57.1	41.2	"
aggravated assault	136,184	227,632	371,768	36.6	61.2	"
arrests for property crimes:						
burglary	72,780	167,100	245,564	29.6	68.0	"
larceny-theft	334,046	667,528	1,032,467	32.4	64.7	"
motor vehicle theft	45,203	67,316	115,948	39.0	58.1	"
arson	3,440	10,114	13,814	24.9	73.2	"

SOURCE: U.S. Federal Bureau of Investigation, Crime in the United States, 1997, p. 240, table 43 (data from the Uniform Crime Reporting program). J 1.14/7:997

NOTES: 'All Races' includes other races not shown separately. Crime index crimes are made up of the four violent crimes (murder and nonnegligent manslaughter, rape, robbery, and aggravated assault), and four property crimes (burglary, larceny-theft, motor vehicle theft, and arson) which are tracked by the FBI.

UNITS: Number of arrests; percent distribution as a percent of total, 100.0%

Table 5.19 Arrests, by Offense Charged, Persons Under 18 Years of Age, 1985

	number of arrests			percent distribution		
	Black	White	All Races	Black	White	All Races
All arrests	407.8	1,317.8	1,758.8	23.2%	74.9%	100.0%
Arrests for crime index crimes	187.1	452.4	653.4	28.6	69.2	"
arrests for violent crimes	37.8	33.5	72.3	52.4	46.3	"
arrests for property crimes	149.2	418.9	581.1	25.7	72.1	"
arrests for violent crimes:						
murder and nonnegligent homicide	0.6	0.6	1.3	50.7	48.2	"
forcible rape	2.4	2.3	4.8	50.6	48.3	"
robbery	20.1	9.6	30.0	66.8	32.1	"
aggravated assault	14.7	20.9	36.2	40.7	57.8	"
arrests for property crimes:						
burglary	32.6	109.9	144.8	25.5	75.9	"
larceny-theft	103.1	273.1	385.8	27.7	07.8	"
motor vehicle theft	12.6	30.1	43.6	28.9	69.1	"
arson	0.9	5.8	6.9	13.6	84.7	"

SOURCE: U.S. Department of Justice, Bureau of Justice Statistics, Sourcebook of Criminal Justice Statistics, 1986, p. 301, table 4.8, (data from the Uniform Crime Reporting program). J 29.9/6:986

NOTES: 'All Races' includes other races not shown separately. Crime index crimes are made up of the four violent crimes (murder and nonnegligent homicide, rape, robbery, and aggravated assault), and four property crimes (burglary, larceny-theft, motor vehicle theft, and arson) which are tracked by the FBI.

UNITS: Arrests in thousands of arrests; percent distribution as a percent of total, 100.0%

Table 5.20 Arrests, by Offense Charged, Persons Under 18 Years of Age, 1997

	number of arrests			percent distribution		
	Black	White	All Races	Black	White	All Races
All arrests	520,417	1,387,992	1,966,735	26.5%	70.6%	100.0%
Arrests for crime index crimes	168,222	388,550	576,036	29.2	67.5	"
arrests for violent crimes	38,196	46,146	86,367	44.2	53.4	"
arrests for property crimes	130,026	342,404	489,669	26.6	69.9	"
arrests for violent crimes:						
murder and nonnegligent manslaughter	997	697	1,731	57.6	40.3	"
forcible rape	1,603	2,129	3,791	42.3	56.2	"
robbery	15,529	11,835	28,051	55.4	42.2	"
aggravated assault	20,067	31,485	52,794	38.0	59.6	"
arrests for property crimes:						
burglary	21,892	65,867	90,346	24.2	72.9	"
larceny-theft	89,524	243,734	346,193	25.9	70.4	"
motor vehicle theft	17,281	27,348	46,223	37.4	59.2	"
arson	1,329	5,455	6,907	19.2	79.0	"

SOURCE: U.S. Federal Bureau of Investigation, Crime in the United States, 1997, p. 241, table 43 (data from the Uniform Crime Reporting program). J 1.14/7:997

NOTES: 'All Races' includes other races not shown separately. Crime index crimes are made up of the four violent crimes (murder and nonnegligent manslaughter, rape, robbery, and aggravated assault), and four property crimes (burglary, larceny-theft, motor vehicle theft, and arson) which are tracked by the FBI.

UNITS: Number of arrests; percent distribution as a percent of total, 100.0%

Table 5.21 Arrests in Cities, by Offense Charged, 1985

	number of arrests			percent distribution		
	Black	White	All Races	Black	White	All Races
All arrests	2,325.6	5,443.9	7,916.9	29.4%	68.8%	100.0%
Arrests for crime index crimes	614.5	1,067.6	1,716.6	35.8	62.2	"
arrests for violent crimes	171.7	158.8	335.3	51.2	474.	"
arrests for property crimes	442.8	908.8	1,381.3	32.1	65.8	"
arrests for violent crimes:						
murder and nonnegligent homicide	6.3	4.9	11.3	55.6	42.8	"
forcible rape	12.4	10.9	23.7	52.4	46.2	"
robbery	65.5	36.6	103.2	63.5	35.5	"
aggravated assault	87.9	106.4	197.0	44.4	54.0	"
arrests for property crimes:						
burglary	91.6	186.9	282.6	32.4	66.1	"
larceny-theft	315.4	658.2	997.3	31.6	66.0	"
motor vehicle theft	32.5	54.8	89.0	36.5	61.6	"
arson	3.2	9.0	12.5	26.1	72.2	"

SOURCE: U.S. Department of Justice, Bureau of Justice Statistics, Sourcebook of Criminal Justice Statistics, 1986, p. 304, table 4.10, (data from the Uniform Crime Reporting program). J 29.9/6:986

NOTES: 'All Races' includes other races not shown separately. Crime index crimes are made up of the four violent crimes (murder and nonnegligent homicide, rape, robbery, and aggravated assault), and four property crimes (burglary, larceny-theft, motor vehicle theft, and arson) which are tracked by the FBI.

UNITS: Arrests in thousands of arrests; percent distribution as a percent of total, 100.0%

Table 5.22 Arrests in Cities, by Offense Charged, 1997

	number of arrests			percent distribution		
	Black	White	All Races	Black	White	All Races
All arrests	2,675,786	5,200,103	8,070,225	33.2%	64.4%	100.0%
Arrests for crime index crimes	566,471	941,459	1,549,374	36.6	60.8	"
arrests for violent crimes	175,461	210,934	394,153	44.5	53.5	"
arrests for property crimes	391,010	730,525	1,155,221	33.8	63.2	"
arrests for violent crimes:						
murder and nonnegligent manslaughter	6,168	3,550	9,868	62.5	36.0	"
forcible rape	7,311	8,752	16,384	44.6	53.4	"
robbery	47,023	32,415	80,813	58.2	40.1	"
aggravated assault	114,959	166,217	287,088	40.0	57.9	"
arrests for property crimes:						
burglary	60,487	114,377	178,828	33.8	64.0	"
larceny-theft	288,400	558,848	874,077	33.0	63.9	"
motor vehicle theft	39,145	49,826	91,669	42.7	54.4	"
arson	2,978	7,474	10,647	28.0	70.2	"

SOURCE: U.S. Federal Bureau of Investigation, Crime in the United States, 1997, p. 249, table 49 (data from the Uniform Crime Reporting program). J 1.14/7:997

NOTES: 'All Races' includes other races not shown separately. Crime index crimes are made up of the four violent crimes (murder and nonnegligent manslaughter, rape, robbery, and aggravated assault), and four property crimes (burglary, larceny-theft, motor vehicle theft, and arson) which are tracked by the FBI.

UNITS: Number of arrests; percent distribution as a percent of total, 100.0%

Table 5.23 Prisoners Under Jurisdiction of Federal and State Correctional Authorities, 1994, 1995

	Black	White	All Races
December 31, 1994			
Total	501,672	464,167	1,054,774
federal institutions	33,448	58,403	95,034
state institutions	468,224	405,764	959,740
December 31, 1995			
Total	544,005	455,021	1,126,287
federal institutions	37,055	60,261	100,250
state institutions	506,950	394,760	1,026,037

SOURCE: U.S. Department of Justice, Bureau of Justice Statistics, Sourcebook of Criminal Justice Statistics, 1995, p. 562, table 6.26; 1996, p. 524, table 6.26.. J 29.9/6:(YEAR)

NOTES: 'All Races' includes other races not shown separately.

UNITS: Number of prisoners under jurisdictional authority.

Table 5.24 Criminal History Profile of Prisoners Under Sentence of Death, 1997

	Black	White	All Races
U.S. Total	1,393	1,613	3,335
Prior felony convictions			
Yes	895	939	2,011
No	393	552	1,068
Not reported	0	0	256
Prior homicide convictions			
Yes	125	127	281
No	1,234	1,457	2,980
Not reported	0	0	74
Legal status at time of capital offense			
Charges pending	86	121	225
Probation	132	141	301
Parole	270	237	578
Prison escapee	10	25	38
Prison inmate	35	35	76
Other status	12	16	30
None	691	872	1,721
Not reported	0	0	366

SOURCE: U.S. Department of Justice, Bureau of Justice Statistics, Capital Punishment, 1997, p. 10, table 9. J 29.11:997

NOTES: 'All Races' includes other races not shown separately. 'White' excludes Hispanic persons.

UNITS: Number of jail inmates. Percent of all jail inmates of given race/ethnic group.

Table 5.25 Jail Inmates, 1990-1997

	Black	White	All Races
1990	42.5%	41.8%	100%
1991	43.4	41.1	100
1992	44.1	40.1	100
1993	44.2	39.3	100
1994	43.9	39.1	100
1995	43.5	40.1	100
1996	41.1	41.6	100
1996	41.1	41.6	100
1997	42.0	40.6	100

SOURCE: U.S. Department of Justice, Bureau of Justice Statistics, Prison and Jail Inmates 1997, p. 6, table 7 J 29.11/5:997

NOTES: 'All Races' includes other races not shown separately.

UNITS: Percent of local jail inmates.

Table 5.26 Type of Offense by Juvenile Offenders, 1995

	Black	White	All Races
All offenses	30.5%	65.8%	100%
Person	38.4	58.2	100
Property	25.8	69.9	100
Drug	33.6	64.2	100
Public order	32.5	64.2	100

SOURCE: U.S. Department of Justice, Bureau of Justice Statistics, Sourcebook of Criminal Justice Statistics, 1997, p. 440, table 5.74. (Howard Snyder et al., "Easy Access to Juvenile Court Statistics 1986-95" Washington, DC: U.S. Department of Justice, Office of Juvenile Justice and Delinquency Prevention, 1997). J 29.9/6:997

NOTES: 'All Races' includes other races not shown separately. Cases disposed by juvenile courts.

UNITS: Percent of all offenses committed by juvenile offenders, as disposed by juvenile courts.

Table 5.27 Juvenile Court Cases, by Type of Case and Outcome, 1995

	Black	White	All Races
Type of offense			
Total	100%	100%	100%
crimes against persons	27.7	19.5	"
crimes against property	43.0	54.0	"
drug law violations	10.2	9.1	"
offenses against public order	19.0	17.4	"
Case outcome			
Delinquency cases			
detained prior to court disposition	27.4%	14.6%	18.7%
petitioned	60.4	52.1	54.7
Petitioned cases			
adjudicated delinquent	53.4	57.6	56.4
waived to adult court	1.6	0.8	1.0
Adjudicated cases			
placed out of home	31.5	26.2	28.1
placed on probation	52.0	54.6	53.5
dismissed	7.2	3.9	4.9
other	9.3	15.4	13.5

SOURCE: U.S. Department of Justice, Bureau of Justice Statistics, Sourcebook of Criminal Justice Statistics, 1997, p. 440, table 5.75, p. 441, table 5.76. (Howard Snyder et al., "Easy Access to Juvenile Court Statistics 1986-95" Washington, DC: U.S. Department of Justice, Office of Juvenile Justice and Delinquency Prevention, 1997). J 29.9/6:997

NOTES: 'All Races' includes other races not shown separately. Data based on national estimates of delinquency cases disposed by juvenile courts.

UNITS: Percent, as a percent of total shown, 100.0%.

Table 5.28 Prisoners Under Sentence of Death, and Elapsed Time from Sentence to Execution, 1980 - 1998

	Black	White	All Races
Prisoners under sentence of death			
1980	268	425	697
1986	750	1,006	1,781
1987	821	1,138	1,984
1988	845	1,223	2,124
1989	903	1,310	2,213
1990	940	1,368	2,346
1991	979	1,449	2,465
1992	1,029	1,508	2,575
April, 1993	1,075	1,385	2,737
April, 1994	1,138	1,423	2,848
April, 1995	1,217	1,455	3,009
April, 1996	1,272	1,493	3,122
April, 1998	1,420	1,611	3,387
Average elapsed time (in months) from sentence to execution			
1986	102	77	86
1987	96	78	86
1988	89	72	80
1989	112	78	95
1990	91	97	95
1991	107	124	116
1992	135	104	114
1993	121	112	113
1994	132	117	122
1995	144	128	134
1996	153	112	125
1997	147	126	133

SOURCE: U.S. Bureau of the Census, Statistical Abstract of the United States, 1989, p. 187, table 325. C 3.134:989

U.S. Department of Justice, Bureau of Justice Statistics, Sourcebook of Criminal Justice Statistics, 1993, p. 666, table 6.108, p. 667, table 6.110; 1994, p. 587, table 6.70, 1995, p. 604, table 6.74, 1997, p. 527, table 6.76. J 29.9/6:9(date)

U.S. Department of Justice, Bureau of Justice Statistics, Bureau of Justice Statistics Bulletin: Capital Punishment, 1997, p. 12, table 12. J 29.11:997

NOTES: 'All Races' includes other races not shown separately. Some figures for yearend 1991 have been revised since last publication.

UNITS: Number of prisoners under sentence of death; Average elapsed time from sentence to execution in months.

Table 5.29 Prisoners Executed Under Civil Authority, 1930 - 1995

	Black	White	All Races
1930-1939			
All executions	816	827	1,667
for murder	687	803	1,514
for rape	115	10	125
for other offenses	14	14	28
1940-1949			
All executions	781	490	1,284
for murder	595	458	1,064
for rape	179	19	200
for other offenses	7	3	20
1950-1959			
All executions	376	336	717
for murder	280	316	601
for rape	89	13	102
for other offenses	7	7	14
1960-1964			
All executions	91	90	181
for murder	66	79	145
for rape	22	6	28
for other offenses	3	5	8
1965-1967	2	8	10
1968-1976	0	0	0
1977-1980	0	3	3
1981	0	1	1
1982	1	1	2
1983	1	4	5
1984	8	13	21

continued on the next page

Table 5.29 continued

	Black	White	All Races
1985	7	11	18
1986	7	11	18
1987	12	13	25
1988	5	6	11
1989	8	8	16
1990	7	16	23
1991	7	7	14
1992	11	19	31
1993	14	23	38
1994	11	20	31
1995	22	33	56

SOURCE: U.S. Department of Justice, Bureau of Justice Statistics, Sourcebook of Criminal Justice Statistics,1996, p. 568, table 6.73. J29.9/6:996
U.S. Department of Justice, Bureau of Justice Statistics, Bureau of Justice Statistics Bulletin: Capital Punishment, 1992, p. 671, table 6.128; J 29.11:992

NOTES: 'All Races' includes other races not shown separately. Since 1965 the only executions that have taken place have been for murder. 'Other offenses' include executions for kidnapping, armed robbery, burglary, espionage, and aggravated assault.

UNITS: Number of prisoners executed under civil authority.

Table 5.30 Attitudes Toward Crime and Safety, 1996

Question: I want to ask you how much you worry about each of the following situations. Do you worry very frequently, somewhat frequently, seldom, or never about...?

	Black	White	Total
Getting murdered:			
very frequently	23.6%	6.3%	10.6%
somewhat frequently	17.3	12.2	12.4
seldom	30.9	41.4	38.4
never	28.2	40.1	38.6
Getting beaten up, knifed or shot:			
very frenquently	25.5%	9.0%	12.5%
somewhat frequently	17.3	20.1	20.3
seldom	34.5	43.2	40.2
never	22.7	27.7	27.1
Yourself or someone in your family getting sexually assaulted:			
very frequently	31.8%	14.2%	18.1%
somewhat frequently	20.0	31.1	29.0
seldom	22.7	34.7	32.1
never	25.5	20.0	20.8
Your home being burglarized:			
very frenquently	22.7%	17.6%	20.4%
somewhat frequently	30.9	28.9	28.9
seldom	31.8	36.7	34.1
never	14.5	16.9	16.7

SOURCE: U.S. Department of Justice, Bureau of Justice Statistics, Sourcebook of Criminal Justice Statistics, 1997, p. 126, table 2.40. Data provided by Survey Research Program, College of Criminal Justice, Sam Houston State University) J 29.9/6:997

NOTES: The National Opinion Survey on Crime and Justice - 1996 was designed and commissions by the College of Criminal Justice's Survey Research Program at Sam Houston State University. The data were collected by the Public Policy Research Institute of Texas A&M University through telephone interviews conducted from May 16 to June 9, 1996. A total of 1,085 interviews were conducted from a stratified random sample of all working telephone numbers in the United States. The data presented are weighted estimates adjusted according to U.S. Bureau of the Census racial/ethnic group and gender population figures for 1990.

UNITS: Percent of persons taking survey who answered with given response.

Table 5.31 Attitudes Toward the Death Penalty, 1996

Question: Are you in favor of the death penalty for persons convicted of murder?

	Black	White	All Races
Yes	58.6%	77.2%	73.4%
No	32.4	16.5	19.9
Don't know/refused	9.0	6.3	6.7

Question: If you knew that murderers would be given a true life sentence without the possibility of parole, would you continue to favor the death penalty?

	Black	White	All Races
Yes	61.5%	77.5%	75.7%
No	35.4	18.2	20.1
Don't know	3.1	3.8	3.9

SOURCE: U.S. Department of Justice, Bureau of Justice Statistics, Sourcebook of Criminal Justice Statistics, 1997, p. 139, tables 2.58 and 2.59. Data provided by the Survey Research Program, College of Criminal Justice, Sam Houston State University. 29.9/6:997

NOTES: The National Opinion Survey on Crime and Justice - 1996 was designed and commissions by the College of Criminal Justice's Survey Research Program at Sam Houston State University. The data were collected by the Public Policy Research Institute of Texas A&M University through telephone interviews conducted from May 16 to June 9, 1996. A total of 1,085 interviews were conducted from a stratified random sample of all working telephone numbers in the United States. The data presented are weighted estimates adjusted according to U.S. Bureau of the Census racial/ethnic group and gender population figures for 1990.

UNITS: Percent of persons taking survey who answered with given response.

Table 5.32 HIV-Positive Local Jail Inmates, 1995-96

	Black	White	All Races
Tested inmates who reported results	125,259	110,023	289,991
male	110,453	98,745	258,019
female	14,806	11,278	31,972
HIV-positive	2.6%	1.4%	2.2%
male	2.5	1.3	2.1
female	3.2	2.1	2.4

SOURCE: U.S. Department of Justice, Bureau of Justice Statistics, HIV in Prisons and Jails, 1995, p. 8, table 7.

NOTES: 'All Races' includes other races not shown separately.

UNITS: Percent of inmates tested for HIV (Human Immunodeficiency Virus) and reporting the results.

Chapter 6: The Labor Force, Employment & Unemployment

Table 6.01 Labor Force Participation of the Civilian Noninstitutional Population 16 Years Old and Over, by Age, 1980 - 1997

	Black	White	All Races
1980			
civilian noninstitutional population			
all persons 16 years old and over	17,824	146,122	167,745
- persons 16-19 years old	2,289	13,854	16,543
- persons 20 years old and over	15,535	132,268	151,202
- persons 65 years old and over	2,030	22,050	24,350
civilian labor force			
all persons 16 years old and over	10,865	93,600	106,940
- persons 16-19 years old	891	8,312	9,378
- persons 20 years old and over	9,975	85,286	97,561
- persons 65 years old and over	257	2,759	3,054
labor force participation rate			
all persons 16 years old and over	61.0%	64.1%	63.8%
- persons 16-19 years old	38.9	60.0	56.7
- persons 20 years old and over	64.1	64.5	64.5
- persons 65 years old and over	13.0	12.5	12.5

continued on the next page

Table 6.01 continued

	Black	White	All Races
1985			
civilian noninstitutional population			
all persons 16 years old and over	19,664	153,679	178,206
- persons 16-19 years old	2,160	11,900	14,506
- persons 20 years old and over	17,504	141,780	163,700
- persons 65 years old and over	2,259	24,352	26,977
civilian labor force			
all persons 16 years old and over	12,364	99,926	115,461
- persons 16-19 years old	889	6,841	7,901
- persons 20 years old and over	11,476	93,085	107,560
- persons 65 years old and over	252	2,605	2,907
labor force participation rate			
all persons 16 years old and over	62.9%	65.0%	64.8%
- persons 16-19 years old	41.2	57.5	54.5
- persons 20 years old and over	65.6	65.7	65.7
- persons 65 years old and over	11.2	10.7	10.8

continued on the next page

Table 6.01 continued

	Black	White	All Races
1990			
civilian noninstitutional population			
all persons 16 years old and over	21,300	160,415	188,049
- persons 16-19 years old	2,150	11,095	13,794
- persons 20 years old and over	19,150	149,320	174,255
- persons 65 years old and over	2,506	26,643	29,730
civilian labor force			
all persons 16 years old and over	13,493	107,177	124,787
- persons 16-19 years old	831	6,374	7,410
- persons 20 years old and over	12,662	100,803	117,377
- persons 65 years old and over	279	3,189	3,535
labor force participation rate			
all persons 16 years old and over	63.3%	66.8%	66.4%
- persons 16-19 years old	38.6	57.5	53.7
- persons 20 years old and over	59.4	62.8	62.4
- persons 65 years old and over	11.1	12.0	11.9

continued on the next page

Table 6.01 continued

	Black	White	All Races
1997			
civilian noninstitutional population			
all persons 16 years old and over	24,003	169,993	203,133
- persons 16-19 years old	2,412	12,181	15,365
- persons 65 years old and over	2,653	28,514	31,989
civilian labor force			
all persons 16 years old and over	15,529	114,693	136,297
- persons 16-19 years old	933	6,720	7,932
- persons 65 years old and over	265	3,517	3,887
labor force participation rate			
all persons 16 years old and over	64.7%	67.5%	67.1%
- persons 16-19 years old	38.7	55.2	51.6
- persons 65 years old and over	10.0	12.3	12.2

SOURCE: U.S. Department of Labor, Bureau of Labor Statistics, Handbook of Labor Statistics, 1989, pp. 13-30, tables 3-5. L 2.3/5:989
U.S. Department of Labor, Bureau of Labor Statistics, *Employment and Earnings*, January, 1991, pp. 164-166, table 3; January, 1998, pp. 164-166, table 3 (data from the Current Population Survey). L2.41/2:(vol)/1:(year)

NOTES: 'All Races' includes other races not shown separately.

UNITS: Civilian noninstitutional population and civilian labor force in thousands of persons; participation rate as a percent (the civilian noninstitutional population divided by the civilian labor force).

Table 6.02 Labor Force Participation of the Civilian Noninstitutional Population 16 Years Old and Over, by Sex and Age, 1980 - 1997

	Black		White		All Races	
	male	female	male	female	male	female
1980						
civilian noninstitutional population						
all persons 16 years old and over	7,944	9,880	69,634	76,489	79,398	88,348
- persons 16-19 years old	1,110	1,180	6,941	6,914	8,260	8,283
- persons 20 years old and over	6,834	8,700	62,694	69,575	71,138	80,065
- persons 65 years old and over	822	1,208	9,027	13,022	9,979	14,372
civilian labor force						
all persons 16 years old and over	5,612	5,253	54,473	39,127	61,453	45,487
- persons 16-19 years old	479	412	4,424	3,888	4,999	4,381
- persons 20 years old and over	5,134	4,841	50,049	35,239	56,455	41,106
- persons 65 years old and over	138	119	1,727	1,032	1,893	1,161
labor force participation rate						
all persons 16 years old and over	70.3%	53.1%	78.2%	51.2%	77.4%	51.5%
- persons 16-19 years old	43.2	34.9	63.7	56.2	60.5	52.9
- persons 20 years old and over	75.1	55.6	79.8	50.6	79.4	51.3
- persons 65 years old and over	16.9	10.2	19.1	7.9	19.0	8.1

continued on the next page

Table 6.02 continued

	Black		White		All Races	
	male	female	male	female	male	female
1985						
civilian noninstitutional population						
all persons 16 years old and over	8,790	10,873	73,373	80,306	84,469	93,736
- persons 16-19 years old	1,059	1,101	5,987	5,912	7,275	7,231
- persons 20 years old and over	7,731	9,773	67,386	74,394	77,195	86,506
- persons 65 years old and over	902	1,357	10,010	14,342	11,084	15,913
civilian labor force						
all persons 16 years old and over	6,126	6,144	56,472	43,455	64,411	51,050
- persons 16-19 years old	440	417	3,576	3,265	4,134	3,767
- persons 20 years old and over	5,686	5,727	52,895	40,190	60,277	47,283
- persons 65 years old and over	118	127	1,595	1,010	1,750	1,156
labor force participation rate						
all persons 16 years old and over	70.8%	56.5%	77.0%	54.1%	76.3%	54.5%
- persons 16-19 years old	44.6	37.9	59.7	55.2	56.8	52.1
- persons 20 years old and over	74.4	58.6	78.5	54.0	78.1	54.7
- persons 65 years old and over	13.9	9.4	15.9	7.0	15.8	7.3

continued on the next page

Table 6.02 continued

	Black		White		All Races	
	male	female	male	female	male	female
1990						
civilian noninstitutional population						
all persons 16 years old and over	9,567	11,773	77,082	83,332	89,650	98,399
- persons 16-19 years old	1,065	1,085	5,600	5,495	6,947	6,847
- persons 20 years old and over	8,502	10,648	71,482	77,837	82,703	91,552
- persons 65 years old and over	1,012	1,493	11,129	15,514	12,392	17,337
civilian labor force						
all persons 16 years old and over	6,708	6,785	58,298	47,879	68,234	56,554
- persons 16-19 years old	433	398	3,329	3,046	3,866	3,544
- persons 20 years old and over	6,275	6,387	54,969	44,833	64,368	53,010
- persons 65 years old and over	131	148	1,865	1,325	2,033	1,502
labor force participation rate						
all persons 16 years old and over	70.1%	57.8%	76.9%	57.5%	76.1%	57.5%
- persons 16-19 years old	40.6	36.7	59.4	55.4	55.7	51.8
- persons 20 years old and over	73.8	60.0	78.3	57.6	77.8	57.9
- persons 65 years old and over	13.0	9.9	16.8	8.5	16.4	8.7

continued on the next page

Table 6.02 continued

	Black		White		All Races	
	male	female	male	female	male	female
1997						
civilian noninstitutional population						
all persons 16 years old and over	10,763	13,241	82,577	87,417	97,715	105,418
- persons 16-19 years old	1,188	1,225	6,257	5,924	7,836	7,528
- persons 65 years old and over	1,045	1,608	12,067	16,447	13,469	18,520
civilian labor force						
all persons 16 years old and over	7,354	8,175	62,639	52,054	73,261	63,036
- persons 16-19 years old	444	489	3,513	3,207	4,095	3,837
- persons 65 years old and over	134	131	2,094	1,422	2,298	1,590
labor force participation rate						
all persons 16 years old and over	68.3%	61.7%	75.9%	59.5%	75.0%	59.8%
- persons 16-19 years old	37.4	39.9	56.1	54.1	52.3	51.0
- persons 65 years old and over	12.9	8.2	17.4	8.6	17.1	8.6

SOURCE: U.S. Department of Labor, Bureau of Labor Statistics, Handbook of Labor Statistics, 1989, pp. 13-30, tables 3-5. L 2.3/5:989
U.S. Department of Labor, Bureau of Labor Statistics, *Employment and Earnings*, January, 1991, pp. 164-166, table 3; January, 1998, pp. 164-166, table 3 (data from the Current Population Survey). L2.41/2:(vol)/1:(year)

NOTES: 'All Races' includes other races not shown separately.

UNITS: Civilian noninstitutional population and civilian labor force in thousands of persons; participation rate as a percent (the civilian noninstitutional population divided by the civilian labor force).

Table 6.03 Civilian Labor Force and Civilian Labor Force Participation Rates: Projections for 2006

	Black	White	All Races
2006			
civilian labor force			
total	17.2%	123.6%	148.8%
men	8.0	66.0	78.2
women	9.2	57.6	70.6
labor force participation rate			
total	64.9%	68.1%	67.6%
men	69.6	74.3	73.6
women	61.3	62.0	61.4

SOURCE: U.S. Bureau of the Census, Statistical Abstract of the United States, 1998, p. 403, table 645 (data from U.S. Department of Labor, Bureau of Labor Statistics) C 3.134:998

NOTES: 'All Races' includes other races not shown separately.

UNITS: Civilian labor force population 16 years old and over in millions of persons; labor force participation rate as a percent (the civilian noninstitutional population divided by the civilian labor force).

Table 6.04 Employed Members of the Civilian Labor Force, by Sex and Age, 1980 - 1997

	Black		White		All Races	
	male	female	male	female	male	female
1980						
all employed persons 16 years old and over	4,798	4,515	51,127	36,587	57,186	42,177
- persons 16-19 years old	299	248	3,708	3,314	4,085	3,625
- persons 20 years old and over	4,498	4,267	47,419	33,275	53,101	38,492
- persons 65 years old and over	126	113	1,684	1,001	1,835	1,125
1990						
all employed persons 16 years old and over	5,915	6,051	56,432	45,654	64,435	53,479
- persons 16-19 years old	294	279	2,856	2,662	3,237	3,024
- persons 20 years old and over	5,621	5,780	53,576	42,992	61,198	50,455
- persons 65 years old and over	125	139	1,812	1,288	1,972	1,455
1997						
all employed persons 16 years old and over	6,607	7,362	59,998	49,859	69,685	59,873
- persons 16-19 years old	282	349	3,011	2,796	3,401	3,260
- persons 65 years old and over	127	122	2,037	1,374	2,229	1,532

SOURCE: U.S. Department of Labor, Bureau of Labor Statistics, Handbook of Labor Statistics, 1989, pp. 63-68, table 15, (data from the Current Population Survey). L 2.3/5:989

U.S. Department of Labor, Bureau of Labor Statistics, *Employment and Earnings*, January, 1991, pp. 164-166, table 3; January, 1998, pp. 164-166, table 3 (data from the Current Population Survey). L2.41/2:(vol)/1:(year)

NOTES: 'All Races' includes other races not shown separately. Data covers members of the civilian labor force.

UNITS: Employed members of the civilian labor force in thousands of persons, by age group as shown.

Table 6.05 Employment Status of Families, 1997

	Black	White	All Races
Total families	8,308	58,514	69,714
With employed member(s)	6,409	48,378	57,289
Some usually work full time	5,810	45,069	53,226
With no employed member	1,899	10,135	12,425
With unemployed member(s)	1,104	3,566	4,913
Some member(s) employed	631	2,632	3,445
Some usually work full time	553	2,353	3,070

SOURCE: U.S. Department Labor, Bureau Labor Statistics; "Employment Characteristics of Families, 1997 (Table) 1. Employment and unemployment in families, by race and Hispanic origin, 1996-97 annual averages"; (accessed: 19 November 1998); <http://stats.bls.gov/news.release/famee.t0l.htm>

NOTES: 'All Races' includes other races not shown separately.

UNITS: Number of families in thousands of families.

Table 6.06 Self-employed Persons, 1997

	Black	White	All Races
1997			
worked at home	135	3,868	4,125
percent who worked less than 8 hours	29.2%	30.5%	30.4%
8 hours or more			
total	70.8	69.5	69.6
35 hours or more	47.0	29.0	29.3
mean hours:			
worked at home	29.1	22.9	23.0
total at work on primary job	42.7	36.9	37.3

SOURCE: U.S. Department of Labor, Bureau of Labor Statistics, "Table 5: Home-based businesses: Self-employed persons by selected characteristics, May 1997;" pp. 1-2, table 5. <http://stats.bls.gov/news.release/homey.t05.htm> accesses 19 November, 1998.

NOTES: Data refer to employed persons in nonagricultural industries who reported work in a home-based business during the survey reference week as part of their primary job. Detail for the above race and Hispanic-origin groups will not sum to totals because data for the "other races" group are not presented and Hispanics are included in both the white and black population groups. Data reflect revised population controls used in the Current Population Survey effective with January 1997 estimates.

UNITS: Numbers in thousands of persons. Percent as a percent of persons working at home.

Table 6.07 Unemployed Jobseekers by Active Job Search Methods Used, 1997

	Black	White	All Races
Total unemployed	1,560	4,836	6,739
Total jobseekers	1,438	4,059	5,808
Methods used as a percent of total jobseekers			
Employer directly	64.7%	65.1%	65.0%
Sent out resumes or filled out applications	46.5	49.2	48.4
Placed or answered ads	15.2	17.4	16.9
Friends or relatives	14.7	16.3	16.1
Public employment agency	23.0	17.5	18.7
Private employment agency	7.2	6.8	6.9
Other	6.2	8.8	8.1

SOURCE: U.S. Department of Labor, Bureau of Labor Statistics, *Employment and Earnings*, January, 1998, p. 200, table 33, (data from the Current Population Survey). L 2.41/2:40/1:998

NOTES: 'All Races' includes other races not shown separately. "Jobseekers" does not include persons on temporary layoff.

UNITS: Persons in thousands of persons.

Table 6.08 Employed Black Persons as Percent of All Employed Persons in the Civilian Labor Force, by Selected Occupation, 1997

1997	
All occupations	10.8%
Managerial and professional specialty	7.3
executive, administrative and managerial	6.9
Professional specialty	7.8
architects	1.7
engineers	3.9
mathematical and computer scientists	7.5
natural scientists	5.1
physicians	4.2
dentists	2.6
health assessment and treatment occupations	8.4
college and university teachers	6.5
teachers, except college and university	10.2
lawyers and judges	2.8
writers, artists, entertainers, and athletes	5.0
Technicians, sales, and administrative support	10.5
technical and related support	9.7
health technologists	13.0
engineering and related technologists and technicians	7.4
science technicians	9.4
Sales occupations	8.1
Administrative support, including clerical	12.8
computer equipment operators	15.4
secretaries, stenographers, typists	9.8

continued on the next page

Table 6.08 continued

Service occupations	17.6%
private household	16.2
protective service	18.7
fire fighting and fire prevention	11.9
police and detectives	18.1
guards	21.6
Service occupations (except private household and protective service)	17.5
food preparation and service occupations	11.6
health service occupations	30.8
cleaning and building service occupations	21.5
personal service occupations	14.3
Precision production, craft and repair	8.1
mechanics and repairers	7.9
construction trades	7.1
precision production occupations	9.7
Operators, fabricators, and laborers	15.1
machine operators, assemblers, and inspectors	14.8
Transportation and material moving occupations	15.2
Handlers, equipment cleaners, helpers, and laborers	15.5
Farming, forestry, and fishing	4.5
farm operators and managers	1.2

SOURCE: U.S. Department of Labor, Bureaù of Labor Statistics, *Employment and Earnings*, January, 1998, pp. 174-178, table 11 (data from the Current Population Survey). L 2..41/2:408/1:998

NOTES: Only selected subcategories of occupational groups displayed.

UNITS: Employed Black persons as a percent of all employed persons, by occupation.

Table 6.09 Employed Black Persons as Percent of All Employed Persons in the Civilian Labor Force, by Industry Group, 1997

	1997
All industries	10.8%
agriculture	3.4
mining	4.2
construction	6.8
manufacturing	10.4
transportation, communications, and other public utilities	14.9
wholesale and retail trade	8.9
wholesale trade	6.3
retail trade	9.4
finance, insurance and real estate	9.7
services	12.1
public administration	16.5

SOURCE: U.S. Department of Labor, Bureau of Labor Statistics, *Employment and Earnings*, January, 1998, pp. 187-191, table 18 (data from the Current Population Survey). L 2.41/2:40/1:998

NOTES: Only selected subcategories of industry groups are displayed.

UNITS: Employed Black persons as a percent of all employed persons, by industry group.

Table 6.10 Full-Time and Part-Time Status of Employed Persons in Nonagricultural Industries, 1980 - 1997

	Black	White	All Races
1980			
All employed persons in nonagricultural industries	8,502	79,614	90,209
full-time	6,998	64,835	73,590
part-time	1,504	14,780	16,619
part time for economic reasons	601	3,375	4,064
1985			
All employed persons in nonagricultural industries	9,711	85,857	98,303
full-time	7,951	69,713	79,931
part-time	1,760	16,144	18,372
part time for economic reasons	875	4,322	5,334
1990			
All employed persons in nonagricultural industries	11,184	93,886	108,697
full-time	9,358	76,697	89,081
part-time	1,826	17,188	19,616
part time for economic reasons	721	3,989	4,860

continued on the next page

Table 6.10 continued

	Black	White	All Races
1992			
All employed persons in nonagricultural industries	11,142	93,383	108,457
full-time	9,194	75,604	88,012
part-time	1,948	17,779	20,345
part time for economic reasons	907	4,975	6,116
1993			
All employed persons in nonagricultural industries	11,408	94,835	110,340
full-time	9,428	76,814	89,597
part-time	1,980	18,021	20,743
part time for economic reasons	914	4,951	6,106
1997			
All employed persons in nonagricultural industries	13,247	102,063	120,770
full-time	10,287	76,478	91,021
part-time	2,960	25,585	29,749
part time for economic reasons	632	3,058	3,879

SOURCE: U.S. Department of Labor, Bureau of Labor Statistics, Handbook of Labor Statistics, 1989, pp. 121-123, table 23, (data from the Current Population Survey). L 2.3/5:989

U.S. Department of Labor, Bureau of Labor Statistics, *Employment and Earnings*, January, 1991, p. 201, table 32; p. 202, table 33; January, 1993, p. 211, table 32; p. 212, table 33; January, 1994, p. 222, table 33; January, 1998, p. 194, table 22 (data from the Current Population Survey). L 2.41/2:(vol)/1:(year)

NOTES: 'All Races' includes other races not shown separately. Economic reasons for persons who are employed part-time are: slack work; material shortages; repairs to plant or equipment; start or termination of a job during the week; and inability to find full time work.

UNITS: Employed members of the civilian labor force in thousands of persons, by status, as shown.

Table 6.11 Unemployment Rates for the Civilian Labor Force, by Age, 1980 - 1997

	Black	White	All Races
1980			
unemployment rate			
all ages	14.3%	6.3%	7.1%
- persons 16-19 years old	38.5	15.5	17.8
- persons 20 years old and over	12.1	5.4	6.1
- persons 65 years old and over	6.9	2.7	3.1
1985			
unemployment rate			
all ages	15.1%	6.2%	7.2%
- persons 16-19 years old	40.2	15.7	18.6
- persons 20 years old and over	13.1	5.5	6.4
- persons 65 years old and over	7.0	2.9	3.2
1990			
unemployment rate			
all ages	11.3%	4.7%	5.5%
- persons 16-19 years old	31.3	13.4	15.5
- persons 20-24 years old	19.9	7.2	8.8
- persons 25-54 years old	9.0	3.9	4.5
- persons 55-64 years old	4.6	3.2	3.3
- persons 65 years old and over	5.3	2.8	3.0

continued on the next page

Table 6.11 continued

	Black	White	All Races
1997			
unemployment rate			
all ages	10.0%	4.2%	4.9%
- persons 16-19 years old	32.4	13.6	16.0
- persons 20-24 years old	18.3	6.9	8.5
- persons 25-54 years old	7.6	3.3	3.9
- persons 55-64 years old	4.2	2.7	2.9
- persons 65 years old and over	6.1	3.0	3.3

SOURCE: U.S. Department of Labor, Bureau of Labor Statistics, Handbook of Labor Statistics, 1989, pp. 136-141, table 28, (data from the Current Population Survey). L 2.3/5:989
U.S. Department of Labor, Bureau of Labor Statistics, *Employment and Earnings*, January, 1991, pp. 164-166, table 3; January, 1998, pp. 164-166, table 3 (data from the Current Population Survey). L2.41/2:(vol)/1:(year)

NOTES: 'All Races' includes other races not shown separately. Data covers members of the civilian labor force.

UNITS: Unemployment rate, by age group as shown.

Table 6.12 Unemployment Rates for the Civilian Labor Force, by Sex and Age, 1980 - 1997

	Black		White		All Races	
	male	female	male	female	male	female
1980						
unemployment rate						
all ages	14.5%	14.0%	6.1%	6.5%	6.9%	7.4%
- persons 16-19 years old	37.5	39.8	16.2	14.8	18.3	17.2
- persons 20 years old and over	12.4	11.9	5.3	5.6	5.9	6.4
- persons 65 years old and over	8.7	4.9	2.5	3.0	3.1	3.1
1985						
unemployment rate						
all ages	15.3	14.9%	6.1%	6.4%	7.0%	7.4%
- persons 16-19 years old	41.0	39.2	16.5	14.8	19.5	17.6
- persons 20 years old and over	13.2	13.1	5.4	5.7	6.2	6.6
- persons 65 years old and over	8.9	5.2	2.7	3.1	3.1	3.3
1990						
unemployment rate						
all ages	11.3%	10.8%	4.8%	4.6%	5.6%	5.4%
- persons 16-19 years old	31.1	30.0	14.2	12.6	16.3	14.7
- persons 20-24 years old	19.9	19.7	7.6	6.8	9.1	8.5
- persons 25-54 years old	9.0	8.7	3.9	3.9	4.5	4.5
- persons 55-64 years old	4.6	3.7	3.6	2.7	3.8	2.8
- persons 65 years old and over	5.3	5.8	2.8	2.8	3.0	3.1

continued on the next page

Table 6.12 continued

	Black		White		All Races	
	male	female	male	female	male	female
1997						
unemployment rate						
all ages	10.2%	9.9%	4.2%	4.2%	4.9%	5.0%
- persons 16-19 years old	36.5	28.7	14.3	12.8	16.9	15.0
- persons 20-24 years old	19.8	17.1	7.3	6.4	8.9	8.1
- persons 25-54 years old	7.2	7.9	3.3	3.5	3.7	4.1
- persons 55-64 years old	4.2	4.1	2.9	2.4	3.1	2.7
- persons 65 years old and over	5.5	6.6	2.7	3.4	3.0	3.6

SOURCE: U.S. Department of Labor, Bureau of Labor Statistics, Handbook of Labor Statistics, 1989, pp. 151-153, table 37, (data from the Current Population Survey). L 2.3/5:989

U.S. Department of Labor, Bureau of Labor Statistics, *Employment and Earnings*, January, 1991, pp. 164-166, table 3; January, 1998, pp. 164-166, table 3 (data from the Current Population Survey). L2.41/2:(vol)/1:(year)

NOTES: 'All Races' includes other races not shown separately. Data covers members of the civilian labor force.

UNITS: Unemployment rate, by age group as shown.

Table 6.13 Unemployment, by Reason for Unemployment, 1980 - 1997

	Black	White	All Races
1980			
Total	1,553	5,884	7,637
job losers	na .	3,100	3,947
job leavers	na	733	891
reentrants to the labor force	424	1,447	1,927
new entrants to the labor force	239	603	872
1985			
Total	1,864	6,191	8,312
job losers	890	3,146	4,139
job leavers	110	727	877
reentrants to the labor force	546	1,635	2,256
new entrants to the labor force	317	682	1,039
1990			
Total	1,527	5,091	6,874
job losers	678	2,534	3,322
job leavers	187	787	1,014
reentrants to the labor force	461	1,346	1,883
new entrants to the labor force	201	423	654
1997			
Total	1,560	4,836	6,739
job losers	616	2,284	3,037
job leavers	138	623	795
reentrants to the labor force	634	1,576	2,338
new entrants to the labor force	172	354	569

SOURCE: U.S. Department of Labor, Bureau of Labor Statistics, Handbook of Labor Statistics, 1989, pp. 151-153, table 37, (data from the Current Population Survey). L 2.3/5:989

U.S. Department of Labor, Bureau of Labor Statistics, *Employment and Earnings*, January, 1991, p. 176, table 12; January, 1998, p. 200, table 28 (data from the Current Population Survey). L2.41/2:(vol)/1:(year)

NOTES: 'All Races' includes other races not shown separately. Data covers members of the civilian labor force.

UNITS: Unemployed members of the civilian labor force in thousands of persons, by reason for unemployment as shown.

Table 6.14 Duration of Unemployment, by Region of Residence, 1992 and 1996

	Black	White	All Races
1992			
Northeast			
less than 5 weeks	22.3%	25.9%	25.5%
5-14 weeks	27.1	27.9	27.8
15 weeks and over	50.6	46.1	46.7
27 weeks and over	31.6	28.0	28.5
52 weeks and over	20.2	14.5	15.5
Midwest			
less than 5 weeks	39.5%	36.2%	37.0%
5-14 weeks	30.8	30.4	30.5
15 weeks and over	29.7	33.4	32.5
27 weeks and over	17.0	18.5	18.2
52 weeks and over	11.1	10.0	10.2
South			
less than 5 weeks	37.1%	38.7%	38.0%
5-14 weeks	29.0	29.7	29.6
15 weeks and over	33.8	31.7	32.4
27 weeks and over	19.0	18.1	18.4
52 weeks and over	11.5	9.4	10.1
West			
less than 5 weeks	29.5%	38.3%	37.3%
5-14 weeks	36.4	29.0	29.7
15 weeks and over	34.0	32.7	33.0
27 weeks and over	21.3	18.1	18.4
52 weeks and over	12.4	9.4	9.6
1996			
Northeast			
less than 5 weeks	22.5%	33.1%	30.8%
5-14 weeks	28.2	31.9	30.9
15 weeks and over	49.5	35.2	36.4
27 weeks and over	32.2	19.2	22.2
52 weeks and over	20.9	10.8	13.1

continued on the next page

Table 6.14 continued

	Black	White	All Races
1996			
Midwest			
less than 5 weeks	30.5%	41.3%	39.1%
5-14 weeks	33.4	32.8	32.7
15 weeks and over	36.0	25.9	28.1
27 weeks and over	19.3	12.1	13.7
52 weeks and over	11.5	6.5	7.5
South			
less than 5 weeks	33.3%	41.3%	38.5%
5-14 weeks	34.0	31.3	32.3
15 weeks and over	32.8	27.4	29.3
27 weeks and over	18.3	14.0	15.5
52 weeks and over	9.1	6.5	7.6
West			
less than 5 weeks	25.6%	37.5%	36.2%
5-14 weeks	34.6	30.1	30.4
15 weeks and over	40.3	33.0	34.0
27 weeks and over	25.3	18.8	19.4
52 weeks and over	12.9	10.4	10.9

SOURCE: U.S. Department of Labor, Bureau of Labor Statistics, Geographic Profile of Employment and Unemployment, 1992, pp. 33-34, table 11; 1996, pp. 33-34, table 11. L 2.3/12:(year)

NOTES: 'All Races' includes other races not shown separately.

UNITS: Duration of unemployment by region as a percent of total unemployment in each region, 100.0%.

Table 6.15 Labor Force Status of the Civilian Noninstitutional Population 16 - 24 Years of Age, by School Enrollment, 1980 and 1997

	Black	White	All Races
1980			
All persons enrolled in school	2,028	13,242	15,713
civilian labor force	595	6,687	7,454
- employed	406	5,889	6,433
- unemployed	189	798	1,021
all persons enrolled in school below college level	1,281	6,566	8,049
civilian labor force	294	3,095	3,458
- employed	174	2,579	2,801
- unemployed	120	516	657
all persons enrolled in school on college level	747	6,678	7,664
civilian labor force	300	3,592	3,996
- employed	230	3,310	3,632
- unemployed	70	282	364
persons not enrolled in school	2,864	18,103	21,390
civilian labor force	2,055	15,121	17,464
- employed	1,451	13,318	15,021
- unemployed	604	1,803	2,443

continued on the next page

Table 6.15 continued

	Black	White	All Races
1997			
All persons enrolled in school	2,619	14,376	18,140
civilian labor force	924	7,519	8,841
- employed	732	6,862	7,957
- unemployed	192	657	884
all persons enrolled in school below college level	1,511	6,756	na
civilian labor force	406	2,951	na
- employed	278	2,575	na
- unemployed	128	376	na
all persons enrolled in school on college level	1,109	7,620	9,373
civilian labor force	519	4,568	5,372
- employed	455	4,287	5,016
- unemployed	64	281	356
persons not enrolled in school	2,337	11,881	14,825
civilian labor force	1,710	9,980	12,152
- employed	1,333	9,095	10,853
- unemployed	377	885	1,299

SOURCE: U.S. Bureau of the Census, Statistical Abstract of the United States, 1998 p. 407, table 651 (data from U.S. Department of Labor, Bureau of Labor Statistics). C 3.134:998

NOTES: 'All Races' includes other races not shown separately.

UNITS: Civilian noninstitutional population, civilian labor force, employed and unemployed, in thousands of persons.

Table 6.16 Educational Attainment of Persons 16 Years and Over, by Labor Force Status and Sex, 1997

	Black		White		All Races	
	male	female	male	female	male	female
High school graduate or more						
In civilian labor force	79.7%	84.9%	84.1%	88.7%	83.8%	88.1%
Employed	82.1	87.0	85.2	89.6	85.0	89.2
Unemployed	62.7	65.6	63.9	66.4	64.3	68.5
Not in labor force	45.6	52.0	61.9	67.5	59.5	65.5
Bachelor's degree or more						
In civilian labor force	13.2%	15.5%	26.4%	25.7%	25.8%	24.7%
Employed	14.3	16.5	27.4	26.4	26.8	25.6
Unemployed	5.5	6.4	9.7	10.4	9.3	9.7
Not in labor force	3.8	6.0	14.2	11.8	13.0	11.4

SOURCE: U.S. Bureau of the Census, Current Population Reports: Educational Attainment in the United States: March 1997, Series P-20, #505, pp. 35-37, table 6. <www.census.gov/prod/3/98pubs/p20-505u.pdf>, accessed 15 October 1998.

NOTES: 'All Races' includes other races not shown separately.

UNITS: Percent distribution as a percent of total, 100.0%.

Table 6.17 Unemployment Rates of the Civilian Labor Force 25 - 64 Years of Age, by Educational Attainment, 1980 - 1997

	Black	White	All Races
1980			
Total	9.6%	4.4%	5.0%
less than 4 years of high school	11.7	7.8	8.4
4 years of high school only	9.5	4.6	5.1
1-3 years of college	9.0	3.9	4.3
4 or more years of college	4.0	1.8	1.9
1985			
Total	12.0%	5.3%	6.1%
less than 4 years of high school	15.3	10.6	11.4
4 years of high school only	13.0	6.1	6.9
1-3 years of college	10.6	3.9	4.7
4 or more years of college	5.4	2.1	2.4
1990			
Total	8.6%	3.8%	4.4%
less than 4 years of high school	13.3	7.6	8.5
4 years of high school only	9.5	4.2	4.9
1-3 years of college	6.8	3.2	3.7
4 or more years of college	3.0	2.1	2.2
1997			
Total	8.1%	3.9%	4.4%
less than a high school diploma	16.6	9.4	10.4
high school graduate, no college	8.2	4.6	5.1
less than a bachelor's degree	6.1	3.4	3.8
college graduate	4.4	1.8	2.0

SOURCE: U.S. Bureau of the Census, Statistical Abstract of the United States, 1992, p. 400, table 637; 1998, p. 425, table 681 (data from U.S. Department of Labor, Bureau of Labor Statistics). C 3.134:(year)

NOTES: 'All Races' includes other races not shown separately. 1997 data is for persons 25 years old and over.

UNITS: Unemployment rates (percent of the civilian labor force that is unemployed) as a percent of the total civilian labor force.

Table 6.18 Self-Employed Workers, 1980 - 1997

	Black	White	All Races
1980	342	8,116	8,642
1983	345	8,581	9,140
1984	365	8,763	9,338
1985	379	8,659	9,269
1986	380	8,706	9,328
1987	403	8,956	9,624
1988	414	9,199	9,917
1989	411	9,291	10,008
1990	461	9,377	10,160
1991	475	9,512	10,341
1992	452	9,215	10,017
1993	468	9,486	10,335
1994	458	8,179	9,003
1995	488	8,105	8,902
1996	481	8,106	8,971
1997	471	8,153	9,056

SOURCE: U.S. Bureau of the Census, Statistical Abstract of the United States, 1989, p. 380, table 627 (data from U.S. Department of Labor, Bureau of Labor Statistics, *Employment and Earnings*). C 3.134:989
U.S. Department of Labor, Bureau of Labor Statistics, *Employment and Earnings*, January, 1991, p. 210, table 41; January, 1992, p. 210, table 41; January, 1993, p. 220, table 41; January, 1994, p. 230, table 41; January, 1998, p. 180, table 12 (data from the Current Population Survey). L2.41/2:(vol)/1:(year)

NOTES: 'All Races' includes other races not shown separately.

UNITS: Self-employed workers in thousands of persons.

Table 6.19 Labor Force Participation Rates for Wives in Married Couple Families, by Age of Own Youngest Child, 1980 - 1997

	Black	White	All Races
1980			
All wives in married couple families	59.3%	49.3%	50.2%
wives with no children under 18	51.2	45.5	46.0
wives with children under 18	65.6	53.2	54.3
with children under 6	63.4	43.5	45.3
with children under 3	57.7	40.0	41.5
- 1 year or under	52.9	37.7	39.0
- 2 years old	71.0	46.1	48.1
with children 3-5	72.3	49.4	51.7
- 3 years old	73.4	48.4	51.5
- 4 years old	66.4	49.8	51.4
- 5 years old	77.8	50.4	52.4
with children 6-13 years	71.8	61.4	62.6
with children 14-17 years	58.4	60.6	60.5
1990			
All wives in married couple families	64.7%	57.6%	58.2%
wives with no children under 18	52.9	50.8	51.1
wives with children under 18	75.6	65.6	66.3
with children under 6	73.1	57.8	58.9
with children under 3	67.5	54.9	55.5
- 1 year or under	64.4	53.3	53.9
- 2 years old	75.4	60.3	60.9
with children 3-5	80.4	62.5	64.1
- 3 years old	74.5	62.3	63.1
- 4 years old	80.6	63.2	65.1
- 5 years old	86.2	62.0	64.5
with children 6-13 years	77.6	72.6	73.0
with children 14-17 years	78.8	74.9	75.1

continued on the next page

Table 6.19 continued

	Black	White	All Races
1993			
All wives in married couple families	64.8%	58.9%	59.4%
wives with no children under 18	53.8	52.2	52.4
wives with children under 18	75.3	66.9	67.5
with children under 6	70.9	58.6	59.6
with children under 3	65.6	56.7	57.3
- 1 year or under	64.8	56.8	57.5
- 2 years old	74.5	56.5	58.1
with children 3-5	78.1	61.6	63.1
- 3 years old	79.4	60.2	61.6
- 4 years old	79.3	64.3	65.7
- 5 years old	77.5	61.4	63.1
with children 6-13 years	80.6	74.5	74.7
with children 14-17 years	75.7	75.6	75.6
1997			
All wives in married couple families	69.2%	61.5%	62.1%
wives with no children under 18	57.4	53.8	54.2
wives with children under 18	80.1	70.6	71.1
with children under 6	78.1	62.9	63.6
with children under 3	73.7	61.1	61.3
- 1 year or under	69.5	58.9	59.5
- 2 years old	81.5	66.5	66.6
with children 3-5	82.8	65.5	67.0
- 3 years old	79.4	64.6	65.1
- 4 years old	79.5	63.2	64.6
- 5 years old	78.7	70.0	71.2
with children 6-13 years	81.3	76.2	76.5
with children 14-17 years	82.9	80.0	80.1

SOURCE: U.S. Bureau of the Census, Statistical Abstract of the United States, 1992, p. 388, table 621; 1994, p. 402, table 627; 1998, p. 409, table 655 (data from the Current Population Survey). C 3.134:(year)

NOTES: 'All Races' includes other races not shown separately. Civilian noninstitutional population, 16 years old and over.

UNITS: Participation rates in percent.

Table 6.20 Workers Paid Hourly Rates With Earnings at or Below the Minimum Wage, 1997

	Black	White	All Races
Number of workers			
All workers paid hourly rates	9,562	58,395	71,081
at or below $5.15 per hour	1,116	4,863	6,237
at $5.15 per hour	423	1,632	2,115
below $5.15 per hour	693	3,231	4,122
Percent of all workers paid hourly rates			
All at or below $5.15 per hour	11.7%	8.3%	8.8%
at $5.15 per hour	4.4	2.8	3.0
below $5.15 per hour	7.2	5.5	5.8
Median hourly earnings	$8.06	$8.97	$8.84

SOURCE: U.S. Bureau of the Census, Statistical Abstract of the United States, 1998, p. 438, table 700 (data from the U.S. Bureau of Labor Statistics). C 3.134:998

NOTES: 'All Races' includes other races not shown separately. Workers 16 years and over.

UNITS: Number of workers in thousands; 'percent of all workers paid hourly rates' in percent, as a percent of total, 100.0%; median hourly earnings of workers paid hourly rates in dollars per hour.

Table 6.21 Union Membership, 1997

	Black	White	All Races
Men			
total employed	6,201	50,941	59,825
members of unions			
number	1,251	8,171	9,763
as a percent of total employed	20.2%	16.0%	16.3%
represented by unions			
total	1,378	8,859	10,619
as a percent of total employed	22.2%	17.4%	17.7%
Women			
total employed	7,145	45,163	54,708
members of unions			
number	1,143	4,917	6,347
as a percent of total employed	16.0%	10.9%	11.6%
represented by unions			
total	1,309	5,679	7,304
as a percent of total employed	18.3%	12.6%	13.4%

SOURCE: U.S. Department of Labor, Bureau of Labor Statistics, *Employment and Earnings*, January 1998, p. 215, table 40, (data from the Current Population Survey). L 2.41/2:40/1:998

NOTES: 'All Races' includes other races not shown separately. 'Members of unions' includes members of a labor union or an employee association similar to a union. 'Represented by unions' includes members of a labor union or an employee association similar to a union as well as workers who report no union affiliation but whose jobs are covered by a union or an employee association contract.

UNITS: Total employed, members of unions and represented by unions in thousands of persons 16 years old and older; percent as shown.

Chapter 7: Earnings, Income, Poverty & Wealth

Table 7.01 Money Income of Households, 1980 - 1997

	Black	White	All Races
Median income			
1980	$19,383	$33,645	$31,891
1985	20,411	34,306	32,530
1986	20,391	35,394	33,665
1987	20,445	35,821	33,999
1988	20,554	36,055	34,106
1989	21,612	36,340	34,547
1990	21,177	35,413	33,952
1991	20,464	34,350	32,780
1992	19,811	34,023	32,361
1993	20,033	33,804	32,041
1994	21,027	34,028	32,264
1996	23,482	37,161	35,492
1997	25,050	38,972	37,005
Mean income			
1980	$25,156	$39,459	$37,929
1985	26,631	41,676	40,033
1986	27,358	43,324	41,592
1987	27,606	44,088	42,281
1988	28,158	44,432	42,615
1989	28,678	45,465	43,647
1990	28,136	44,122	42,411
1991	27,249	43,005	41,263
1992	26,883	42,880	41,027
1993	27,926	44,393	42,489
1994	29,259	45,034	43,133
1996	32,460	48,994	47,123
1997	32,963	51,902	49,692

SOURCE: U.S. Bureau of the Census, Current Population Reports: Income, Poverty, and Valuation of Noncash Benefits: 1994, Series P-60, #189, pp. B-2 - B-3, table B-1. C3.186/2:994

U.S. Bureau of the Census, Current Population Reports: Money Income in the United States: 1996, Series P-60, #197, p. 5, table 2 C3.186/2:996; 1997, Series P-60, #200, p. 5, table 2 , <www.census.gov/prod/3/98pubs/p60-200.pdf accessed 15 October 1998.

NOTES: 'All Races' includes other races not shown separately.

UNITS: Median and mean money income in 1994 CPI-U-XI adjusted dollars, as shown.

Table 7.02 Money Income of Households, by Selected Household Characteristic, 1985, 1990, 1997

	Black	White	All Races
1985			
Number of households	9,797	76,576	88,458
percent of households with current dollar incomes of:			
under $2,500	17.6%	6.7%	7.6%
$5,000-$7,499	10.6	6.4	6.8
$7,500-$9,999	8.2	5.3	5.6
$10,000-$12,499	7.9	5.8	6.0
$12,500-$14,999	6.2	5.4	5.4
$15,000-$19,999	12.4	10.8	10.9
$20,000-$24,999	8.4	10.1	10.0
$25,000-$34,999	12.9	17.5	17.0
$35,000-$49,999	9.9	16.5	15.8
$50,000 and over	5.8	15.8	14.8
mean income	$19,335	$30,259	$29,066
Mean income by:			
occupation of the householder			
managerial, professional specialty	$36,191	$47,731	$47,042
technical, sales, administrative support	23,570	34,467	33,437
service workers	17,324	23,651	22,169
farming, forestry, fishing	12,001	20,183	19,756
precision production, craft, repair	27,996	32,388	32,110
operators, fabricators, laborers	23,037	28,015	27,314
work experience of the householder			
worked at full time jobs	$26,198	$36,779	$35,756
worked 50-52 weeks	28,394	39,304	38,307
type of household			
family households	$21,673	$34,605	$33,182
married couple families	28,258	36,991	36,350
non-family households	13,708	19,187	18,559
single person households	11,995	16,550	15,997

continued on the next page

Table 7.02 continued

	Black	White	All Races
1990			
Number of households	10,671	80,968	94,312
percent of households with current dollar incomes of:			
under $5,000	14.1%	4.0%	5.2%
$5,000-$9,999	16.7	8.8	9.7
$10,000-$14,999	11.6	9.2	9.5
$15,000-$24,999	19.1	17.7	17.7
$25,000-$34,999	13.5	16.1	15.8
$35,000-$49,999	13.1	18.0	17.5
$50,000-$74,999	8.1	15.8	14.9
$75,000-$99,999	2.7	5.7	5.4
$100,000 and over	1.1	4.7	4.3
mean income	$24,814	$38,912	$37,403
median income	$18,676	$31,231	$29,943
Median income by:			
type of residence			
nonfarm	$18,734	$31,216	$29,901
farm	na	31,819	21,589
inside metropolitan area	20,121	33,460	31,823
outside metropolitan area	13,119	24,887	23,709
type of household			
family households	$21,899	$37,219	$35,707
married couple families	33,893	40,433	39,996
non-family households	11,789	18,449	17,690
male householder living alone	13,126	20,900	19,964
female householder living alone	7,674	13,094	12,548
age of householder			
15-24 years old	$ 9,816	$19,662	$18,002
25-34 years old	18,339	31,859	30,359
35-44 years old	26,011	40,423	38,561
45-54 years old	26,910	44,098	41,922
55-64 years old	19,226	34,249	32,365
65 years old and over	9,902	17,539	16,855

continued on the next page

Table 7.02 continued

	Black	White	All Races
1990 - continued			
size of household			
one person	$ 10,156	$15,981	$15,344
two persons	20,122	32,561	31,358
three persons	21,474	38,930	36,765
four persons	25,683	43,363	41,473
five persons	24,342	40,715	39,275
six persons	26,742	40,420	38,159
seven or more persons	22,361	40,822	36,108
number of earners			
no earners	$ 5,870	$12,395	$11,159
one earner	17,040	25,801	24,575
two earners or more	36,404	45,705	44,887
work experience of the householder			
all civilian householders	$18,471	$31,242	$29,945
worked	25,683	37,441	36,329
worked year-round full-time	31,042	42,010	40,976
did not work	7,249	15,144	13,820
housing tenure			
owner occupied	$27,377	$36,810	$36,298
renter occupied	13,929	21,962	20,722

continued on the next page

Table 7.02 continued

	Black	White	All Races
1997			
Number of households	12,474	86,106	102,528
number of households with current dollar incomes of:			
under $5,000	925	2,415	3,531
$5,000-$9,999	1,747	5,773	7,765
10,000-$14,999	1,316	6,716	8,326
$15,000-$24,999	2,238	12,549	15,244
$25,000-$34,999	1,766	11,350	13,586
$35,000-$49,999	1,859	14,170	16,698
$50,000-$74,999	1,637	16,190	18,531
$75,000-$99,999	570	8,183	9,186
$100,000 and over	415	8,762	9,661
median income	$25,050	$38,972	$37,005
mean income	$32,963	$51,902	$49,692
Median income by:			
type of residence			
inside metropolitan area	$25,720	$41,576	$39,381
outside metropolitan area	20,184	31,110	30,057
type of household			
family households	$29,915	$47,454	$45,347
married couple families	45,372	52,199	51,681
non-family households	17,073	22,380	21,705
male householder living alone	19,459	30,009	27,592
female householder living alone	15,341	17,997	17,613
age of householder			
15-24 years old	$15,056	$24,423	$22,583
25-34 years old	26,148	40,477	38,174
35-44 years old	27,711	49,695	46,359
45-54 years old	33,761	54,879	51,875
55-64 years old	27,350	43,052	41,356
65 years old and over	14,241	21,374	20,761

continued on the next page

Table 7.02 continued

	Black	White	All Races
1997 - continued			
size of household			
one person	$15,258	$19,288	$18,762
two persons	26,870	40,954	39,343
three persons	28,047	50,269	47,115
four persons	35,529	55,819	53,165
five persons	36,525	52,493	50,407
six persons	32,050	48,974	46,465
seven or more persons	30,799	46,044	42,343
number of earners			
no earners	$ 8,172	$15,324	$14,142
one earner	21,319	31,412	29,780
two earners or more	47,602	58,947	57,525
work experience of the householder			
all civilian householders	$25,050	$38,972	37,005
worked	31,461	47,973	45,877
worked year-round full-time	36,928	53,045	51,336
did not work	10,523	19,342	18,143
housing tenure			
owner occupied	$35,679	$46,578	$45,821
renter occupied	18,533	25,954	24,514

SOURCE: U.S. Bureau of the Census, Current Population Reports: Money Income of Households in the United States; March 1985, Series P-60, #156, p. 7, table 2; pp. 9-14, table 4; pp. 19-20, table 6. March 1990, Series P-60, #174, pp. 13-15, table 1; p. 16, table 2. C3.186/2:(year)
U.S. Bureau of the Census, Current Population Reports: Money Income in the United States: 1997, Series P-60, #200, pp. 1-3, table 1, p. 5, table 2. <www.census.gov/prod/3/98pubs/p60-200.pdf> accessed 15 October 1998.

NOTES: 'All Races' includes other races not shown separately. Number of households as of March of the following year. 'Occupation of the householder' represents the longest job held by the householder.

UNITS: Number of households in thousands; mean and median income in current dollars.

Table 7.03 Money Income of Families, 1980 - 1997

	Black	White	All Races
Median income			
1980	$24,717	$42,717	$40,999
1985	25,039	43,484	41,371
1986	25,780	45,117	43,139
1987	26,005	45,755	43,756
1988	26,224	46,013	43,674
1989	26,158	46,564	44,284
1990	26,308	45,332	43,414
1991	25,392	44,524	42,351
1992	24,141	44,238	41,839
1993	23,927	43,652	41,051
1994	26,748	44,277	42,001
1995	27,350	44,913	42,769
1996	27,131	45,783	43,271
1997	28,602	46,754	44,568
Mean income			
1980	$30,825	$48,636	$45,754
1985	31,860	51,275	49,140
1986	33,356	53,328	51,143
1987	33,586	54,436	52,112
1988	34,347	54,692	52,380
1989	34,190	56,179	53,723
1990	33,836	54,685	52,377
1991	32,490	53,352	50,951
1992	32,008	53,118	50,588
1993	33,362	55,055	52,450
1994	35,550	56,001	53,435
1995	35,819	56,445	54,082
1996	35,737	57,486	54,908
1997	36,504	59,587	56,902

SOURCE: U.S. Bureau of the Census, Current Population Reports: Money Income in the United States: 1997, Series P-60, #200, pp. B-8 - B-9, table B-4. <www.census.gov/prod/3/98pubs/p60-200.pdf>,accessed 15 October 1998.

NOTES: 'All Races' includes other races not shown separately.

UNITS: Median and mean money income in 1997 CPI-U-XI adjusted dollars, as shown.

Table 7.04 Money Income of Families, by Selected Family Characteristic, 1985

	Black	White	All Races
Families			
Number of families	6,921	54,991	63,558
percent of families with incomes:			
under $2,500	4.2%	1.6%	1.9%
$2,500-$4,499	9.3	2.1	2.9
$5,000-$7,499	9.4	3.6	4.2
$7,500-$9,999	7.7	3.9	4.3
$10,000-$12,499	7.9	4.8	5.2
$12,500-$14,999	6.4	4.9	5.0
$15,000-$19,999	13.0	10.3	10.5
$20,000-$24,999	9.0	10.4	10.3
$25,000-$34,999	14.3	19.2	18.6
$35,000-$49,999	11.8	19.7	18.8
$50,000 and over	7.0	19.6	18.3
median income	$16,786	$29,152	$27,735
mean income	$21,359	$34,375	$32,944
Mean family income by:			
occupation of the householder			
managerial, professional specialty	$38,870	$52,649	$51,820
technical, sales, administrative support	24,732	38,798	37,436
service occupations	19,485	26,604	24,846
farming, forestry, fishing	16,185	21,305	21,285
precision production, craft, repair	30,315	33,691	33,507
operators, fabricators, laborers	24,223	29,449	28,725
work experience of the householder			
worked at full time jobs	$28,022	$39,510	$38,437
worked 50-52 weeks	30,281	41,992	40,968

continued on the next page

Table 7.04 continued

	Black	White	All Races
Mean family income - continued			
type of family			
married couple families	$28,163	$36,911	$36,267
wife in paid labor force	33,120	41,818	41,058
wife not in paid labor force	19,306	31,934	30,650
male householder, no wife present	18,205	29,041	27,525
female householder, no husband present	13,050	19,468	17,647
type of income			
wages and salaries	$21,651	$31,277	$30,258
non-farm self-employment	10,165	14,565	14,420
farm self employment	na	4,593	4,557
property income	1,042	3,486	3,327
- interest income	722	2,440	2,328
transfer payments and all other income	5,491	7,776	7,469
- social security or railroad retirement income	5,801	7,684	7,488
-public assistance and supplemental income	3,475	3,416	3,498

SOURCE: U.S. Bureau of the Census, Current Population Reports: Money Income of Households Families and Persons in the United States; March 1985, Series P-60, #156, pp. 26-29, tables 9, 10; pp. 40-46, tables 13, 14; pp. 56-64, table 17; pp. 86-88, table 25. C3.186:P-60/156

NOTES: 'All Races' includes other races not shown separately. Number of families as of March of the following year. 'Occupation of the householder' represents the longest job held by the householder. 'Property income' includes interest, dividends, net rental income, income from trusts and estates, and net royalty income.

UNITS: Number of families and families with income, in thousands of families; percent as a percent as shown; mean and median income in current dollars.

Table 7.05 Money Income of Families, by Selected Family Characteristic, 1990

	Black	White	All Races
Families			
Number of families	7,471	58,803	66,322
percent of families with current dollar incomes of:			
under $5,000	11.5%	2.5%	3.6%
$5,000-$9,999	14.1	4.7	5.8
$10,000-$14,999	11.3	7.0	7.5
$15,000-$24,999	19.5	16.0	16.4
$25,000-$34,999	14.0	16.5	16.2
$35,000-$49,999	15.0	20.8	20.0
$50,000-$74,999	9.8	19.3	18.2
$75,000-$99,999	3.4	7.3	6.9
$100,000 and over	1.3	5.9	5.4
mean income	$27,554	$44,532	$42,652
median income	$21,423	$36,915	$35,353
Median income by:			
type of residence			
nonfarm	$21,467	$36,974	$35,376
farm	na	34,476	34,171
inside metropolitan area	22,924	40,086	37,893
outside metropolitan area	15,677	29,693	28,272
type of family			
married couple families	$33,784	$40,331	$39,895
wife in paid labor force	40,038	47,247	46,777
wife not in paid labor force	20,333	30,781	30,265
male householder, no wife present	21,848	30,570	29,046
female householder, no husband present	12,125	19,528	16,932

continued on the next page

Table 7.05 continued

	Black	White	All Races
Median income by:			
age of householder			
15-24 years old	$ 7,218	$18,234	$16,219
25-34 years old	17,130	33,457	31,497
35-44 years old	27,025	42,632	41,061
45-54 years old	30,847	49,249	47,165
55-64 years old	25,442	40,416	39,035
65 years old and over	16,585	25,864	25,049
size of family			
two persons	$19,020	$31,734	$30,428
three persons	20,602	38,858	36,644
four persons	25,758	43,352	41,451
five persons	22,455	41,037	39,452
six persons	26,926	40,387	38,379
seven or more persons	22,501	39,845	35,363
number of earners			
no earners	$ 6,305	$17,369	$15,047
one earner	16,308	27,670	25,878
two earners or more	36,741	46,261	45,462

SOURCE: U.S. Bureau of the Census, Current Population Reports: Money Income of Households, Families, and Persons in the United States: March 1990, Series P-60, #174, pp. 52-54, table 13; p. 56, table 14. C3.186/2:990

NOTES: 'All Races' includes other races not shown separately. Number of families as of March of the following year.

UNITS: Number of families and families with income, in thousands of families; percent as a percent as shown; mean and median income in current dollars.

Table 7.06 Money Income of Families, by Selected Family Characteristic, 1997

	Black	White	All Races
Families			
Number of families	8,408	59,515	70,884
with current dollar incomes of:			
under $5,000	577	1,262	1,929
$5,000-$9,999	851	1,923	2,887
$10,000-$14,999	824	3,047	4,054
$15,000-$24,999	1,486	7,454	9,250
$25,000-$34,999	1,193	7,552	9,079
$35,000-$49,999	1,302	10,527	12,357
$50,000-$74,999	1,344	13,172	15,112
$75,000-$99,999	480	6,973	7,826
$100,000 and over	352	7,605	8,391
median income	$28,602	$46,754	$44,568
mean income	$36,504	$59,587	$56,902
Median income by:			
type of residence			
inside metropolitan area	$29,737	$50,410	$47,315
outside metropolitan area	24,619	37,305	36,149
type of family			
married couple families	$45,372	$52,098	$51,591
wife in paid labor force	51,702	61,441	60,669
wife not in paid labor force	28,757	36,343	36,027
male householder, no wife present	25,654	34,802	32,960
female householder, no husband present	16,879	22,999	21,023

continued on the next page

Table 7.06 continued

	Black	White	All Races
Median income by:			
age of householder			
15-24 years old	$13,556	$22,431	$20,820
25-34 years old	24,620	41,890	39,979
35-44 years old	28,148	52,753	50,424
45-54 years old	41,903	61,852	59,959
55-64 years old	36,415	51,598	50,241
65 years old and over	23,420	31,167	30,660
size of family			
two persons	$25,061	$39,492	$37,562
three persons	26,060	50,149	46,783
four persons	34,644	56,022	53,350
five persons	36,984	53,696	51,101
six persons	31,197	48,079	45,473
seven or more persons	32,544	45,816	42,001
number of earners			
no earners	$ 9,012	$21,516	$19,731
one earner	19,597	32,811	30,204
two earners or more	48,750	60,291	58,972

SOURCE: U.S. Bureau of the Census, Current Population Reports: Money Income in the United States: 1997, Series P-60, #200, pp. 13-15, table 4; p. 17, table 5. <www.census.gov/prod/3/98pubs/p60-200.pdf>, accessed 15 October 1998.

NOTES: 'All Races' includes other races not shown separately. Number of families as of March of the following year.

UNITS: Number of families and families with income, in thousands of families; mean and median income in current dollars.

Table 7.07 Median Weekly Earnings of Families, by Type of Family and Number of Earners, 1985, 1990, 1993

	Black	White	All Races
1985			
All families with earners	$378	$543	$522
married couple families	487	589	582
with one earner	257	395	385
with two or more earners	622	723	715
families maintained by women	259	311	297
families maintained by men	360	475	450
1990			
All families with earners	$459	$681	$653
married couple families	601	745	732
with one earner	304	473	455
with two or more earners	748	892	880
families maintained by women	314	382	363
families maintained by men	397	539	514
1993			
All families with earners	$490	$739	$707
married couple families	674	816	804
with one earner	344	492	481
with two or more earners	846	984	973
families maintained by women	334	415	393
families maintained by men	413	547	523

SOURCE: U.S. Department of Labor, Bureau of Labor Statistics, Handbook of Labor Statistics, 1989, p. 200, table 44 (data from the Current Population Survey). L 2.3/5:989

U.S. Department of Labor, Bureau of Labor Statistics, *Employment and Earnings*, January, 1991, p. 219, table 52; January, 1994, p. 239, table 52 (data from the Current Population Survey). L 2.41/2:37/1:(year)

NOTES: 'All Races' includes other races not shown separately. Data excludes families in which there is no wage or salary earner, or in which the husband, wife, or other person maintaining the family is either self-employed or in the armed forces.

UNITS: Median weekly earnings in dollars.

Table 7.08 Money Income of Persons 15 Years Old and Older, by Selected Characteristic, 1985

	Black		White		All Races	
	male	female	male	female	male	female
Number of persons	9,309	11,263	76,617	82,345	88,474	96,354
persons with incomes:						
under $2,000	909	1,301	5,180	14,024	6,304	15,848
$2,000-$2,999	400	871	1,808	4,420	2,297	5,425
$3,000-$3,999	407	993	2,190	4,856	2,671	5,958
$4,000-$4,999	479	946	2,095	4,635	2,642	5,693
$5,000-$5,999	351	540	2,169	4,201	2,595	4,848
$6,000-$6,999	353	556	2,278	3,992	2,708	4,648
$7,000-$8,499	584	707	3,402	5,006	4,132	5,855
$8,500-$9,999	365	416	2,896	3,779	3,353	4,288
$10,000-$12,499	737	788	5,895	6,579	6,859	7,576
$12,500-$14,999	598	530	4,527	4,672	5,245	5,339
$15,000-$17,499	673	531	4,940	4,359	5,739	5,012
$17,500-$19,999	453	363	3,869	2,980	4,423	3,432
$20,000-$24,999	672	483	7,521	4,839	8,410	5,513
$25,000-$29,999	454	336	6,374	2,759	7,018	3,194
$30,000-$34,999	301	135	5,324	1,437	5,767	1,633
$35,000-$49,999	289	99	7,730	1,450	8,211	1,585
$50,000-$74,999	80	14	3,421	484	3,588	509
$75,000 and over	32	4	1,603	169	1,669	177
median income	$10,768	$ 6,277	$17,111	$ 7,357	$16,311	$ 7,217
mean income	$13,376	$ 9,001	$21,523	$10,317	$20,652	$10,173
Mean income by:						
occupation						
managerial, professional specialty	$25,575	$18,273	$34,711	$17,763	$34,201	$17,857
technical, sales, administrative support	16,026	11,645	24,050	10,988	23,293	11,076
service occupations	10,270	6,800	13,161	5,935	12,549	6,104
farming, forestry, fishing	4,800	na	8,241	3,865	8,024	3,762
precision production, craft, repair	$16,314	$11,217	$20,593	$12,998	$20,277	$12,595
operators, fabricators, laborers	13,808	9,649	16,378	9,528	15,971	$9,548
work experience						
worked at full time jobs	$16,618	$12,988	$24,531	$14,556	$23,767	$14,364
worked 50-52 weeks	19,940	15,448	28,140	17,249	27,414	17,028

continued on the next page

Table 7.08 continued

	Black		White		All Races	
	male	female	male	female	male	female
educational attainment						
less than 8 years of school	$ 7,962	$ 4,684	$10,593	$ 5,809	$10,016	$ 5,582
high school graduates	15,392	10,155	21,584	10,121	20,916	10,120
1-3 years of college	18,658	12,687	25,768	12,763	24,987	12,754
4 or more years of college	27,210	19,587	38,460	18,367	37,570	18,410
type of income						
wages and salaries	$14,446	$10,668	$21,848	$11,295	$21,056	$11,239
non-farm self-employment	10,222	5,565	16,083	5,885	15,834	5,867
farm self employment	na	na	4,234	1,654	4,184	1,695
property income	709	708	1,866	2,021	1,794	1,937
- interest income	505	483	1,305	1,454	1,254	1,395
transfer payments and all other income	4,777	3,641	6,812	4,428	6,572	4,318
- social security or railroad retirement	4,757	3,620	5,803	4,330	5,701	4,261
-public assistance and supplemental income	2,383	2,922	2,526	2,881	2,560	2,919

SOURCE: U.S. Bureau of the Census, Current Population Reports: Money Income of Households in the United States; March 1985, Series P-60, #156, pp. 107-109, table 31; pp. 135-138, table 35; pp. 141-143, table 37; pp. 160-163, tables 40, 41. C3.186:P-60/156

NOTES: 'All Races' includes other races not shown separately. Number of persons as of March of the following year. Data is based on persons living in households. Persons with incomes under $2,000 includes those with a loss. Occupation represents the longest job held by the person during the year. Educational attainment covers persons 25 years old and older; income covers persons 15 years old and older. 'Property income' includes interest, dividends, net rental income, income from trusts and estates, and net royalty income.

UNITS: Number of persons and persons by income in thousands of persons; median and mean income in dollars.

Table 7.09 Money Income of Persons 15 Years Old and Older, by Selected Characteristic, 1990

	Black		White		All Races	
	male	female	male	female	male	female
Number of persons	10,074	12,124	79,555	85,012	92,240	100,680
persons with incomes:						
under $5,000	1,866	3,455	8,539	22,062	10,820	26,337
$5,000-$9,999	1,643	2,561	9,249	16,358	11,312	19,563
$10,000-$14,999	1,323	1,487	9,529	11,652	11,253	13,566
$15,000-$24,999	1,859	1,793	16,679	15,162	19,166	17,516
$25,000-$34,999	1,112	883	12,707	7,547	14,185	8,707
$35,000-$49,999	716	392	10,531	3,895	11,604	4,457
$50,000-$74,999	237	83	5,973	1,382	6,433	1,535
$75,000 and over	64	32	3,274	509	3,446	565
median income	$12,868	$ 8,328	$21,170	$10,317	$20,293	$10,070
mean income	$16,985	$12,049	$27,142	$14,138	$26,041	$13,913
Mean income by:						
work experience						
worked at full time jobs	$20,729	$16,992	$30,498	$19,269	$29,524	$19,010
worked 50-52 weeks	24,021	19,976	34,300	22,198	33,334	21,977
educational attainment						
less than 8 years of school	$13,719	$ 7,565	$15,057	$ 8,598	$14,914	$ 8,602
high school graduates	18,879	14,146	25,520	13,955	24,727	13,999
1-3 years of college	23,877	17,499	31,235	17,148	30,340	17,188
4 or more years of college	33,404	26,195	45,709	25,230	44,864	25,388
age						
15-24 years old	$ 7,254	$ 6,105	$ 8,915	$ 7,161	$ 8,693	$ 6,998
25-34 years old	16,948	12,436	25,442	15,317	24,365	14,955
35-44 years old	23,266	17,271	35,723	17,724	34,468	17,667
45-54 years old	24,268	16,963	38,632	17,845	37,182	17,831
55-64 years old	18,585	11,234	33,396	14,159	31,899	13,834
65 years old and over	10,954	7,136	20,918	11,864	20,011	11,441

continued on the next page

Table 7.09 continued

	Black		White		All Races	
	male	female	male	female	male	female
Mean income by:						
marital status						
single	$11,997	$10,306	$16,902	$14,504	$16,112	$13,656
married	21,648	13,711	32,362	13,828	31,488	13,858
spouse present	22,457	14,261	32,627	13,805	31,888	13,883
spouse absent	16,790	11,910	25,396	14,255	23,158	13,508
widowed	10,873	8,985	18,528	13,822	17,440	13,190
divorced	19,120	16,781	26,830	19,448	25,787	19,058

SOURCE: U.S. Bureau of the Census, Current Population Reports: Money Income of Households, Families, and Persons in the United States: March 1990, Series P-60, #174, pp. 104-105, table 24; p. 108, table 25; pp. 112-119, table 26; pp. 124-127, table 28; pp. 128-149, table 29; pp. 160-163, table 31. C3.186/2:990

NOTES: 'All Races' includes other races not shown separately. Number of persons as of March of the following year. Data is based on persons living in households. Persons with incomes under $5,000 includes those with a loss. Educational attainment covers persons 25 years old and older; income covers persons 15 years old and older. Single persons are those who were never married.

UNITS: Number of persons and persons with income, in thousands of persons; percent as a percent as shown; mean and median income in current dollars.

Table 7.10 Money Income of Persons 15 Years Old and Older, by Selected Characteristic, 1997

	Black		White		All Races	
	male	female	male	female	male	female
Number of persons	11,283	13,715	85,219	89,489	101,123	108,168
persons with incomes:						
under $5,000	1,254	2,046	6,903	15,500	8,578	18,456
$5,000-$9,999	1,605	2,779	7,527	15,597	9,598	19,077
$10,000-$14,999	1,264	1,661	8,979	11,890	10,695	14,123
$15,000-$24,999	2,062	2,697	14,962	16,060	17,800	19,472
$25,000-$34,999	1,459	1,407	12,678	9,898	14,740	11,813
$35,000-$49,999	1,176	858	12,602	6,950	14,367	8,207
$50,000-$74,999	635	414	9,829	3,727	10,938	4,351
$75,000 and over	216	99	6,921	1,730	7,451	1,947
median income	$18,096	$13,048	$26,115	$13,792	$25,212	$13,703
mean income	$22,781	$17,310	$36,282	$19,792	$34,794	$19,511

SOURCE: U.S. Bureau of the Census, Current Population Reports, Money Income in the United States: 1997, Series P-60, #200, pp. 30-32, table 8. <www.census.gov/prod/3/98pubs/p60-28900.pdf>, accessed 15 October 1998.

NOTES: 'All Races' includes other races not shown separately. Number of persons as of March of the following year. Data is based on persons living in households. Persons with incomes under $5,000includes those with a loss. Educational attainment covers persons 25 years old and older; income covers persons 15 years old and older. Single persons are those who were never married.

UNITS: Number of persons and persons with income, in thousands of persons; mean and median income in current dollars.

Table 7.11 Median Weekly Earnings of Full-Time Wage and Salary Workers, by Sex and Age, 1985, 1990, 1997

	Black		White		All Races	
	male	female	male	female	male	female
1985						
All full-time wage and salary workers	$304	$252	$417	$281	$406	$277
workers 16-24 years old	199	193	245	212	240	210
workers 25 years old and over	325	265	459	300	442	296
- workers 25-54 years old	326	268	457	303	441	298
- workers 55 years old and over	323	241	476	286	455	281
1990						
All full-time wage and salary workers	$360	$308	$497	$355	$485	$348
workers 16-24 years old	na	na	na	na	283	254
workers 25 years old and over	na	na	na	na	514	370
1997						
All full-time wage and salary workers	$432	$375	$595	$444	$579	$431
workers 16-24 years old	na	na	na	na	317	292
workers 25 years old and over	na	na	na	na	615	462

SOURCE: U.S. Bureau of the Census, Statistical Abstract of the United States, 1991, p. 415, table 678, (data from *the Current Population Survey*). C 3.134:991

U.S. Department of Labor, Bureau of Labor Statistics, *Employment and Earnings*, January, 1998, p. 208, table 37 (data from the Current Population Survey). L 2.41/2:38/1:998

NOTES: 'All Races' includes other races not shown separately.

UNITS: Median weekly earning in dollars.

Table 7.12 Median Income of Year-Round, Full-Time Workers, by Sex, 1980 - 1997

	Black		White		All Races	
	male	female	male	female	male	female
1980	$23,094	$18,193	$32,658	$19,224	$31,729	$19,088
1981	22,932	17,439	32,243	18,854	31,548	18,687
1982	22,752	17,805	31,703	19,313	30,932	19,099
1983	22,754	17,876	31,577	19,814	30,822	19,601
1984	22,464	18,527	32,357	20,125	31,352	19,958
1985	22,791	18,656	32,678	20,596	31,548	20,372
1986	23,476	18,861	33,189	21,022	32,330	20,779
1987	23,618	19,453	32,764	21,088	32,044	20,886
1988	24,159	19,614	32,292	21,133	31,613	20,880
1989	23,111	19,675	32,293	21,409	30,924	21,236
1990	22,665	19,365	31,002	21,521	29,711	21,278
1991	22,740	19,284	31,177	21,420	30,307	21,172
1992	22,369	19,819	31,012	21,659	30,358	21,440
1993	23,566	20,315	31,832	22,979	31,077	22,469
1994	24,405	20,628	32,440	23,894	31,612	23,265
1995	24,798	21,079	33,515	24,264	32,199	23,777
1996	27,136	21,990	34,741	25,358	33,538	24,935
1997	26,897	22,764	36,118	26,470	35,248	26,029

SOURCE: U.S. Bureau of the Census, Current Population Reports: Money Income of Households, Families, and Persons in the United States: March 1992, Series P-60, #184, p. B 36, table B-17; 1996, Series P-60, #197, pp.28-29, table 7. C3.186/2:(year)

U.S. Bureau of the Census, Current Population Reports: Income Poverty, and Valuation of Noncash Benefits: 1994, Series P-60, #189, pp. 15-16, table 5. C3.186/2:994

U.S. Bureau of the Census, Current Population Reports: Money Income in the United States: 1997, Series P-60, #200, pp. 28-29, table 7. <www.census.gov/prod/3/98pubs/p60-200.pdf>, accessed 15 October 1998.

NOTES: 'All Races' includes other races not shown separately. Data covers the earnings of wage and salary workers who usually worked 35 or more hours per week for 50 to 52 weeks during the year. Data prior to 1989 are for civilian workers only.

UNITS: Median money earnings.

Table 7.13 Per Capita Money Income in Current and Constant Dollars, 1980 - 1992

	Black	White	All Races
Current dollars			
1980	$ 4,804	$ 8,233	$ 7,787
1985	6,840	11,671	11,013
1986	7,207	12,352	11,670
1987	7,645	13,143	12,391
1988	8,271	13,896	13,123
1989	8,747	14,896	14,056
1990	9,017	15,265	14,387
1991	9,170	15,510	14,617
1992	9,296	15,981	15,033
Constant dollars			
1980	$ 8,190	$14,035	$13,275
1985	8,919	15,218	14,360
1986	9,226	15,812	14,939
1987	9,442	16,232	15,303
1988	9,809	16,480	15,563
1989	9,897	16,854	15,904
1990	9,679	16,386	15,444
1991	9,446	15,977	15,057
1992	9,296	15,981	15,033

SOURCE: U.S. Bureau of the Census, Current Population Reports: Money Income of Households, Families, and Persons in the United States: March 1992, Series P-60, #184, p. B 38, table B-19. C3.186/2:992

NOTES: 'All Races' includes other races not shown separately.

UNITS: Median money income per capita in current and constant dollars, as shown.

Table 7.14 Families Below the Poverty Level, 1980 - 1997

	Black	White	All Races
Number below the poverty level			
1980	1,826	4,195	6,217
1985	1,983	4,983	7,223
1986	1,987	4,811	7,023
1987	2,117	4,567	7,005
1989	2,077	4,409	6,784
1990	2,193	4,622	7,098
1991	2,343	5,022	7,712
1992	2,484	5,255	8,144
1993	2,499	5,452	8,393
1994	2,212	5,312	8,053
1995	2,127	4,994	7,532
1996	2,206	5,059	7,708
1997	1,985	4,990	7,324
Percent below the poverty level			
1980	28.9%	8.0%	10.3%
1985	28.7	9.1	11.4
1986	28.0	8.6	10.9
1987	29.4	8.1	10.7
1989	27.8	7.8	10.3
1990	29.3	8.1	10.7
1991	30.4	8.8	11.5
1992	31.1	9.1	11.9
1993	31.3	9.4	12.3
1994	27.3	9.1	11.6
1995	26.4	8.5	10.8
1996	26.1	8.6	11.0
1997	23.6	8.4	10.3

SOURCE: U.S. Bureau of the Census, Current Population Reports: Poverty in the United States, 1997, Series P-60, #201, pp. C-8-C-12, table C-3. <www.census.gov/prod/3/98pubs/p60-201.pdf>, accessed 15 October 1998.

NOTES: 'All Races' includes other races not shown separately. Families as of March of the following year.

UNITS: Number below the poverty level in thousands of families; percent as a percent of all families, by race, as shown.

Table 7.15 Families Below the Poverty Level by Type of Family and Presence of Related Children, 1997

	Black	White	All Races
Total Families	8,408	59,515	70,884
Families below poverty level	1,985	4,990	7,324
Married-couple families	312	2,312	2,821
Male householder, no wife present	110	373	508
Female householder, no husband present	1,563	2,305	3,995
Total families with children under 18 years	5,647	30,060	37,427
Families below poverty level	1,721	3,895	5,884
Married-couple families	205	1,516	1,863
Male householder, no wife present	80	310	407
Female householder, no husband present	1,436	2,069	3,614

SOURCE: U.S. Bureau of the Census, Current Population Reports: Poverty in the United States 1997, Series P-60, #201, pp. C-8 - C-12, table C-3, <www.census.gov/prod/3/98pubs/p60-201.pdf>, accessed 15 October 1998

NOTES: 'All Races' includes other races not shown separately.

UNITS: Number in thousands of families

Table 7.16 Persons Below the Poverty Level, 1980 - 1997

	Black	White	All Races
Number below the poverty level			
1980	8,579	19,699	29,272
1985	8,926	22,860	33,064
1986	8,983	22,183	32,370
1987	9,520	21,195	32,221
1988	9,356	20,715	31,745
1989	9,302	20,785	31,528
1990	9,837	22,326	33,585
1991	10,242	23,747	35,708
1992	10,827	25,259	38,014
1993	10,877	26,226	39,265
1994	10,196	25,379	38,059
1995	9,872	24,423	36,425
1996	9,694	24,650	36,529
1997	9,116	24,396	35,574
Percent below the poverty level			
1980	32.5%	10.2%	13.0%
1985	31.3	11.4	14.0
1986	31.1	11.0	13.6
1987	32.4	10.4	13.4
1988	31.3	10.1	13.0
1989	30.7	10.0	12.8
1990	31.9	10.7	13.5
1991	32.7	11.3	14.2
1992	33.4	11.9	14.8
1993	33.1	12.2	15.1
1994	30.6	11.7	14.5
1995	29.3	11.2	13.8
1996	28.4	11.2	13.7
1997	26.5	11.0	13.3

SOURCE: U.S. Bureau of the Census, Current Population Reports: Poverty in the United States, 1997, Series P-60, #201 pp. C-2- C-3, table C-1 <www.census.gov/prod/3/98pubs/p60-201.pdf>, accessed 15 October 1998.

NOTES: 'All Races' includes other races not shown separately.

UNITS: Number below the poverty level in thousands of persons; percent as a percent of all persons, by race, as shown.

Table 7.17 Children Below the Poverty Level, 1980 - 1997

	Black	White	All Races
Number below the poverty level			
1980	3,961	7,181	11,543
1985	4,157	8,253	13,010
1986	4,148	8,209	12,876
1987	4,385	7,788	12,843
1988	4,296	7,435	12,455
1989	4,375	7,599	12,590
1990	4,550	8,232	13,431
1991	4,755	8,848	14,341
1992	5,106	8,399	15,294
1993	5,125	9,752	15,727
1994	4,906	9,346	15,289
1995	4,761	8,981	14,665
1996	4,519	9,044	14,623
1997	4,225	8,990	14,113
Percent below the poverty level			
1980	42.3%	13.9%	18.3%
1985	43.6	16.2	20.7
1986	43.1	16.1	20.5
1987	45.1	15.3	20.3
1988	43.5	14.5	19.5
1989	43.7	14.8	19.6
1990	44.8	15.9	20.6
1991	45.9	16.8	21.8
1992	46.6	17.4	22.3
1993	46.1	17.8	22.7
1994	43.8	16.9	21.8
1995	41.9	16.2	20.8
1996	39.9	16.3	20.5
1997	37.2	16.1	19.9

SOURCE: U.S. Bureau of the Census, Current Population Reports: Poverty in the United States, 1997, Series P-60, #201, pp. C-5-C-6, table C-2. <www.census.gov/prod/3/98pubs/p60-201.pdf, >accessed 15 October 1998

NOTES: 'All Races' includes other races not shown separately.

UNITS: Number below the poverty level in thousands of children; percent as a percent of all children, by race, as shown

Table 7.18 Persons 65 Years Old and Over Below Poverty Level, 1970 - 1996

	Black	White	All Races
Number below the poverty level			
1970	735	4,011	4,793
1979	740	2,911	3,682
1985	717	2,698	3,456
1990	860	2,707	3,658
1991	880	2,802	3,781
1992	887	2,992	3,983
1993	702	2,939	3,755
1994	700	2,846	3,663
1995	629	2,572	3,318
1996	661	2,667	3,428
Percent below the poverty level			
1970	47.7%	22.6%	24.6%
1979	36.3	13.3	15.2
1985	31.5	11.0	12.6
1990	33.8	10.1	12.2
1991	33.8	10.3	12.4
1992	33.3	10.9	12.9
1993	28.0	10.7	12.2
1994	27.4	10.2	11.7
1995	25.4	9.0	10.5
1996	25.3	9.4	10.8

SOURCE: U.S. Bureau of the Census, Statistical Abstract of the United States, 1994, p. 476, table 731; 1998, p. 478, table 759, C 3.134:9(year)

NOTES: 'All Races' includes other races not shown separately. Persons as of March of following year.

UNITS: Number below the poverty level in thousands of persons; percent as a percent of all persons, by race, as shown.

Table 7.19 Income of Households from Specified Sources, 1992

	Black	White	All Races
All households	11,190	82,083	96,391
one or more members received:			
Social Security	25.1%	28.5%	27.7%
AFDC or other non-SSI cash assistance	15.5	3.7	5.2
SSI	10.2	3.2	4.1
food stamps	25.0	6.6	8.8
housing assistance	14.5	3.3	4.6
free or reduced-price school lunches	20.5	5.5	7.4
employer subsidized health insurance	43.4	54.3	52.9
Medicare	23.1	26.6	25.9
Medicaid	30.9	10.1	12.8
Mean household income from:			
Social Security	$6,597	$8,980	$8,708
AFDC or other non-SSI cash assistance	3,379	3,444	3,489
SSI	3,415	3,651	3,666
food stamps	1,791	1,430	1,564
housing assistance	2,129	1,957	2,022
free or reduced-price school lunches	558	547	553
employer subsidized health insurance	2,777	3,163	3,139
Medicare	2,305	3,652	3,511
Medicaid	1,297	1,696	1,595

SOURCE: U.S. Bureau of the Census, Current Population Reports: Measuring the Effect of Benefits and Taxes on Income and Poverty: 1992, Series P-60-186RD, pp. 52-54, table 7. C 3.186/P-60/186RD

NOTES: 'All Races' includes other races not shown separately.

UNITS: Number of households in thousands. Percent as a percent of all households, 100.0%. Mean amount of income from specified source per household receiving that source.

Table 7.20 Income of Persons from Specified Sources, 1997

	Black	White	All Races
All persons, 15 years and over	21,631	161,752	191,615
Number with income from:			
Earnings	16,266	121,516	144,429
Unemployment compensation	818	4,962	6,042
Workers' compensation	220	1,740	2,043
Social Security	3,784	33,217	37,743
SSI (Supplemental Security Income)	1,341	3,488	5,111
Public assistance (total)	1,264	2,288	3,758
Veterans' benefits	291	2,007	2,353
Survivors benefits	196	2,172	2,405
Disability benefits	249	1,212	1,508
Pensions	1,088	13,209	14,611
Interest	6,239	92,812	102,933
Dividends	1,191	30,596	32,885
Rents, royalties, estates or trusts	595	11,519	12,592
Education	1,139	6,245	7,817
Child support	800	4,139	5,034
Alimony	16	383	409
Mean income, total from:	$19,756	$27,989	$27,022
Earnings	21,447	29,700	28,754
Unemployment compensation	2,692	2,613	2,626
Workers' compensation	6,370	5,791	5,838
Social Security	7,431	8,480	8,359
SSI (Supplemental Security Income)	4,509	4,370	4,444
Public assistance (total)	3,249	3,108	3,240
Veterans' benefits	6,601	7,157	7,047
Survivors benefits	12,249	9,847	10,004
Disability benefits	8,336	10,771	10,213
Pensions	11,061	12,274	12,220
Interest	923	1,959	1,869
Dividends	2,208	2,910	2,883
Rents, royalties, estates or trusts	2,478	4,487	4,316
Education	3,732	3,628	3,732
Child support	2,721	3,826	3,643
Alimony	na	10,401	9,923

SOURCE: U.S. Bureau of the Census, Current Population Reports: Money Income in the United States: 1997, Series P60-200, p. 42, table 11. <www.census.gov/prod/3/98pubs/p60-200.pdf>, accessed 15 October 1998.

NOTES: 'All Races' includes other races not shown separately. Persons 15 years old and older as of March the following year

UNITS: Number of persons in thousands, mean income in dollars.

Table 7.21 Child Support Payments Agreed to or Awarded Custodial Parents, 1991

	Black	White	All Races
All Custodial Parents	2,886	8,319	11,502
Child support agreed to or awarded	1,009	5,035	6,190
Supposed to receive child support	834	4,357	5,326
Received payments	577	3,340	4,006
Full Payments	357	2,330	2,742
Partial Payments	220	1,011	1,265
Did not receive payments	257	1,017	1,320
All Custodial Mothers	2,698	6,966	9,918
Child support agreed to or awarded	958	4,459	5,542
Supposed to receive child support	791	3,976	4,883
Received payments	553	3,094	3,728
Full Payments	340	2,162	2,552
Partial Payments	213	932	1,176
Did not receive payments	238	882	1,156
All Custodial Fathers	188	1,352	1,584
Child support agreed to or awarded	51	576	648
Supposed to receive child support	43	381	443
Received payments	24	246	278
Full Payments	17	168	189
Partial Payments	7	78	89
Did not receive payments	19	135	164

SOURCE: U.S. Department of Commerce, Current Population Reports, Consumer Income, Series P60-187, Child Support for Custodial Mothers and Fathers: 1991, pp. 13- 16, table 1. C3.186:P-60/187

NOTES: 'All Races' includes other races not shown separately.

UNITS: Numbers in thousands. Persons 15 years and older with own children under 21 years of age present from absent parents as of spring 1992.

Chapter 8: Special Topics

Table 8.01 Social Security Benefits and Beneficiaries, 1980, 1990, 1996

	Black	White	All Races
1980			
Beneficiaries			
total	3,576,014	31,431,133	35,584,955
retired workers	1,533,904	17,780,617	19,562,085
disabled workers	432,449	2,376,823	2,858,680
wives	229,177	3,147,297	3,436,099
husbands	3,719	36,728	41,328
children	645,162	3,501,249	4,606,517
widowed mothers and fathers	115,235	428,822	562,316
widows (nondisabled)	288,931	3,935,175	4,262,607
widowers (nondisabled)	2,208	17,870	20,328
widows (disabled)	20,168	104,847	126,679
widowers (disabled)	139	747	901
parents	1,921	12,052	14,779
special age-72 beneficiary	2,986	88,098	91,808
wife of special age-72 beneficiary	15	808	828
Average monthly benefit			
total	$236.00	$308.60	$300.20
retired workers	281.60	346.90	341.40
disabled workers	325.30	379.70	370.70
wives	119.00	168.30	164.20
husbands	111.50	132.10	130.00
children	154.00	200.00	187.60
widowed mothers and fathers	196.60	261.70	246.20
widows (nondisabled)	244.80	316.90	311.00
widowers (nondisabled)	210.00	243.20	239.40
widows (disabled)	169.80	212.60	205.40
widowers (disabled)	131.50	148.10	145.70
parents	247.00	282.60	276.00
special age-72 beneficiary	104.90	104.90	104.90
wife of special age-72 beneficiary	52.60	52.60	52.60

continued on the next page

Table 8.01 continued

	Black	White	All Races
1990			
Beneficiaries			
total	3,707,980	34,846,200	39,814,330
retired workers	1,904,140	22,287,520	24,826,230
disabled workers	489,450	2,335,560	3,011,130
wives	187,660	3,046,270	3,329,830
husbands	4,170	28,610	36,570
children	544,780	1,745,840	3,193,070
widowed mothers and fathers	55,290	233,640	305,080
widows (nondisabled)	388,010	4,501,160	4,963,820
widowers (nondisabled)	4,200	28,380	33,790
widows (disabled)	19,060	77,510	100,150
widowers (disabled)	390	1,130	1,630
parents	800	4,190	5,840
special age-72 beneficiary	310	6,790	7,190
Average monthly benefit			
total	$443.10	$558.60	$544.50
retired workers	505.80	612.60	602.60
disabled workers	531.70	603.00	587.00
wives	226.20	306.80	300.10
husbands	175.60	189.30	183.90
children	na	na	na
widowed mothers and fathers	350.80	432.70	409.00
widows (nondisabled)	442.40	569.10	557.70
widowers (nondisabled)	384.00	417.40	411.00
widows (disabled)	341.40	404.40	389.50
widowers (disabled)	213.40	233.20	228.50
parents	425.50	506.10	491.00
special age-72 beneficiary	167.50	166.80	166.80

continued on the next page

Table 8.01 continued

	Black	White	All Races
1996			
Beneficiaries			
total	4,501,500	37,822,600	43,737,470
retired workers	2,132,220	24,158,810	26,899,170
disabled workers	783,100	3,308,290	4,386,040
wives	177,180	2,891,170	3,160,690
husbands	5,780	24,270	34,260
children	881,170	2,634,260	3,811,600
widowed mothers and fathers	49,760	170,790	241,490
widows (nondisabled)	427,360	4,463,800	4,979,740
widowers (nondisabled)	5,240	31,060	37,940
widows (disabled)	37,890	134,510	178,050
widowers (disabled)	1,010	2,740	3,970
parents	740	2,430	3,830
special age-72 beneficiary	50	470	690
Average monthly benefit			
total	$544.80	$692.90	$672.80
retired workers	629.10	757.50	744.90
disabled workers	645.30	724.00	704.80
wives	280.10	379.20	370.70
husbands	201.70	217.70	212.70
children	311.00	378.50	356.30
widowed mothers and fathers	422.60	548.50	513.70
widows (nondisabled)	562.70	724.70	708.60
widowers (nondisabled)	484.70	528.00	520.00
widows (disabled)	417.50	494.40	475.70
widowers (disabled)	316.40	312.90	308.80
parents	554.90	640.10	615.40
special age-72 beneficiary	199.00	199.00	199.00

SOURCE: U.S. Department of Health & Human Services, Social Security Administration, Social Security Bulletin, Annual Statistical Supplement, 1982, pp. 112-123, table 70; 1991, pp. 149-159, table 5.A1; 1997, pp. 183-193, table 5.A1. SSA 1.22/2:(year)

NOTES: 'All Races' includes other races not shown separately.

UNITS: Beneficiaries in number of beneficiaries, average monthly benefit in current dollars.

Table 8.02 Selected Characteristics of Farms and Farm Operators, 1992

	Black farms	All farms
Characteristics of farms		
Farms and land in farms		
farms (number)	18,816	1,925,300
land in farms (acres)	2,310,349	945,531,506
harvested cropland (acres)	761,281	295,936,976
Farms by size		
1-9 acres	2,338	166,496
10-49 acres	6,327	387,711
50-139 acres	6,069	445,055
140-219 acres	1,844	233,628
220-499 acres	1,518	333,111
500 acres or more	677	359,299
Owned and rented land in farms		
owned land in farms		
farms	16,762	1,708,395
acres	1,380,905	540,695,158
rented or leased land in farms		
farms	7,238	813,564
acres	929,444	404,836,348
Market value of agricultural products sold, (in thousands of dollars)		
total	$365,617	$162,608,334
crops (including nursery and greenhouse crops)	208,060	75,228,255
livestock, poultry and their products	157,557	87,380,078
Farms by value of sales		
less than $1,000	3,565	212,580
$2,500-$9,999	4,045	210,187
$2,500-$9,999	6,639	483,750
$10,000-$19,999	1,898	232,067
$20,000-$24,000	433	69,737
$25,000 or more	2,236	716,979

continued on the next page

Table 8.02 continued

	Black farms	All farms
Farms by Standard Industrial Classification		
cash grains (011)	2,497	405,008
field crops except cash grains (013)	3,556	250,338
cotton (0131)	490	20,447
tobacco (0132)	1,956	90,826
sugarcane and sugarbeets; Irish potatoes; field crops except cash grains not elsewhere classified (0133, 0134, 0139)	1,110	139,065
vegetables and melons (016)	689	29,605
fruits and tree nuts (017)	368	89,514
horticultural specialties (018)	160	39,712
general farms, primarily crop (019)	520	48,847
livestock, except dairy, poultry and animal specialties (021)	10,028	808,283
beef cattle, except feedlots (0212)	7,518	612,203
dairy farms (024)	303	113,412
poultry and eggs (025)	209	35,066
animal specialties (027)	310	80,504
general farms, primarily livestock and animal specialties (029)	176	25,011
Characteristics of the farm operator		
Residence		
on farm operated	10,477	1,378,701
not on farm operated	5,733	408,560
not reported	2,606	138,039
Principal occupation		
farming	8,284	1,053,150
other	10,532	872,150
Days of work off farm		
none	6,947	801,881
any	9,773	992,773

continued on the next page

Table 8.02 continued

	Black farms	All farms
Characteristics of the farm operator - continued		
Days of work off farm - continued		
1-99 days	1,653	165,180
100-199 days	1,834	162,023
200 days or more	6,286	665,570
Years on present farm		
2 years or less	952	94,711
3 or 4 years	1,133	133,079
5 to 9 years	2,040	258,767
10 years or more	7,915	1,112,827
average on present farm	19.3	19.5
Age		
under 25 years old	93	27,906
25-34 years old	772	178,826
35-44 years old	2,745	381,746
45-54 years old	3,574	429,333
55-59 years old	2,129	213,315
60-64 years old	2,358	216,524
65-69 years old	2,319	188,165
70 years old and over	4,826	289,475
average age	58.7	53.3
Sex		
male	16,986	1,780,144
female	1,830	145,156

SOURCE: U.S. Bureau of the Census, 1992 Census of Agriculture, Vol. 1 Geographic Area Series, Pt. 51, U.S. Summary and State Data, pp. 23-24, table 17. C 3.31/4:992/v. 1/ pt. 51

NOTES: 'All farms' includes farms owned/operated by persons of all races.

UNITS: Farms, farms by size, farms by organization, farms by value of sales, farms by Standard Industrial Classification, in number of farms; land in farms and harvested crop lands in acres; market value of agricultural products sold in thousands of dollars. Characteristics of farm operators in number of farm operators.

Table 8.03 Black Owned Firms, by Major Industry Group, 1987 and 1992

	all firms		firms with paid employees			
	firms	sales & receipts	firms	sales & receipts	employees	annual payroll
1987						
All industries	424.2	$19,762.9	70.8	$14,130.4	220.5	$2,761.1
agricultural services, forestry and fishing	7.3	216.7	1.7	144.3	3.1	38.0
mining	0.3	54.1	0.5	46.0	0.4	7.0
construction	36.8	2,174.4	11.1	1,669.0	27.4	424.7
manufacturing	8.0	1,023.1	2.6	927.1	13.7	244.0
transportation and public utilities	37.0	1,573.3	5.0	786.1	9.9	154.0
wholesale trade	5.5	1,327.5	1.3	1,169.6	6.2	115.9
retail trade	66.2	5,889.7	14.3	4,861.5	62.5	571.5
finance, insurance, and real estate	27.0	804.3	2.5	464.4	5.9	94.7
services	209.5	6,120.1	30.0	3,888.2	89.7	1,077.4
industries not classified	26.5	579.7	2.4	174.3	1.6	33.8
1992						
All industries	620,912	$32,197,361	64,478	$22,589,676	345,193	$4,806,624
agricultural services, forestry and fishing	9,820	265,089	1,491	159,119	3,904	45,547
mining	490	65,621	51	46,000	293	6,454
construction	43,381	2,651,356	8,798	1,962,727	28,545	447,362
manufacturing	10,469	1,319,193	1,958	1,155,011	12,977	251,322
transportation and public utilities	49,095	2,498,102	4,072	1,305,091	20,308	308,376
wholesale trade	7,550	2,944,321	1,510	2,745,412	8,649	203,544
retail trade	86,840	6,967,644	12,096	5,591,522	82,931	760,051
finance, insurance, and real estate	40,924	3,777,171	3,194	2,771,537	17,606	380,056
services	332,981	11,057,136	30,081	6,773,932	169,248	2,393,563
industries not classified	39,363	651,727	1,226	79,325	731	10,350

SOURCE: U.S. Bureau of the Census, 1987 Economic Censuses MB87-1 Survey of Minority-Owned Business Enterprises: Black, pp.7-8, table 1, 1992 Economic Censuses MB92-1 Survey of Minority-Owned Business Enterprises: Black, pp. 9-10, table 1. C 3.258:(year)

NOTES: Data from the 1987 and 1992 Economic Censuses.

UNITS: 1987 data: Firms in thousands of firms; sales and receipts in millions of dollars; employees in thousands of employees; annual payroll in millions of dollars.
1992 data: Firms in number of firms; sales and receipts in thousands of dollars; employees in number of employees; annual payroll in thousands of dollars

Table 8.04 Black Owned Firms, by State, 1992

	all firms		firms with paid employees			
	firms	sales & receipts	firms	sales & receipts	employees	annual payroll
United States	620,912	$2,197,361	64,478	$2,589,676	345,193	$,806,624
Alabama	14,707	534,692	1,989	343,331	6,827	81,710
Alaska	739	39,137	78	28,871	855	10,633
Arizona	2,936	137,721	328	99,734	1,274	16,326
Arkansas	5,738	232,850	646	160,875	1,952	21,691
California	68,968	5,478,365	6,875	4,155,861	43,292	732,136
Colorado	4,372	295,305	431	242,385	2,955	43,655
Connecticut	5,714	292,369	544	188,098	2,400	40,466
Delaware	2,060	156,880	243	125,503	2,352	22,763
District of Columbia	10,111	451,861	787	313,107	4,277	88,431
Florida	40,371	2,265,451	4,435	1,601,641	22,978	320,116
Georgia	38,264	1,677,083	4,095	1,103,546	18,744	253,026
Hawaii	717	27,382	42	16,794	211	2,513
Idaho	152	24,532	28	23,079	119	2,311
Illinois	28,433	1,773,293	2,694	1,272,218	17,972	345,569
Indiana	8,349	710,971	1,260	599,379	6,894	95,907
Iowa	1,106	75,521	141	64,082	604	8,734
Kansas	3,078	92,295	291	50,991	1,088	13,012
Kentucky	5,097	250,855	522	198,117	2,452	29,686
Louisiana	20,312	774,132	2,086	487,065	8,626	90,944
Maine	235	25,439	45	21,925	293	3,244
Maryland	35,758	1,241,530	2,543	734,155	31,450	227,305
Massachusetts	7,225	427,948	567	307,974	3,692	83,650
Michigan	19,695	1,268,426	2,147	860,556	13,727	202,061
Minnesota	2,785	283,392	332	211,664	2,845	44,532
Mississippi	14,067	504,945	1,891	300,535	5,699	54,676
Missouri	9,973	403,289	1,089	276,594	4,879	56,084
Montana	113	6,504	15	5,311	124	1,626
Nebraska	1,350	61,523	154	46,833	950	9,621
Nevada	1,736	113,338	161	84,299	1,570	20,320
New Hampshire	326	46,369	46	40,182	228	5,101
New Jersey	20,137	1,239,325	1,970	880,252	9,989	199,195
New Mexico	925	60,631	96	45,190	591	7,122

continued on the next page

Table 8.04 continued

	all firms		firms with paid employees			
	firms	sales & receipts	firms	sales & receipts	employees	annual payroll
New York	51,312	$2,267,600	4,033	$1,385,469	16,070	$301,625
North Carolina	29,221	893,369	3,479	530,720	11,166	115,873
North Dakota	117	7,845	14	5,201	105	1,024
Ohio	22,690	1,096,178	2,328	807,206	11,604	147,470
Oklahoma	4,621	190,517	510	134,555	2,027	24,574
Oregon	1,447	100,644	196	83,726	1,066	16,038
Pennsylvania	15,917	1,133,581	1,922	870,766	12,366	223,020
Rhode Island	857	65,252	110	50,353	1,154	16,541
South Carolina	18,343	672,514	2,485	435,256	9,464	105,246
South Dakota	111	10,307	20	9,160	91	860
Tennessee	14,920	555,015	1,686	326,870	5,955	65,861
Texas	50,008	2,339,221	4,861	1,604,853	23,745	285,195
Utah	354	45,246	54	41,444	269	5,445
Vermont	139	7,202	33	5,691	109	1,358
Virginia	26,100	1,211,173	2,958	892,170	20,992	267,017
Washington	4,575	257,073	595	200,651	3,601	46,716
West Virginia	1,093	42,228	127	32,941	559	7,379
Wisconsin	3,446	323,743	488	278,266	2,858	40,322
Wyoming	97	5,301	10	4,230	85	897

SOURCE: U.S. Bureau of the Census, 1992 Economic Censuses MB92-1 Survey of Minority-Owned Business Enterprises: Black, p. 10, table 2. C 3.258:92-1

NOTES: Data from the 1992 Economic Censuses.

UNITS: Firms in number of firms; sales and receipts in thousands of dollars; employees in number of employees; annual payroll in thousands of dollars.

Table 8.05 Summary of Results of the 1996 Consumer Expenditure Survey

	Black consumer units	White consumer units	All consumer units
Number of consumer units	12,355	91,856	104,212
income before taxes	$27,190	$39,419	$38,014
income after taxes	$25,712	$36,052	$34,864
Average number in consumer unit:			
persons	2.9	2.5	2.5
children under 18 years old	1.1	0.6	0.7
persons 65 and over	0.2	0.3	0.3
earners	1.2	1.4	1.3
vehicles	1.2	2.0	1.9
Average annual expenditures			
Total	$24,926	$34,994	$33,797
food	3,630	4,844	4,698
food at home	2,568	2,918	2,876
- cereals and bakery products	377	457	447
cereals and cereal products	157	167	166
bakery products	220	290	281
- meats, poultry, fish, and eggs	873	718	737
beef	231	213	215
pork	213	149	157
other meats	95	99	99
poultry	184	139	144
fish and seafood	112	85	88
eggs	37	34	34
- dairy products	212	326	312
fresh milk and cream	94	138	132
other dairy products	118	188	180
- fruits and vegetables	424	499	490
fresh fruits	121	158	153
fresh vegetables	119	151	147
processed fruits	110	110	110
processed vegetables	73	81	80

continued on the next page

Table 8.05 continued

	Black consumer units	White concumer units	All consumer units
food at home - continued			
- other food at home	$ 683	$ 918	$ 889
sugar and other sweets	97	117	114
fats and oils	84	83	83
miscellaneous foods	295	404	391
nonalcoholic beverages	192	260	252
- food prepared by consumer unit on out of town trips	16	54	49
food away from home	1,062	1,926	1,823
alcoholic beverages	162	329	309
housing	$ 8,525	$11,046	$10,747
shelter	4,772	6,237	6,064
- owned dwellings	2,055	4,015	3,783
mortgage interest and charges	1,204	2,237	2,114
property taxes	451	1,005	939
maintenance, repair, insurance, other	401	773	729
- rented dwellings	2,581	1,767	1,864
- other lodging	137	455	417
utilities, fuels and public services	2,438	2,335	2,347
- natural gas	344	284	291
- electricity	923	905	907
- fuel oil and other fuels	55	115	108
- telephone	887	757	772
- water and other public services	231	273	268
household operations	355	545	522
- personal services	246	260	259
- other household expenses	109	284	263
housekeeping supplies	297	486	464
- laundry and cleaning supplies	111	120	119
- other household products	118	217	205
- postage and stationary	68	149	140

continued on the next page

Table 8.05 continued

	Black consumer units	White consumer units	All consumer units
household furnishings and equipment	$ 663	$ 1,443	$ 1,350
- household textiles	48	80	76
- furniture	195	337	321
- floor coverings	23	111	101
- major appliances	105	170	162
- small appliances, misc. housewares	45	90	84
- misc. household equipment	247	656	607
apparel and services	$ 2,050	$ 1,711	$ 1,752
- men and boys	447	420	423
men, 16 years old and over	301	334	330
boys, 2-15 years old	145	86	93
- women and girls	735	716	718
women, 16 years old and over	563	613	607
girls, 2-15 years old	172	102	111
- children under 2 years old	108	79	82
- footwear	498	271	298
- other apparel and services	263	226	230
transportation	$ 4,323	$ 6,659	$ 6,382
- vehicle purchases	1,766	2,956	2,815
cars and trucks (new) net outlay	672	1,281	1,209
cars and trucks (used) net outlay	1,094	1,632	1,568
other vehicles	0	43	38
- gasoline and motor oil	759	1,125	1,082
- other vehicle expenses	1,531	2,129	2,058
vehicle finance charges	263	277	276
maintenance and repairs	467	669	645
vehicle insurance	540	719	698
vehicle rental, license and other charges	262	464	440
- public transportation	269	449	427

continued on the next page

Table 8.05 continued

	Black consumer units	White consumer units	All consumer units
health care	$ 1,014	$ 1,872	$ 1,770
- health insurance	557	863	827
- medical services	222	587	543
- drugs	182	319	303
- medical supplies	54	103	97
entertainment	$ 882	$ 1,963	1,834
- fees and admissions	171	498	459
- televisions, radios, sound equipment	482	572	561
- pets, toys, playground equipment	151	360	335
- other entertainment equipment, supplies and services	77	533	479
personal care products and services	$ 609	$ 500	$ 513
reading	75	171	159
education	322	551	524
tobacco products and smoking supplies	187	264	255
miscellaneous	588	891	855
cash contributions	599	986	940
personal insurance and pensions	1,960	3,208	3,060
- life and other personal insurance	342	355	353
- pensions and Social Security	1,618	2,854	2,707
Sources on income and personal taxes			
Money income before taxes	$ 27,190	$ 39,419	$ 38,014
wages and salaries	21,965	30,546	29,560
self employment income	608	2,540	2,318
Social Security, private and government retirement	2,667	4,551	4,334

continued on the next page

Table 8.05 continued

	Black consumer units	White consumer units	All consumer units
Money income before taxes - continued			
interest, dividends, rental income, other property income	$ *121	$ 844	$ 761
unemployment, workers' compensation, veterans benefits	142	222	213
public assistance, supplemental security income, food stamps	1,335	321	437
regular contributions for support	224	245	243
other income	127	150	148
Personal taxes	$ 1,478	$ 3,367	$ 3,150
federal income taxes	1,056	2,542	2,372
state income taxes	372	703	665
other taxes	50	121	113
Income after taxes	$ 25,712	$ 36,052	$ 34,864

SOURCE: U.S. Department of Labor, Bureau of Labor Statistics, Consumer Expenditure Survey, 1996, table 7, accessed 15 October 1998, <ftp://ftp.bls.gov/pub/special.requests/ce/standard/1996/tenracar.txt>

NOTES: 'All consumer units' includes consumer units of all races. *Data are likely to have large sampling errors.

UNITS: Number of consumer units in thousands; average numbers as shown; average annual expenditures by category, average income by source of income, and addenda, averages in current dollars.

Table 8.06 Occupied Housing Units, by Tenure, 1980 and 1995

	Black householder	White householder	Householders of all races
1980			
All households	8,382	68,810	80,390
owner occupied			
number	3,724	46,671	51,795
percent	44.4%	67.8%	64.4%
renter occupied	4,657	22,139	28,595
1995			
All households	11,773	81,611	97,693
owner occupied			
number	5,137	56,507	63,544
percent	43.6%	69.2%	65.0%
renter occupied	6,637	25,104	34,150

SOURCE: U.S. Bureau of the Census, Statistical Abstract of the United States, 1998, p. 725, table 1214. C 3.134:998

UNITS: Number of housing units; percent as a percent of total as shown.

Table 8.07 Housing Affordability: Families and Unrelated Individuals, 1991

	Black	White	All Races
Percent that cannot afford a median priced home in their region using conventional, fixed rate, 30 year financing			
All families	78.2%	47.0%	51.3%
married couples	61.3	40.2	42.2
male householder (no wife present)	79.0	64.7	67.8
female householder (no husband present)	92.8	79.4	83.9
Unrelated individuals	90.5	73.9	76.2
Percent that cannot afford a median priced home in their region using FHA, fixed rate, 30 year financing			
All families	76.7%	45.0%	49.4%
married couples	58.3	37.9	39.9
male householder (no wife present)	77.6	63.7	66.7
female householder (no husband present)	92.7	78.6	83.3
Unrelated individuals	90.1	73.1	75.5

continued on the next page

Table 8.07 continued

	Black	White	All Races
Percent that cannot afford a modestly priced home in their region using conventional, fixed rate, 30 year financing			
All families	70.9%	37.9%	42.4%
married couples	51.0	31.1	33.0
male householder (no wife present)	71.2	54.8	57.5
female householder (no husband present)	88.1	70.2	76.1
Unrelated individuals	85.6	63.6	66.6
Percent that cannot afford a modestly priced home in their region using FHA, fixed rate, 30 year financing			
All families	68.4%	34.6%	39.3%
married couples	46.7	27.4	29.4
male householder (no wife present)	68.2	53.4	55.9
female householder (no husband present)	87.2	68.7	74.8
Unrelated individuals	84.6	61.7	64.8

SOURCE: U.S. Bureau of the Census, Current Housing Reports: Who Can Afford to Buy A House in 1991?, p. 2-9, table 2-2; p. 3-8, table 3-2. C 3.215:H121/93-3

NOTES: 'All Races' includes families/unrelated individuals of all races.

UNITS: Percent as a percent of families/unrelated individuals as shown.

Table 8.08 General Mobility, 1996 to 1997

	Black	White	All Races
Total	33,659	217,026	262,976
same house (non-movers)	26,999	182,800	219,585
different house in U.S.	6,600	33,299	42,088
same county	4,847	21,485	27,740
different county	1,752	11,814	14,348
same state	1,044	6,523	7,960
different state	709	5,291	6,389
same region	506	2,504	3,220
different region	203	2,787	3,168
movers from abroad	61	927	1,303

SOURCE: U.S. Bureau of the Census, Geographic Mobility: March 1996 to March 1997, P20-510, pp. 3-5, table 2. <www.census.gov/prod/3/98pubs/p20-510u.pdf>, accessed 15 October 1998.

NOTES: 'All Races' persons individuals of all races. Mobility data from March 1996 to March 1997.

UNITS: Number of persons one year old and over in thousands.

Glossary

ACUTE CONDITION see **CONDITION (HEALTH).**

AGE ADJUSTMENT

Age adjustment, using the direct method, is the application of the age specific rates in a population of interest to a standardized age distribution in order to eliminate the differences in observed rates that result from age differences in population composition. This adjustment is usually done when comparing two or more populations at one point in time, or one population at two or more points in time.

AGGRAVATED ASSAULT see **CRIME.**

ARSON see **CRIME.**

AVERAGE see **MEAN; MEDIAN.**

BED (HOSPITAL; NURSING HOME)

Any bed that is staffed for use by inpatients is counted as a bed in a facility.

BED-DISABILITY DAY see **DISABILITY DAY.**

BIRTH see **LIVE BIRTH.**

BURGLARY see **CRIME.**

CAUSE OF DEATH

For the purpose of national mortality statistics, every death is attributed to one underlying condition, based on information reported on the death certificate and utilizing the international rules (International Classifications of Disease) for selecting the underlying cause of death from reported conditions. Selected causes of death are shown on tables.

CHRONIC CONDITION see **CONDITION (HEALTH).**

CIVILIAN LABOR FORCE

All persons (excluding members of the Armed Forces) who are either employed or unemployed. (The experienced civilian labor force is a subgroup of the civilian labor force, composed of all persons, employed and unemployed, that have worked before.)

Employed persons are those persons 16 years old and over who were either a) "at work"- those who did any work at all as paid employees, or in their own business or profession, or on their own farm, or worked 15 or more hours as unpaid workers on a family farm or in a family business; or b) "with a job but not at work"- those who did not work during the reference period but had jobs or businesses from which they were temporarily absent due to illness, bad weather, industrial dispute, vacation, or other personal reasons. Excluded from the employed are persons whose only activity consisted of work around the house or volunteer work for religious, charitable, and similar organizations.

Employed persons are classified as either **full-time workers**, those who worked 35 hours or more per week; or **part-time workers**, those who worked less than 35 hours per week.

Unemployed persons are those who were neither "at work" nor "with a job, but not at work" and who were a) looking for work, and b) available to accept a job. Also included as unemployed are persons who are waiting to be called back to a job from which they have been laid off. The unemployed are divided into four groups according to reason for unemployment:

--**job losers** (including those who have been laid off)
--**job leavers** who have left their job voluntarily
--**reentrants**, persons who have worked before and are reentering the labor force
--**new entrants** to the labor force looking for work

CIVILIAN NONINSTITUTIONAL POPULATION see **POPULATION.**

CIVILIAN POPULATION see **POPULATION.**

COLLEGE

A postsecondary school which offers a general or liberal arts education, usually leading to an associate, bachelor's, master's, doctor's, or first professional degree. Junior colleges and community colleges are included. See also **Institution of Higher Education; University.**

COMMUNITY HOSPITAL

All non-federal short term hospitals, excluding hospital units of institutions, whose services are available to the public. **Short term hospitals** are those where the average length of stay is less than 30 days.

CONDITION (HEALTH)

A health condition is a departure from a state of physical or mental well-being. Based on duration, there are two categories of conditions: acute and chronic.

An **acute condition** is one that has lasted less than three months, and has involved either a physician visit (medical attention) or restricted activity.

A **chronic condition** is any condition lasting three months or more, or is one classified as chronic regardless of the time of onset. See also **Health Limitation of Activity.**

CONSOLIDATED METROPOLITAN STATISTICAL AREA (CMSA)

A geographic area concept introduced in June, 1984, which, in combination with Metropolitan Statistical Area (MSA), and Primary Metropolitan Statistical Area (PMSA), replace the Standard Metropolitan Statistical Area (SMSA) concept. CMSAs are designated in accordance with criteria established by the federal Office of Management and Budget (OMB). In general CMSAs are MSAs with a population of one million or more, and which have component PMSAs. See also **Metropolitan Statistical Area.**

CONSUMER EXPENDITURE SURVEY

A survey of current consumer expenditures reflecting the buying habits of American consumers. Begun in 1979 and conducted jointly by the U.S. Bureau of Labor Statistics and the U.S. Bureau of the Census, the survey consists of two parts: an interview panel survey in which the expenditures of consumer units are obtained in five interviews conducted every three months, and a diary or recordkeeping survey completed by the participating households for two consecutive one-week periods. See also **Consumer Unit.**

The Consumer Expenditure Survey, which collects data on expenditures, should not be confused with the Consumer Price Index, which measures the average change in prices of consumer goods and services.

CONSUMER UNIT

An entity used as the basis of the Consumer Expenditure Survey. A consumer unit comprises either

--all the members of a particular household who are related by blood, marriage, adoption, or other legal arrangements; or

--a person living alone or sharing a household with others, or living as a roomer in a private home or lodging house or in a permanent living quarters in a hotel or motel, but who is financially independent; or

--two or more persons living together who pool their income to make joint expenditure decisions.

A consumer unit may or may not be a household.

CRIME

A crime is an action which is prohibited by law. Their are two major statistical programs which measure crime in the United States. The first is the Uniform Crime Reporting (UCR) program, administered by the FBI. The Bureau receives monthly and annual reports from most police agencies around the country (covering approximately 97% of the population). These reports contain information on eight major types of crime (called collectively, serious crime), which are known to police. Serious crime consists of four violent crimes (murder and non-negligent manslaughter, which includes willful felonious homicides and is based on police investigations rather than determinations of a medical examiner; forcible rape, which includes attempted rape; robbery, which includes stealing or taking anything of value by force or violence, or by threat of force or violence, and includes attempted robbery; and aggravated assault which includes intent to kill), and four property crimes (burglary, which includes any unlawful entry to commit a felony or theft and includes attempted burglary and burglary followed by larceny; larceny, which includes theft of property or articles of value without use of force, violence, or fraud, and excludes embezzlement, con games, forgery, etc.; motor vehicle theft, which includes all cases where vehicles are driven away and abandoned, but excludes vehicles taken for temporary use and returned by the taker; and arson, which includes any willful or malicious burning or attempt to burn, with or without the intent to defraud, of a dwelling house, public building, motor vehicle, aircraft, or personal property of another.)

The second approach to the measurement of crime is through the National Crime Survey (NCS) administered by the Bureau of Justice Statistics. The survey is based on a representative sample of approximately 49,000 households, inhabited by about 102,000 persons age 12 and over. Although the categories of crime are similar to those used by the FBI in the UCR, the NCS is based on reports of victimization directly by victims, as opposed to crimes reported to police as in the UCR. As might be imagined, not all crimes are reported or known to police, therefore NCS estimates of crime tend to be significantly higher than UCR figures. The NCS also differs from the UCR in that only crimes whose victims can be interviewed are included (hence there are no homicide statistics), and only victims who are 12 years old or older are counted. The two central concepts in the NCS are victimization, which is the specific criminal act as it affects a single victim, and a criminal incident, which is a specific criminal act involving one or more victims. Thus in regard to personal crime, there are more victimizations, than incidents.

DEATH see **CAUSE OF DEATH; INFANT MORTALITY**.

DISABILITY

The presence of a physical, mental, or other health condition which has lasted six or more months and which limits or prevents a particular type of activity. See also **Work Disability.**

DISABILITY DAY

A day on which a person's usual activity is reduced because of illness or injury. There are four types of disability days (which are not mutually exclusive). They are

--a **restricted-activity day**, a day on which a person cuts down on his or her usual activities because of illness or an injury.

--a **bed-disability day,** a day on which a person stays in bed more than half of the daylight hours (or normal waking hours) because of a specific illness or injury. All hospital days are bed-disability days. Bed disability days may also be work-loss days or school loss days.

--a **work-loss day**, a day on which a person did not work at his or her job or business for at least half of his or her normal workday because of a specific illness or injury. Work loss days are determined only for employed persons.

--a **school-loss day**, a day on which a child did not attend school for at least half of his or her normal schoolday because of a specific illness or injury. School-loss days are determined only for children 6 to 16 years of age.

DISPOSABLE INCOME see **INCOME.**

EMPLOYED PERSONS see **CIVILIAN LABOR FORCE.**

EMPLOYMENT STATUS see **LABOR FORCE STATUS.**

ENROLLMENT

The total number of students registered in a given school unit at a given time, generally in the fall of the year. See also **Full-Time Enrollment; Part-Time Enrollment.**

EVER MARRIED PERSONS see MARITAL STATUS.

EXPERIENCED CIVILIAN LABOR FORCE

That portion of the Civilian Labor Force, both employed and unemployed, that have worked before. Excludes new entrants to the Civilian Labor Force. See also **Civilian Labor Force.**

EXPERIENCED WORKER see **EXPERIENCED CIVILIAN LABOR FORCE.**

FAMILY

A type (subgroup) of household in which there are two or more persons living together (including the householder) who are related by birth, marriage, or adoption. All such related persons in one housing unit are considered as members of one family. (For example, if the son or daughter of the family householder and that son's or daughter's spouse and/or children are members of the household, they are all counted as part of the householder's family.) However, non-family members who are not related to the householder (such as a roomer or boarder and his or her spouse, or a resident employee and his or her spouse who are living in), are not counted as family members but as unrelated individuals living in a family household. Thus for Census purposes, a housing unit can contain only one household, and a household can contain only one family. See also **Family Type; Household; Householder; Unrelated Individual.**

FAMILY INCOME see **INCOME.**

FAMILY TYPE

Families are classified by type according to the sex of the householder and the presence of a spouse and children. The three main types of households are: **Married Couples,** in which a husband and wife live together (with or without other persons in the household); **Male Householder, No Wife Present,** in which a male householder lives together with other members of his family but without a wife; and **Female Householder, No Husband Present,** in which a female householder lives together with other members of her family but without a husband. See also **Family; Family Household; Household.**

FARM

As defined by the Bureau of the Census (and adopted by the Department of Agriculture), a farm is any place from which $1,000 or more of agricultural products were sold, or would have been sold during a given year. Control of the farm may be exercised through ownership or management, or through a lease, rental or cropping arrangement. In the case of landowners who have one or more tenants or renters, the land operated by each is counted as a separate farm. This definition has been in effect since 1974.

FARMLAND

All land under the control of a farm operator, including land not actually under cultivation or not used for pasture or grazing. Rent free land is included as part of a farm only if the operator has sole use of it. Land used for pasture or grazing on a per head basis that is neither owned nor leased by the farm operator is not included except for grazing lands controlled by grazing associations leased on a per acre basis.

FARM INCOME

Gross farm income comprises cash receipts from farm marketings of crops and livestock, federal government payments made directly to farmers for farm-related activities, rental value of farm homes, value of farm products consumed in farm homes, and other farm-related income such as machine hire and custom work.

FULL-TIME ENROLLMENT (HIGHER EDUCATION)

The number of students enrolled in higher education courses with a total credit load equal to at least 75% of the normal full-time course load.

FULL-TIME WORKERS see **CIVILIAN LABOR FORCE.**

HEALTH LIMITATION OF ACTIVITY

A characteristic of persons with chronic conditions. Each person identified as having a chronic condition is classified as to the extent to which his or her activities are limited by the condition as follows:

--persons unable to carry on a major activity (that is the principal activity of a person of his or her age-sex group: for persons 1-5 years of age, it refers to ordinary play with other children; for persons 6-16 years of age, it refers to school attendance; for persons 17 years of age and over, it usually refers to a job, housework, or school attendance.)

--persons limited in the amount or kind of major activity performed.

--persons not limited in major activity, but otherwise limited.

--persons not limited in activity.

See also **Condition (Health).**

HEALTH MAINTENANCE ORGANIZATION (HMO)

A prepaid health plan delivering comprehensive care to members through designated providers, having a fixed monthly payment for health care services, and requiring members to be in the plan for a specified period of time (usually one year). HMOs are distinguished by the relationship of the providers to the plan. HMO model types are: **Group** -- an HMO that delivers health services through a physician group controlled by the HMO, or an HMO that contracts with one or more independent group practices to provide health services; **Individual Practice Association (IPA)** -- an HMO that contracts directly with physicians in independent practice, and/or contracts with one or more associations of physicians in independent practice, and/or contracts with one or more multispecialty group practices (but the plan is predominantly organized around solo-single specialty practices).

HIGHER EDUCATION see **INSTITUTION OF HIGHER EDUCATION.**

HISPANIC ORIGIN

An aspect of a person's ancestry. The Bureau of the Census in many of its survey asks persons if they are of Hispanic origin. There are four main subcategories of Hispanic origin: Mexican, Puerto Rican, Cuban, and other Hispanic. Hispanic origin is not a racial classification. Persons may be of any race and of Hispanic origin. Hispanic origin is used interchangeably with Spanish and Spanish origin.

HOME OWNERSHIP see **TENURE.**

HOSPITAL see **COMMUNITY HOSPITAL.**

HOSPITAL DAY

A hospital day is a night spent in a hospital by a person admitted as an inpatient.

HOUSEHOLD

The person or persons occupying a housing unit. There are two main types of households: family households, which consist of two or more persons related by birth, marriage, or adoption living together (see also **Family; Family Type**); and non-family households, which consist of a person living alone, or together with unrelated individuals (see Unrelated Individuals). See also **Householder.**

HOUSEHOLD INCOME see **INCOME.**

HOUSEHOLD TYPE see **HOUSEHOLD.**

HOUSEHOLDER

The person in whose name a housing unit is rented or owned.

HOUSING UNIT

A house, apartment, mobile home or trailer, group of rooms, or single room occupied as a separate living quarter, or, if vacant, intended for occupancy as a separate living quarter. Separate living quarters are those in which the occupants live and eat separately from any other persons in the building and which have direct access from the outside of the building or through a common hall.

Both occupied and vacant housing units are counted in many surveys; however, recreational vehicles, boats, caves, tents, railroad cars, and the like are only included if they are occupied as someone's usual place of residence. Vacant mobile homes are included if they are intended for occupancy on the site where they stand. Vacant mobile homes on dealer's sales lots, at the factory, or in storage yards are excluded.

Most housing unit data is for year-round housing units which comprises all occupied housing units plus vacant housing units intended for year round use. Vacant units held for seasonal use or migratory labor are excluded. See also **Occupancy Status, Rooms, Specified Owner-Occupied Housing Units, Tenure, Value (Housing).**

HOUSING TENURE see **TENURE.**

INCIDENT see **CRIME.**

INCOME

The term income has different definitions depending on how it is modified and in what situation it is used. Like many government statistical terms, income can be viewed hierarchically.

Personal income is the current income received by persons from all sources, minus their personal contributions for social insurance. Persons include individuals (including owners of unincorporated firms), non-profit institutions serving individuals, private trust funds, and private non-insured welfare funds. Personal income includes transfers (payments not resulting from current production) from government and business such as Social Security benefits, public assistance, etc., but excludes transfers among persons. Also included are certain non-monetary types of income, chiefly estimated net rental value to owner-occupants of their homes, the value of services furnished without payment by financial intermediaries, and food and fuel produced and consumed on farms.

Disposable personal income is personal income less personal tax and non-tax payments. It is income available to persons for spending and saving. Personal tax and non-tax payments are tax payments (net of refunds) by persons (excluding contributions for social insurance) that are not chargeable to business expenses, and certain personal payments to general government that are treated like taxes. Personal taxes include income, estate and gift, personal property, and motor vehicle licenses. Non-tax payments include passport fees, fines and penalties, donations, tuition and fees paid to schools and hospitals mainly operated by the government.

Money income is a smaller less inclusive category than personal income. Money income is the sum of the amounts received from wages and salaries, self-employment income (including losses), Social Security, Supplemental Security Income, public assistance, interest, dividends, rents, royalties, estate or trust income, veterans payments, unemployment and workers' compensation payments, private and government retirement and disability pensions, alimony, child support, and any other source of money income which was regularly received. Capital gains or losses and lump-sum or one-time payments, such as life insurance settlements, are excluded. Also excluded are non-cash benefits such as food stamps, health benefits, housing subsidies, rent-free housing, and the goods produced and consumed on farms. Money income is reported for households and various household types as well as for unrelated individuals. (In regard to family money income it should be noted that only the amount received by all family members 15 years old and over is counted, and excludes income received by household members not related to the householder.) It is reported in aggregate, median, mean, and per capita amounts. Money income is also used for determining the poverty status of families and unrelated individuals.

INFANT MORTALITY

The deaths of live-born children who do not reach their first birthday. Infant mortality is usually expressed as a rate per 1,000 live births.

INPATIENT DAYS (HOSPITALS)

The number of adult and pediatric days of care rendered during a given period. See also Hospital Day.

INSTITUTION OF HIGHER EDUCATION

An institution which offers programs of study beyond the secondary school level terminating in an associate, baccalaureate, or higher degree. See also **College; University.**

JAIL

A facility, usually operated by a local law enforcement agency, holding persons detained pending adjudication and/or persons committed after adjudication to a sentence of one year or less.

LABOR FORCE STATUS

A term which refers to whether or not a person is in the labor force, and, if in the labor force, whether he or she is employed or unemployed, a full-time worker or a part-time worker, etc. Persons are in the labor force if they are in the civilian labor force or in the Armed Forces.

The civilian labor force consists of both employed and unemployed persons, full-time and part-time workers. Generally, persons outside the labor force consist of full-time homemakers, students who do not work, retired persons, and inmates of institutions. "Discouraged workers," those who do not have a job and have not been seeking one, are also considered to be not in the labor force. See also **Civilian Labor Force.**

LARCENY see **CRIME.**

LIMITATION OF ACTIVITY see **HEALTH LIMITATION OF ACTIVITY.**

LIVE BIRTH

The live birth of an infant, defined as the complete expulsion or extraction from its mother of a product of conception, irrespective of the duration of the pregnancy, which, after such separation, breathes or shows any evidence of life such as heartbeat, umbilical cord pulsation, or definite movement of voluntary muscles, whether or not the umbilical cord has been cut or the placenta is attached. Each such birth is considered live born.

MARITAL STATUS

All persons 15 years of age and older are classified by the Bureau of the Census according to marital status. The Bureau defines two broad categories of marital status: **Single** - all those persons who have never been married (including persons whose marriage has been annulled), and **Ever married** - which is composed of the now married, the widowed, and the divorced. **Now married** persons are those who are legally married (as well as some persons who have common law marriages, along with some unmarried couples who live together and report their marital status as married), and whose marriage has not ended by widowhood or divorce. The now married are sometimes further subdivided: married, spouse present; separated; married, spouse absent; married, spouse absent, other. **Married, spouse present** covers married couples living together. **Separated** includes those persons legally separated or otherwise absent from their spouse because of marital discord (such as persons who have been deserted or who have parted because they no longer want to live together but who have not obtained a divorce). Separated includes persons with a limited divorce. **Married, spouse absent** covers those households where the both the husband and the wife were not counted as members of the same household, (or where both husband and wife lived together in group quarters). **Married, spouse absent, other**, includes those married persons whose spouse was not counted as a member of the same household, besides those who are separated. Included are persons whose spouse was employed and living away from home, absent in the armed forces, or was an inmate of an institution. **Widowed** includes widows and widowers who have not remarried. **Divorced** includes persons who are legally divorced and have not remarried.

MARRIED COUPLES see **FAMILY TYPE.**

MARRIED PERSONS see **MARITAL STATUS.**

MEAN

The arithmetic average of a set of values. It is derived by dividing the sum of a group of numerical items by the total number of items. Mean income (of a population), for example, is defined as the value obtained by dividing the total or aggregate income by the population. Thus, the mean income for families is obtained by dividing the aggregate of all income reported by persons in families by the total number of families. See also **Median.**

MEDIAN

In general, a value that divides the total range of values into two equal parts. For example, to say that the median money income of families in the United States in 1985 was $27,735 indicates that half of all families had incomes larger than that value, and half had less. See also **Mean.**

MEDICAID

A federally funded but state administered and operated program which provides medical benefits to certain low income persons in need of medical care. The program, authorized in 1965 by Title XIX of the Social Security Act, categorically covers participants in the Aid to Families with Dependent Children (AFDC) program, as well as some participants in the Supplemental Security Income (SSI) program, along with those other people deemed medically needy in each participating state. Each state determines the benefits covered, rates of payment to providers, and methods of administering the program.

MEDICARE

A federally funded nationwide health insurance program providing health insurance protection to people 65 years of age and over, people eligible for social security disability payments for more than two years, and people with end-state renal disease, regardless of income. The program was enacted July 30, 1965, as title XVIII, Health Insurance for the Aged, of the Social Security Act, and became effective on July 1, 1966. It consists of two separate but coordinated programs: hospital insurance (Part A), and supplementary medical insurance (Part B).

METROPOLITAN AREA see **CONSOLIDATED METROPOLITAN STATISTICAL AREA; METROPOLITAN STATISTICAL AREA; PRIMARY METROPOLITAN STATISTICAL AREA; STANDARD CONSOLIDATED STATISTICAL AREA; STANDARD METROPOLITAN STATISTICAL AREA**

METROPOLITAN STATISTICAL AREA (MSA)

A geographic concept introduced in June, 1984, to replace the Standard Metropolitan Statistical Area (SMSA). In general, an MSA is a geographic area consisting of a large population nucleus, together with adjacent communities that have a high degree of economic and social integration with that nucleus. MSAs are designated in accordance with a detailed 16 section criteria established by the federal Office of Management and Budget (OMB). In general, MSAs are a county based concept which must include a city that, with contiguous, densely settled territory, constitutes a Census Bureau defined urbanized area having at least 50,000 population. (However, if an MSA's largest city has less than 50,000 population, the MSA as a whole must have a total population of at least 100,000). Adjacent MSAs are consolidated into a single MSA if certain conditions relating to commuting to work, size, and geographic proximity are met. See also **Consolidated Metropolitan Statistical Area; New England County Metropolitan Area; Primary Metropolitan Statistical Area.**

NEW ENGLAND COUNTY METROPOLITAN AREA (NECMA)

A geographic concept developed for the New England states (Massachusetts, Connecticut, Rhode Island, Maine, New Hampshire, Vermont) to present data that is only available on a county-level basis . Unlike the rest of the country, Metropolitan Statistical Areas (MSAs) in the New England states are officially defined in terms of cities and towns instead of counties. As a result New England MSA data may not be directly comparable to MSA data in the rest of the country. NECMAs are county-based geographic areas (which follow the same general guidelines of MSAs in other parts of the country) and thus provide a basis of comparison with other states. NECMAs do not replace the MSAs in New England, but supplement them.

MOBILE HOME see **HOUSING UNIT.**

MONEY INCOME see **INCOME.**

MURDER see **CRIME.**

NATIONAL CRIME SURVEY

A twice yearly survey of 49,000 households comprising over 102,000 inhabitants 12 years of age and older. Administered by the Bureau of Justice Statistics, the survey measures criminal victimization by surveying victims directly. It differs from the FBI Uniform Crime Report (UCR) which is based on crimes reported to police. See also **Crime.**

NURSING HOME

A facility with three or more beds providing adults with nursing care and/or personal care (such as help with bathing, eating, using toilet facilities, or dressing) and/or supervision over such activities as money management, walking, and shopping.

OCCUPANCY STATUS (HOUSING)

The classification of all housing units as either occupied or vacant. **Occupied housing units** are those that have one or more persons living in them as their usual residence, and include units whose usual occupants are temporarily absent (e.g., on vacation). **Vacant housing units** are those that have no one living in them as their usual residence. Also classified as vacant are housing units that are temporarily occupied solely by persons who have a usual residence elsewhere, newly constructed units completed to the point where all exterior windows and doors are installed and final usable floors are in place, and vacant mobile homes or trailers intended to be occupied on the site on which they stand.

OCCUPATION

The kind of work a person does at a job or business. Occupation is reported for a given survey period, (most frequently the period covered by the survey, the reference period, is the week including March 12). If the person was not at work during the reference period, occupation usually refers to the person's most recent job or business. Persons working at more than one job are asked to identify the job at which he or she works the most hours, which is then counted as his or her occupation.

Occupations are classified according to the Standard Occupational Classification system (SOC), a system promulgated by the federal Office of Management and Budget.

OWNER OCCUPIED HOUSING UNIT see **TENURE.**

PART-TIME ENROLLMENT (HIGHER EDUCATION)

The number of students enrolled in higher education courses with a total credit load of less than 75% of the normal full-time credit load.

PART-TIME WORKERS see **CIVILIAN LABOR FORCE.**

PERSONAL INCOME see **INCOME.**

POPULATION

The number of inhabitants of an area. The total population of the United States is the sum of all persons living within the United States, plus all members of the Armed Forces living in foreign countries, Puerto Rico, Guam, and the U.S. Virgin Islands. Other Americans living abroad (e.g., civilian federal employees and dependents of members of the Armed Forces or other federal employees are not included).

The **resident population of the United States**, is the population living within the geographic United States. This includes members of the Armed Forces stationed in the United States and their families as well as foreigners working or studying here. It excludes foreign military, naval, and diplomatic personnel and their families located here and residing in embassies or similar quarters, as well as Americans living abroad. Resident population is often the denominator when calculating birth and death rates, incidence of disease, and other rates.

The **civilian population** is the resident population excluding members of the Armed Forces. However, families of members of the Armed Forces are included.

The **civilian non-institutional population** is the civilian population not residing in institutions. Institutions include, correctional institutions; detention homes and training schools for juvenile delinquents; homes for the aged and dependent (e.g., nursing homes and convalescent homes); homes for dependent and neglected children; homes and schools for the mentally and physically handicapped; homes for unwed mothers; psychiatric, tuberculosis, and chronic disease hospitals; and residential treatment centers.

POVERTY STATUS

Although the term poverty connotes a complex set of economic, social, and psychological conditions, the standard statistical definition provides for only estimates of economic poverty. These are based on the receipt of money income before taxes and exclude the value of government payments and transfers such as food stamps or Medicare; private transfers, such as health insurance premiums paid by employers; gifts; the depletion of assets; and borrowed money. Thus the term poverty as used by government agencies, classifies persons and families in relation to being above or below a specified income level, or poverty threshold. Those below this threshold are said to be in poverty, or more accurately, as below the poverty level. Poverty thresholds vary by size of family, number of children, and age of householder and are updated annually. Poverty status is also determined for unrelated individuals living in households, but not for those living in group quarters nor for persons in the Armed Forces. The poverty threshold is revised each year according to formula based on the Consumer Price Index.

PRIMARY METROPOLITAN STATISTICAL AREA (PMSA)

This geographic concept, introduced in June, 1984, combines with Metropolitan Statistical Area (MSA) and Consolidated Metropolitan Statistical Areas (CMSA), to replace the Standard Metropolitan Statistical Area (SMSA) concept. PMSAs are designated according to criteria established by the federal Office of Management and Budget. In general PMSAs are those counties with populations of at least 100,000 (60% must be urban), in which less than 50% of its resident workers commute to jobs outside the county. PMSAs are parts of Consolidated Metropolitan Statistical Areas (CMSAs).

PRISON

A confinement facility having custodial authority over adults sentenced to confinement for a period of more than one year. Prisons are usually run by State or federal authorities.

PRIVATE SCHOOL see **SCHOOL.**

PROPERTY CRIME see **CRIME.**

PUBLIC SCHOOL see **SCHOOL.**

RACE

The Bureau of the Census in many of its surveys (most notably in the decennial censuses of population) asks all persons to identify themselves according to race. The concept of race as used by the Bureau reflects the self-identification of the respondents. It is not meant to denote any clear cut scientific or biological definition.

Although it is often reported with racial categories, **Hispanic origin**, or Spanish origin, is not a racial category. Persons may be of any race and of Hispanic origin. Those who describe themselves as Hispanic (or Mexican, Cuban, Chicano, etc.) in response to a question about race, are included by the Bureau in the racial classification, "other." See also **Hispanic Origin.**

RAPE see **CRIME.**

REFERENCE PERSON

Most frequently, the person who responds to a government survey. Most surveys done by the federal government are based on households and begin by asking the initial respondent the name of the person in whose name the housing unit is owned or rented (this person is designated as the householder). Usually the householder is the reference person. Other household members are defined in relation to the householder.

REGION

The Bureau of the Census has divided the United States into four regions. This division is the primary geographic subdivision of the nation for statistical reporting purposes. As a result, almost all federal agencies, along with many private data collectors, have adopted the regional subdivision and use it for presenting statistical data.

The four regions are the **Northeast** (Maine, New Hampshire, Vermont, Massachusetts, Rhode Island, Connecticut, New York, New Jersey, Pennsylvania); the **Midwest** (Ohio, Indiana, Illinois, Michigan, Wisconsin, Minnesota, Iowa, Missouri, North Dakota, South Dakota, Kansas, Nebraska); the **South** (Delaware, Maryland, District of Columbia, Virginia, West Virginia, North Carolina, South Carolina, Georgia, Florida, Kentucky, Tennessee, Alabama, Mississippi, Arkansas, Louisiana, Oklahoma, Texas); and the **West** (Montana, Idaho, Colorado, Wyoming, New Mexico, Arizona, Utah, Nevada, Washington, Oregon, California, Alaska, Hawaii). In this book, all regional data conform to this definition.

REGULAR SCHOOL see **SCHOOL.**

RENTER OCCUPIED HOUSING UNIT see **TENURE.**

RESIDENT POPULATION see **POPULATION.**

RESTRICTED-ACTIVITY DAY see **DISABILITY DAY.**

ROBBERY see **CRIME.**

ROOMS (HOUSING)

The number of whole rooms intended for living purposes in both occupied and vacant housing units. These rooms include living rooms, dining rooms, kitchens, bedrooms, finished recreation rooms, enclosed porches suitable for year-round use, and lodger's rooms. Excluded are strip or Pullman kitchens, bathrooms, open porches, balconies, foyers, halls, half-rooms, utility rooms, unfinished attics or basements, or other space used for storage. A partially divided room, such as a dinette next to a kitchen or living room, is a separate room only if there is a partition from floor to ceiling, but not if the partition consists solely of shelves or cabinets.

RURAL see **URBAN/RURAL POPULATION.**

SCHOOL

Elementary and secondary schools are divisions of the school system consisting of students in one or more grade groups or other identifiable groups, organized as one unit with one or more teachers giving instruction of a defined type, and housed in a school plant of one or more buildings. More than one school may be housed in one school plant as is the case where elementary and secondary programs are housed in the same building.

Regular schools generally are those which advance a person toward a diploma or degree. They include public and private nursery schools, kindergartens, graded schools, colleges, universities, and professional schools.

Public schools are controlled and supported by local, state, or federal government agencies.

Private schools are controlled and supported mainly by religious organizations, private persons, or private organizations.

SCHOOL ENROLLMENT see **ENROLLMENT**.

SCHOOL-LOSS DAY see **DISABILITY DAY**.

SELF-EMPLOYMENT INCOME

A type of money income which comprises net income (gross receipts minus operating expenses) received by persons from an unincorporated business, profession, and/or from the operation of a farm as a farm owner, tenant, or sharecropper. See also **Money Income.**

SEPARATED PERSONS see **MARITAL STATUS**.

SERIOUS CRIME see **CRIME**.

SINGLE PERSON HOUSEHOLDS see **HOUSEHOLD**.

SINGLE PERSONS see **MARITAL STATUS**.

SPECIFIED OWNER-OCCUPIED HOUSING UNITS

Specified owner-occupied units are single family houses on less than ten acres, which have no commercial enterprise or medical practice on the property. Excluded are owner-occupied condominium housing units, mobile homes, trailers, boats, tents, or vans occupied as a usual residence as well as owner-occupied non-condominium units in multi-family buildings. See also **Housing Unit.**

STANDARD CONSOLIDATED STATISTICAL AREA (SCSA)

A large concentration of metropolitan population composed of two or more contiguous Standard Metropolitan Statistical Areas (SMSAs) which together meet certain criteria of population size, urban character, social and economic integration, and/or contiguity of urbanized areas. Each SCSA must have a population of one million or more. The SCSA concept was replaced with the new metropolitan area classifications in June, 1984. See Consolidated Metropolitan Statistical Area; Metropolitan Statistical Area; Primary Metropolitan Statistical Area.

STANDARD METROPOLITAN STATISTICAL AREA (SMSA)

A geographic area concept used until 1984. In general, an SMSA is a large population nucleus and nearby communities which have a high degree of economic and social integration within that nucleus. Each SMSA consists of one or more entire counties (or county equivalents) that meet certain criteria of population, commuting ties, and metropolitan character. In New England, towns and cities rather than counties are the basic units and count as county equivalents. An SMSA includes a city and, generally, the entire surrounding urbanized area and the remainder of the county or counties in which the urbanized area is located. An SMSA also includes those additional outlying counties which meet specified criteria relating to metropolitan character and level of commuting ties.

The SMSA concept was developed in 1949 and has been refined for each succeeding decennial census since 1950. In June, 1984, SMSAs were superseded by three new metropolitan area concepts: Metropolitan Statistical Areas (MSAs), Consolidated Metropolitan Statistical Areas (CMSAs), and Primary Metropolitan Statistical Areas (PMSAs).

TAXES

Compulsory contributions exacted by a government for public purposes (except employee and employer assessments for retirement and social insurance purposes, which are classified as insurance trust revenue). All tax revenue is classified as general revenue and comprises amounts received (including interest and penalties, but excluding protested amounts and refunds) from all taxes imposed by a government.

TENURE

A concept relating to housing units. All occupied housing units are classified as being either owner-occupied or renter occupied. A housing unit is owner-occupied if the owner or co-owner lives in the unit even if the unit is mortgaged or not fully paid for. All other housing units are considered to be renter occupied, regardless of whether or not cash rent is paid for them by a member of the household. See also **Housing Unit.**

UNEMPLOYED PERSONS see **CIVILIAN LABOR FORCE.**

UNEMPLOYMENT see **CIVILIAN LABOR FORCE.**

UNIFORM CRIME REPORTING (UCR) PROGRAM

A program administered by the FBI which collects reports from most police agencies in the nation (covering approximately 95% of the population) on serious crimes known to police (violent crime and property crime), arrests, police officers and related items. The Bureau issues monthly and annual summary reports based on the program. See also **Crime.**

UNIVERSITY

An institution of higher education consisting of a liberal arts college, a diverse graduate program, and usually two or more professional schools or faculties and empowered to confer degrees in various fields of study. See also **Higher Education.**

UNRELATED INDIVIDUAL

An unrelated individual is generally a person living in a household, and is either: 1) a householder living alone or only with persons who are not related to him or her by blood, marriage, or adoption, or; 2) a roomer, boarder, partner, roommate, or resident employee unrelated to the householder. Certain persons living in group quarters (who are not inmates of institutions) are also counted as unrelated individuals.

URBAN/RURAL POPULATION

Urban and rural are type of area concepts rather than specific areas outlined on maps. The urban population comprises all persons living in urbanized areas and in places of 2,500 or more inhabitants outside urbanized areas. The rural population consists of everyone else. Therefore, a rural classification need not imply a farm or sparsely settled areas, since a small city or town is rural when it is outside an urbanized area and has fewer than 2,500 inhabitants. The terms urban and rural are independent of metropolitan and non-metropolitan; both urban and rural areas occur inside and outside metropolitan areas. See also **Urbanized Area.**

URBANIZED AREA

A population concentration of at least 50,000 inhabitants, generally consisting of a central city and the surrounding, closely settled, contiguous territory (suburbs). The urbanized area criteria define a boundary based on a population density of at least 1,000 persons per square mile, but also include some less densely settled areas, such as industrial parks and railroad yards, if they are within areas of dense urban development. The density level of 1,000 persons per square mile corresponds approximately to the contiguously built-up area around a city or cities. The urban fringe is that part of the urbanized area outside of a central city or cities.

Typically, an entire urbanized area is included within an Standard Metropolitan Statistical Area (SMSA) or Metropolitan Statistical Area (MSA). The SMSA (or MSA) is usually much larger in terms of area and includes territory where the population density is less than 1,000. Occasionally more than one urbanized area is located within an SMSA (MSA). In some cases a small part of an urbanized area may extend beyond an SMSA (MSA) boundary, or possibly into an adjacent SMSA (MSA). Urbanized areas sometimes cross state boundaries as well.

VACANCY STATUS see **OCCUPANCY STATUS.**

VALUE (HOUSING UNITS)

In surveys done by the Bureau of the Census, the value of owner-occupied housing units is the respondent's estimate of the current dollar worth of the property; for vacant units, the value is the price asked for the property. A property is defined as the house and the land on which it stands. Respondents are asked by the Bureau to estimate the value of the house and land even if they own only the house, or own the house jointly. Statistics for value are only gathered by the Bureau for owner-occupied condominium units and for specified owner-occupied units (single family houses on less than ten acres, and with no business on the property).

VICTIMIZATION see **CRIME.**

VIOLENT CRIME see **CRIME.**

VOTING AGE POPULATION

All persons over the age of 18 (the voting age for federal elections) in a given geographic area comprise the voting age population. The voting age population does include a small number of persons who, although of voting age, are not eligible to vote (e.g. resident aliens, inmates of institutions, etc.). The voting age population is estimated in even numbered years by the Bureau of the Census.

WAGES AND SALARIES

Wages and salaries are a type (subgroup) of money income and include civilian wages and salaries, Armed Forces pay and allowances, piece-rate payments, commissions, tips, National Guard or Reserve pay (received for training periods), and cash bonuses before deductions for taxes, pensions, union dues, etc. See also **Money Income.**

WIDOWED PERSONS see **MARITAL STATUS.**

WORK DISABILITY

A health condition which limits the kind or amount of work a person can do, or prevents working at a job. A person is limited in the kind of work he or she can do if the person has a health condition which restricts his or her choice of jobs. A person is limited in amount of work if he or she is not able to work at a full-time (35 hours or more per week) job or business. See also **Condition (Health).**

WORK-LOSS DAY see **DISABILITY DAY.**

Index